Doing Research in Counselling and Psychotherapy

Third
Edition

Doing
Research in
Counselling and
Psychotherapy

John McLeod

SAGE

Los Angeles | London | New Delhi
Singapore | Washington DC

Los Angeles | London | New Delhi
Singapore | Washington DC

SAGE Publications Ltd
1 Oliver's Yard
55 City Road
London EC1Y 1SP

SAGE Publications Inc.
2455 Teller Road
Thousand Oaks, California 91320

SAGE Publications India Pvt Ltd
B 1/I 1 Mohan Cooperative Industrial Area
Mathura Road
New Delhi 110 044

SAGE Publications Asia-Pacific Pte Ltd
3 Church Street
#10-04 Samsung Hub
Singapore 049483

Editor: Susannah Trefgarne
Assistant editor: Laura Walmsley
Production editor: Victoria Nicholas
Copyeditor: Audrey Scriven
Proofreader: Derek Markham
Marketing manager: Camille Richmond
Cover design: Shaun Mercier
Typeset by: C&M Digitals (P) Ltd, Chennai, India
Printed in Great Britain by CPI Group (UK) Ltd,
Croydon, CR0 4YY

Library of Congress Control Number: 2014940524

British Library Cataloguing in Publication data

A catalogue record for this book is available from
the British Library

ISBN 978-1-4462-0138-1
ISBN 978-1-4462-0139-8 (pbk)

MIX
Paper from
responsible sources
FSC® C013604
www.fsc.org

At SAGE we take sustainability seriously. Most of our products are printed in the UK using FSC papers and boards.
When we print overseas we ensure sustainable papers are used as measured by the Egmont grading system.
We undertake an annual audit to monitor our sustainability.

Dedication

For Julia

Contents

About the author

John McLeod is Emeritus Professor of Counselling at the University of Abertay, Visiting Professor at the Institute for Integrative Counselling and Psychotherapy, Dublin, and Adjunct Professor of Psychology, University of Oslo. He is committed to promoting the relevance of research as a means of informing therapy practice and improving the quality of services that are available to clients. His enthusiastic search for finding ways to make research interesting and accessible for practitioners has resulted in a teaching award from the students at his own university and an award from the British Association for Counselling and Psychotherapy for his exceptional contribution to research. His writing has influenced a generation of trainees in the field of counselling, counselling psychology and psychotherapy, and his books are widely adopted on training programmes across the world.

How to use this book

This book is aimed at people who are planning to carry out research into some aspect of counselling or psychotherapy. Throughout the book, the words 'counselling', 'psychotherapy' and 'therapy' are used to describe a set of activities and helping processes that are largely similar. Although my own view is that there are important differences between counselling and psychotherapy (McLeod, 2013a), these differences are not particularly manifested in the domain of research. The book should also be relevant to students and practitioners in adjacent fields, such as psychiatry, clinical and counselling psychology, mental health nursing, social work, and life coaching.

For the most part, the book is written as though the reader already has a research project in mind, or has an area of interest that is ready to be converted into a project. Readers who are searching for research ideas may find it valuable to consult McLeod (2013a), which provides an overview of the existing research literature, and examples of the kinds of studies that have been done. Within the present book, Chapter 3 focuses on the process of developing a topic, passionate interest, or germ of an idea, into research questions and a viable research project.

The main chapters are organised along the lines of a cookbook. Each of these chapters explains what is involved in conducting a specific type of study. This does not mean that hybrid or 'fusion' studies are not possible. Anything is possible in research, and there are many ways to combine different methodologies within a single project, or within a programme of research. However, on the basis of my experience as a researcher supervisor, my belief is that combining methodologies is not a good idea for beginners. Ahead of the cookbook chapters, there are some chapters that introduce basic research principles and tools. Following the cookbook chapters, there is a chapter on how to get research published and a chapter on 'what next'.

There are three reasons why I believe that a cookbook, containing recipes for different types of research study, provides a valuable supplement to existing research methods texts that are available. First, I believe that it is useful to learn about research by taking the role of apprentice, and trying to produce something that is similar to existing products that are already considered as worthwhile. Second, successfully completing a research study is greatly assisted by access to insider knowledge in the form of tips and short cuts, and how to avoid pitfalls. Third, I am keen to promote an attitude to research that emphasises the achievement of a finished product that can be shared and celebrated. For me, these are all aspects of good cookbooks.

In my view, it is important for novice researchers to gain knowledge and experience in relation to five different types of research 'product':

- Reviews of the research literature.
- Qualitative interviews that explore the experience of therapy.
- Using basic quantitative skills and methods to evaluate the outcomes of therapy in routine practice.
- Carrying out a systematic case study.
- Using personal experience as a source of research data.

This book offers detailed guidelines on how to carry out publishable research within each of these approaches.

The present book is part of a series of titles on research in counselling and psychotherapy. I have written about general philosophical, methodological and political aspects of therapy research in *An Introduction to Research in Counselling and Psychotherapy* (McLeod, 2013b), and the rationale for specific methodologies in *Case Study Research in Counselling and Psychotherapy* (2010a) and *Qualitative Research in Counselling and Psychotherapy* (2011). The rationale for quantitative research is available in a wide range of texts, cited in McLeod (2013b) and in the present book. In a further book, I intend to write about how research can be used to enhance therapy practice.

Doing Research in Counselling and Psychotherapy is aimed at undergraduate and Master's degree students, as well as practitioners undertaking personal research. While the book may hopefully also be relevant for doctoral students, I would expect someone doing a PhD to be functioning at a more advanced level of understanding of research issues. My goals for students undertaking undergraduate or Master's research projects are that they demonstrate competence in the use of a specific methodology, and are able to reflect on the strengths and limitations of the research approach they have adopted. By contrast, I regard a PhD as a licence to supervise research and apply for research grants. Someone doing a PhD therefore needs to be able not only to demonstrate competence in the use of a methodology, but in addition be able to justify their choice of methodology in the context of the broader field of philosophy and sociology of science, and current debates within the therapy research literature.

The book is written from an interdisciplinary perspective, which views counselling and psychotherapy as applied disciplines that draw their ideas and techniques from the humanities, theology, philosophy, sociology and anthropology, as well as from the more familiar sources in psychology and medicine. Each of these contributor disciplines has much to offer in terms of methodological diversity. Anyone who has had even the slightest involvement with therapy will know that it is a highly complex undertaking. What may on the surface appear to be a simple conversation between client and therapist can be understood at many levels and from many perspectives. This book reflects that multi-faceted reality. There is no one right way to do therapy research.

Each chapter includes a number of personal learning exercises, which are designed to encourage reflection on the issues that are being discussed. These exercises can be carried out on an individual basis, for example in the form of entries in a personal learning journal. Alternatively, they can be used as topics for group discussion. Some exercises may also be suitable for use or adaptation by tutors as assessment tasks or seminar topics within a research methods module or class.

Some passages within the present book have previously been published as part of a second edition of *Doing Counselling Research* (McLeod, 2003) or *Practitioner Research in Counselling* (McLeod, 1999).

Supplementary learning materials are available on a companion website: http://study.sagepub.com/mcleod

Companion Website

Doing Research in Counselling and Psychotherapy, Third Edition, is accompanied by a companion website with free online resources for students and lecturers.

Visit http://**study.sagepub.com/mcleod** to access the following resources:

For students:

- Direct links to **journal articles** that will provide examples and deepen your understanding of topics discussed in the book.
- Weblinks to useful sources of information including open access research tools, websites of key research organisations and more.
- Sample ethical consent forms.

For lecturers:

- Weblinks to useful training resources.
- A full set of reflection tasks for each chapter.
- Research syllabus guidelines for counselling and psychotherapy training programmes.

Acknowledgements

I would like to acknowledge the support I have received from many colleagues who have been willing to share their knowledge and experience around research issues, and all of the students who have allowed me to guide them and accompany me on their research journey. I would also like to thank Susannah Trefgarne and Laura Walmsley at Sage, who have provided invaluable editorial assistance. Finally, I owe the greatest debt to my wife Julia, and to my daughters Kate, Emma and Hannah. Without their love, affection and belief in me, none of this would have been possible.

1

Doing Research in Counselling and Psychotherapy: Basic Principles

Introduction

The aim of this book is to encourage and support the reader to carry out research into counselling, counselling psychology, psychotherapy, or related topics in fields such as social work, mental health and coaching. In preparation for carrying out research, it is important to develop an understanding of the ways in which therapy research has grown and developed, the types of methodological approaches that have been employed, and the social, political and cultural factors that have shaped this enterprise. These themes are addressed in an earlier book – *An Introduction to Research in Counselling and Psychotherapy* (McLeod, 2013a). In the opening chapter of that book, a definition of research is offered and explained: *a systematic process of critical inquiry leading to valid propositions and conclusions that are communicated to interested others.* That same definition functions as the anchor point of the present volume. However, the following chapters adopt a rather different focus. *An Introduction to Research in Counselling and Psychotherapy* looked at therapy research from the outside, from the perspective of a student or practitioner seeking to learn from that body of knowledge. Now, we shift perspective, to consider what therapy research looks like from the inside, from a position of someone actively involved in making a contribution to knowledge.

This opening chapter introduces some key guiding principles, which serve to orient the efforts of anyone undertaking therapy research. These principles can be regarded as an attempt to begin to define what therapy researchers should be trying to accomplish, in terms of practical knowledge that is informed by a specific set of values.

Principle 1: The primary aim of research is to create knowledge products

There is a sense in which any therapist who takes his or her work seriously is engaged in 'research', through activities such as observing what happens in a therapy session, keeping notes, testing hypotheses or hunches about what might be helpful for a client, identifying themes and patterns, reading about the client's problem, and so on. This kind of personal research is essential to good practice. However, it is different from the type of 'research' that is being discussed in this book. What we are concerned with here is an understanding of 'research' that views it as a collective, rather than an individual, undertaking. Throughout human history, but particularly over the past two hundred years, knowledge has advanced through the sharing and dissemination of 'knowledge products' such as books, articles, reports, conference presentations, and so on. What researchers do, is to create knowledge products that take their place in a vast marketplace of knowledge. These products may ultimately be used and traded in ways that are beyond the control or imagination of the person who carried out the study. It might be helpful to regard the distinction between personal research and formal research as similar to the difference between a writer and an author. Many people gain great satisfaction and meaning from the experience of writing. But something different happens when that same work gets published – it becomes part of a collective 'literature'.

Throughout the main chapters of this book, that describe different types of research, there is a strong and consistent emphasis on what needs to be done to arrive at a final end product that will fulfil the standards of the relevant knowledge marketplace. Achieving these standards can be a frustrating experience. The standards that prevail within the various different subdomains of therapy research are socially constructed – they arise from a consensus about what makes sense, what is acceptable, what readers and consumers of research will 'buy'. This consensus can change over time, in response to developments in research methodology.

It is important to acknowledge the powerful social and political forces that underpin the concept of a research marketplace. Open publication of, and access to, new knowledge is a central characteristic of democratic societies. Much anger and resentment is generated in such societies when knowledge is hidden, for example when a drug company conceals evidence of the negative side-effects of a new treatment, or a government analyses data that are collected from the global flow of personal emails. On a smaller scale, a similar kind of expectation of transparency has been a crucial driver of psychotherapy research. We expect approaches to therapy to be backed up by evidence that is independently verifiable. We wonder: if the proponents of a therapy are not willing to provide such evidence, then what are they trying to hide?

It is probable that many readers or users of this book will be novice researchers, who have little or no experience of seeing a research project through to the point of publication as a knowledge product. The majority of novice researchers are university or college students. Unfortunately, in most places it is possible to gain a degree, even a PhD, without publishing the findings of the research that has been carried out. What this means is that there exists a vast amount of potentially useful knowledge that is not readily accessible to others, and remains buried on library shelves or in university websites. Some on-line databases, such as PsychInfo, include abstracts of unpublished dissertations and theses. It is fascinating to scroll through these unpublished works. Many of them are fascinating, imaginative, highly meaningful, and potentially of substantial practical relevance. But, as lengthy documents that have not been subjected to the quality control procedures employed by academic journals and book publishers, they are unlikely ever to be read by more than a handful of people. In a field such as counselling and psychotherapy research, where there are major gaps in almost any area of the research literature, this is a tragic situation.

One of the major implications of viewing research as a matter of 'making things' lies in the area of research training. Many research training courses and modules require students to learn about a wide range of methodological issues, with the assumption that it is necessary to possess a comprehensive knowledge of research methods in order to design a study. It is as if the student needs to be able to develop a research plan from first principles. By contrast, if the task is to create a research product, it makes a lot more sense to adopt an apprenticeship model of training, where the novice researcher basically copies a previous product, under the close supervision of an expert. Apprenticeship learning is based on practice, with occasional time out to learn about underlying principles. The topic of research training is discussed in more detail later in this chapter.

The notion that the purpose of research is *primarily* to generate research products in the form of publications and other means of disseminating findings does not detract from the importance of the role of research involvement in counsellor and psychotherapist development as a whole. There are many ways in which carrying out research can help both trainee and experienced therapists to develop interpersonal skills and awareness, extend and consolidate theoretical understanding, reflect on practice, and gain a deeper appreciation of client needs and issues. These dimensions of learning make a significant contribution to therapist competence and effectiveness.

Exercise 1.1   Reflecting on the type of research product you want to create

Thinking in terms of research products means that it is necessary for a researcher to decide, at the start, what kind of product he or she is trying to manufacture, and where it can be 'sold'. The main outlets for counselling and psychotherapy research consist of:

- brief, non-technical reports in professional journals such as *Therapy Today* or the *Healthcare Counselling and Psychotherapy Journal*;
- conference presentations. Increasingly, abstracts and PowerPoint slides of conference papers are also disseminated on the internet;
- reports produced by counselling agencies or professional organisations;
- papers in research journals or general academic journals, such as *Counselling and Psychotherapy Research, New Zealand Journal of Counselling, Journal of Counseling and Development*, and *Psychotherapy: Theory, Research, Training and Practice*;
- books, and chapters in edited books;
- performances, such as plays, videos and art exhibitions.

In relation to research that you may be planning to carry out, which of these types of product would be most appropriate and realistic? What are the factors that influence you to make this choice? Can you identify specific examples of publications within that type of product, that you might be able to use as a template for your own work? Who do you know, or could consult, who has experience of publishing work of that type, and who might be able to advise you?

Exercise 1.2   Reading research papers

One of the best ways to learn about research is to read articles in research journals. To build an appreciation of research, it is important to read papers that are reports on specific research studies, rather than discussion articles. A specific research report will always include a 'method' section that provides detail on how participants were recruited, and how data were collected. A commitment to read one or two research papers each week will fairly quickly lead to an appreciation of what is possible in research, and the strengths and limitations of different research approaches. It is good to read papers from a position that gives space for an appreciation of the knowledge and information that is being offered, as well as a more critical perspective. Although it is natural to be drawn to studies that reflect one's own personal interests and methodological preferences, it can also be instructive to read papers that fall outside that horizon.

Principle 2: The meaning, significance and value of any research study depend on where it fits within the existing literature

Research is a collective endeavour. Although many research studies are carried out by individual investigators, the reason why research-based knowledge is taken seriously in our society is that it is based on the work of thousands of investigators over many decades. The research community has generated a network of knowledge, where each specific idea, statement or assumption in a research paper is linked to, and supported by, other studies and other theories carried out by different people in different locations. This is what gives research its credibility and persuasive power. The findings of a single study can be intriguing and stimulating. But the findings of a single study will never be taken as a basis for action until they are replicated, or supported by other types of evidence.

The construction of the research literature is organised around a constant process of critical appraisal. Researchers are people who ask awkward questions: Is this true? Is this valid? Are these conclusions justified by the evidence? How can we get better evidence in relation to this issue? The research literature is also organised around a sustained collective effort to answer particular questions. Although there also needs to be space for innovative or maverick researchers who ask new questions, or open up new possibilities, for the most part the research literature reflects a gradual, cumulative progress toward a shared objective. Philosophers and sociologists of science have made a major contribution in developing ways of making sense of how research is organised at a collective level. An introduction to these ideas, along with suggestions for further reading, can be found in McLeod (2013b; see Chapter 3).

One of the main tasks for any new researcher is to become familiar with the research literature around their topic of interest. The process of arriving at an understanding of any subfield within the counselling and psychotherapy literature is a complex and demanding undertaking. It can be helpful to adopt a historical perspective, looking at how knowledge has been built up over time, because in any field of research there are likely to be interesting and potentially significant findings and directions that emerged at various stages but were then never fully exploited or explored. It is also helpful to track the evolution of different research methods that have been used and essential to read the literature from a critical perspective, with a feel for what is missing and what does not 'feel right'. This can be hard, because new researchers generally do not have enough time to immerse themselves in the literature, and may lack confidence in their ability to critically evaluate what they are finding. It can be useful, again, to adopt an apprenticeship model, and work with someone who already knows the literature well.

The importance of the literature is also reflected in the fact that literature reviews are highly significant and highly valued research products in their own right. Chapter 10 of this book looks at what is involved in writing a literature review paper.

Exercise 1.3   Becoming a connoisseur of reviews

Find at least three literature reviews that have been carried out within the area of your topic of interest. These can be stand-alone review papers or reports, or introductory literature review sections within research articles. Make notes on the strengths and limitations of each review. What was helpful or unhelpful in the way that each author or group of authors structured the review that they produced? What have you learned that can guide you in your own literature reviewing?

Principle 3: Developing reliable and practically useful research-based knowledge in the field of counselling and psychotherapy requires the adoption of methodological pluralism

Methodological pluralism is the idea that there are many ways in which reliable, valid, and practically useful knowledge can be attained. Within the field of research in counselling and psychotherapy, there has been a growing acceptance, over the past twenty years, that a pluralistic stance in relation to knowledge is necessary if real progress is to be made in bridging the gap between research and practice. To appreciate the significance of this stance, it is necessary to know a little about the history of therapy research (McLeod, 2013b; see Chapter 2). Historically, therapy research has been dominated by the methods and assumptions of psychology, which have emphasised the use of quantitative, statistical methods to analyse data derived from the experimental manipulation of variables. The dominant role of measurement in psychology arose from the need for psychology in the early years of the twentieth century to establish itself as a scientific discipline. As a result, the first generation of researchers in counselling and psychotherapy, in the 1950s and 1960s, made use of the research tools that they had been taught as psychology students, namely quantitative methods.

What has gradually become apparent, as the psychotherapy research community has grown, and as the research literature became substantial enough to function as a credible source of knowledge for practice, is that quantitative methods could only take us so far. There are many aspects of therapy that are better understood through the use of qualitative methods, such as open-ended interviews, or intensive analysis of patterns within single cases. One of the distinctive characteristics of recent research in therapy has been a search for ways of combining information that has been collected using different methods. However, there are still some influential figures who continue to assert that different sources of knowledge should be organised in a hierarchy of validity/credibility. For these individuals, controlled experiments, such as randomised controlled trials, are at the top of the knowledge hierarchy, while case studies or studies that use qualitative interviews provide only supplementary or supporting evidence. The adoption of a methodologically pluralistic stance involves rejecting the notion that there is a hierarchy of knowledge, in favour of a more nuanced position that argues the choice of method depends on the question that is being asked and the situation in which research is being carried out.

Behind this debate there are important philosophical questions. Quantitative research reflects a particular way of seeing the world, in terms of cause-and-effect relationships between 'variables' or 'factors'. Quantitative research refers to a reality that can be reduced to the deterministic laws of physics, biology and evolution, in which there is no place for human choice and intentionality. By contrast, qualitative research refers to a quite different way of seeing the world, in terms of people interacting together to construct a language and culture that at the same time shape them but can also be shaped by them. Within the 'socially constructed' world of qualitative research, human action is not for the most part 'caused' by physical or biological events and processes. Instead, responses to these events and processes will depend on what they mean to people.

Some researchers have taken the view that the assumptions and realities envisaged in qualitative and quantitative research mean that knowledge derived from these sources is incommensurable. These cannot be combined, because they represent fundamentally different and incompatible ways of seeing the world. This position leads to a basic separation between 'science' on the one hand, and the domain of arts, philosophy and humanities on the other hand. This split has been congenial to some therapists, who have used it as a way of justifying their disregard for science on the grounds that therapy is an art or craft that draws on philosophical and aesthetic insights and that scientific knowledge has no relevance.

In my own view, the existence of distinctive and contrasting world-views and epistemologies associated with the qualitative and quantitative research traditions needs to be taken seriously. We need to understand what is possible, and not possible, within each approach. There are different criteria for good research associated with each approach. For example, on the whole quantitative research produces the most reliable findings if large samples of participants are used. In qualitative research, large numbers of participants usually result in superficial findings, because of the impossibility of capturing and conveying subtleties in meaning. However, counselling and psychotherapy are activities that require paying attention to all aspects of the person. The problems being experienced by a client will always reflect a mix of objective events ('I became depressed because I developed cancer, or lost my job') and the meaning that the person attributes to these events ('my mother died of cancer, and I keep thinking about her'). In addition, clients themselves make sense of their problems in living using a combination of 'scientific reasoning', philosophical analysis and creative expressiveness. The point here is that the practice of therapy requires taking account of different worldviews and epistemologies. It makes sense, therefore, that research into therapy is equally willing to reflect these multiple positions.

The situation in therapy, and by implication in therapy research, is in fact more complicated than this. Clients in therapy (and therapists themselves) draw heavily on knowledge derived from personal experience. Some of this knowledge does not fit at all easily into either the qualitative or quantitative research world-views and epistemologies. These research epistemologies are, in the end, different forms of rationality that reflect the prevailing values of modern secular societies. Personal experience, by contrast, makes use of culturally-shared, commonsense, emotions and 'gut feelings', and knowledge that is derived from spiritual practices. In recent years, therapy practice and research have moved in the direction of embracing these ways of knowing.

I would suggest, therefore, that there is a strong argument to be made that therapy research needs to be pluralistic because good therapy is pluralistic. It seems clear that each time a therapy theory, or programme of therapy research, disregards one of these world-views or epistemologies, it is heading for trouble.

At the same time, at this stage in the development of therapy research, there are some major challenges associated with the adoption of methodological pluralism. One of these challenges is political – the most powerful researchers and research institutions still operate on the basis of a hierarchy of knowledge that places quantitative methods at the top. The second challenge is practical. It takes time and effort to learn how to do research well – any type of research. As a result, researchers tend to specialise in one particular methodology, because they feel more confident and competent when they use that approach. If they become university or college teachers, they then have a tendency to encourage their students to adopt their preferred methodology, thus perpetuating the tendency toward specialisation. In addition, academic departments develop reputations as centres for excellence in particular research approaches. It makes a lot of sense for individual researchers to develop special expertise in particular methodologies. However, if the potential of a methodologically pluralistic perspective on therapy research is be realised, it is necessary for initial research training to enable students to develop a genuine understanding and appreciation of a range of methodologies.

Exercise 1.4   Imagining different ways that a topic could be investigated

Chapters 10 to 14 describe the main methodologies that are currently used in research on counselling and psychotherapy. Identify a research topic that is of interest to you. As you read these later chapters, imagine how this topic might be investigated using each of these approaches. Alternatively, if you have access to a group of colleagues, each member could look at how the topic could be explored using one or two of the methodologies, and then share their ideas with the group as a whole. Once you have generated ideas for a set of possible studies on the same general topic, reflect on the following questions: To what extent, and in what ways, do you find that different methodologies contribute valuable alternative and complementary understandings of the topic? To what extent do different methodologies lead to conflicting understandings of the topic? Is there one approach that clearly seems to be the best way to investigate that topic (and if so, why)?

Principle 4: The purpose of therapy research is to produce practical knowledge that contributes to social justice

There are some branches of scientific inquiry that are driven by a simple human desire to understand and make sense of the world. This type of work is sometimes described as 'blue skies' research. Even when it yields discoveries of practical value, such as new technologies, these are by-products, they do not represent the reason why the work was carried out in the first place. Therapy research is not like this. It is down to earth rather than being up in the sky. Counselling and psychotherapy are forms of practice in contemporary society that aim to help people to achieve learning, personal development and emotional healing. Therapy research always comes back to the central question: 'How does this knowledge help us to do better therapy?' This is one of the reasons why methodological pluralism makes sense within therapy research. It is possible to spend a lifetime thinking about the philosophical implications of what it means to measure human experience as opposed to interpreting the way that people talk about their experience. Yet it is not hard to identify both qualitative and quantitative studies, and personal experience studies, that have something useful to contribute to how to do better therapy.

There are many ways in which the organisation and dissemination of research, across all fields of study, have created barriers between research and practice. Research is largely carried out in universities, which are somewhat inaccessible to ordinary people. Academics primarily write for other academics, and publish in journals that are not read by practitioners. Academic journals are also often hidden behind paywalls. When practitioners do read research articles in academic journals, they are put off by the way in which academic authors emphasise methodological rigour at the expense of practical relevance. Beyond these factors, the academic world is generally structured in terms of 'disciplines': psychology, sociology, biology, and so on. By contrast, practical issues are not generally structured along these lines. A therapy client, for instance, may report psychological, social and biological issues all at the same time.

As with other principles that are discussed in this chapter, there is a lag between the way that research has traditionally been pursued, and an emerging progressive consensus about the preferred direction of travel. Inspired by the ideas of writers such as Fishman (1999) and Flyvbjerg (2001), there has been a movement within therapy research to embrace the principle that the purpose of that research is to generate practical knowledge that makes a difference.

But makes a difference to whom? Accepting that therapy research should aim to produce practical knowledge inevitably leads to further questions about the kind of practical knowledge that is intended. For example, a lot of current research is aimed at demonstrating the effectiveness of specific brand-name therapies such as CBT, psychodynamic or person-centred. The findings from this kind of research have a particular kind of practical outcome – mainly in terms of securing the jobs and careers of therapists who operate within that approach. Other research looks at how to do these therapies in a more effective manner, for example by adding client feedback tools (Lambert, 2007, 2010). This is a more direct form of practical knowledge, but it is still limited to the goal of enhancing a conventional form of therapy. It is possible to think about even more radical types of practical knowledge, which explore ways that people seeking help can be more in control of the therapy choices that are on offer. An example of this kind of research is the action research study by Davidson et al. (2001) in which people with mental health problems designed their own community support programme.

What we see here is that an emphasis on practical knowledge, as opposed to 'academic' outputs, has the effect of opening up the question of who research is for. An increasing proportion of counselling and psychotherapy practitioners and researchers have arrived at the conclusion that both research and practice should be informed by a social justice agenda (Chapman and Schwartz, 2012; McLeod, 2013a; Ratts, 2009; Sperry, 2008). Yes, we are working to help individuals to overcome problems in living and maximise their potential. But unless we do this in a way that takes account of the wider society, all we are doing is papering over the cracks. If therapy is not aligned with other efforts to build a more sustainable and equal society, then it can be accused of impeding these initiatives.

Exercise 1.5   How might your research be used?

Take some minutes to reflect and make notes on the possible practical value of your research. This could be research that you are planning to undertake, or research that has been completed. In what ways might that research make a practical difference? What can you do to draw attention to, and promote, the practical value of your work? What examples have inspired you of therapy research that has had an impact on people's lives? In what way might your research be designed or planned to maximise its practical relevance? In what way might it be written up?

Principle 5: Good therapy research requires paying attention to reflexivity, i.e., the personal meaning of the research for the researcher

A commitment to the development of self-awareness represents a key value for therapists. The majority of therapists participate in personal therapy at some point in their career, as well as a range of other personal development activities (McLeod and McLeod, 2014). Within society, therapists can be viewed as specialists in relationships, emotions and ways of thinking. The practice of therapy involves a capacity to reflect on, and find meaning in, therapist-client interaction. It is not surprising, therefore, that therapy researchers expect each other to be aware of the personal meaning of the research that they undertake. Paying attention to researcher reflexivity comprises one of the distinctive features of all types of therapy research.

Almost everyone who engages in therapy research will have trained as a therapist and been a client in therapy. Therapy researchers therefore have a high level of personal knowledge of the issues they are investigating, and possibly also a high level of personal investment in particular ways of thinking about these issues. One of the most striking examples of the influence of therapist's personal beliefs on the results of research, was documented by Luborsky et al. (1999). They looked at the previous training and theoretical allegiance of lead investigators running randomised controlled trials (RCTs) where two approaches of therapy were compared to discover which of these was more effective with a particular type of client. RCTs hold a special place in the world of therapy research, as a type of investigation in which every possible effort is made to ensure objectivity and eradicate bias. Nevertheless, Luborsky et al. (1999) found that the results of such studies were closely linked to the theoretical allegiance of the lead researcher. For instance, in studies that compared CBT and psychodynamic therapy, if the researcher was an adherent of CBT, that approach would come out on top. If the main researcher was a psychodynamic therapist, then that approach would be found to be more effective.

In an RCT, clients fill in questionnaires and undergo various procedures around which the lead researcher has no direct involvement. In other types of research there may only be one researcher, who interviews the participants, transcribes the recordings of the interviews, analyses the transcripts, and then selects representative quotes for inclusion in the results section of the ensuing article. In such instances, it is easy to see that the study as a whole will be shaped by the way a researcher personally makes sense of the topic being investigated.

These are situations in which the personal meaning of the researcher may get in the way of gaining a satisfactory understanding of the experiences of the subjects of the research, for example clients. There are also other situations in which the personal awareness of the researcher represents a major strength and advantage. For example, personal experience of an issue may help to sensitise a researcher to aspects of that phenomenon, or may make it more likely that research participants will trust the researcher. There are also methodologies that make it possible for researchers to systematically explore, and report on, their personal experience (see Chapter 14).

There are some areas of science in which it is not possible for the researcher to have personal experience of the subject being studied (e.g., geology, evolution, microbiology). There are also other areas where a researcher may be motivated by personal and family experience (such as a cancer researcher whose father died of the disease), but not a way that has led them to want (unconsciously) to arrive at a particular set of conclusions. The prevailing assumption in science, right or wrong, is that scientists are engaged in solving intellectual puzzles, rather than pursuing personal quests. It is hard to see how therapy research can ever be just an intellectual puzzle.

The implication of this set of considerations is not that therapy researchers should necessarily write at length in research papers about their life experiences, feelings and expectations about the topic, and so on. Doing so may be useful in some situations, but in other contexts it will just get in the way of telling the story of what was found. What is needed, really, is a willingness to engage in on-going reflexive self-monitoring, and also engage in conversations with colleagues about what comes up. In other words, to behave like a therapist when being a researcher.

Exercise 1.6   The personal meaning of your own research

Identify a research topic around which you are intending to carry out research, or perhaps have already investigated. Give yourself some time to reflect, answer, or discuss the following questions: What are the points of connection between this topic and your personal life? What makes this topic interesting for you? What is your personal experience of the phenomena you plan to study/have studied? Are there any personal issues that you may be trying to understand through developing an academic knowledge of this topic? In what ways might the personal meaning of the topic: (a) sensitise you to aspects of the questions you are exploring?; (b) contribute to a deeper understanding of the question?; (c) function as a source of bias and error?

Principle 6: To produce genuine knowledge requires commitment to an ethic of care

There is no doubt that rationality constitutes a key value within contemporary society, and that in many respects science represents an arena in which it is allowed its fullest expression. Rationality permeates research – from the level of philosophical logic and mathematical equations that underpin research design and data analysis, through to the structure of scientific papers and the ways that research is written up.

However, in the world of counselling and psychotherapy, research that makes a difference, that is memorable or that inspires readers to change their practice, is not achieved merely through the application of rationality. The essential ingredient of research that makes a difference, alongside logical rigour, can be characterised as commitment to an *ethic of care*. The most obvious way in which therapy researchers take care is in the area of research ethics, by ensuring that no harm comes to research participants. Even here, a lot of the time, the level of care exhibited toward research participants will be the minimum necessary to receive ethical approval for a study to go ahead. It is instructive to read research papers with this question in mind: 'To what extent did this researcher *really* care about what happened to the participants?' There are relatively few studies that pass this test.

A further aspect of care is reflected in the attitude of the researcher toward the work being undertaken. Within university systems, a licence or accreditation to practice as a therapist will depend on completing a research study. In many instances, the student cares passionately about his or her topic. In other instances, the dissertation or thesis, and subsequent published articles, are just hurdles to be negotiated in order to secure a good job as a practitioner. Career research academics do not always care about the research they carry out. There are many occasions when research studies and programmes are undertaken for reasons of career advancement or income generation. Again, it is possible to read research papers with the question in mind, 'To what extent did this researcher demonstrate a passionate interest in the topic of the study?' Some researchers produce work that conveys joy, wonderment, and enchantment, while others do not. These qualities are hard to convey in technical reports in scientific journals, but can be observed (or not observed) when a researcher presents his or her work at a conference, or writes for a more popular readership. Carl Rogers was a good example of a researcher who possessed these qualities, and expressed them in much of his writing. Care is often visible in writing, through flow and aesthetic quality.

Exercise 1.7   Your own personal ethic of care

What are the ethical values that underpin your research? How much do you care about the research you are carrying out? In what ways does this care (or lack of care) exhibit itself in the way you go about your research business? Who do you talk to about your level of care/indifference in relation to your research?

Principle 7: Research is a collaborative activity

There is an image of the seeker after truth that represents an attractive metaphor for many researchers. The seeker after truth sets off alone on a long journey of discovery, or withdraws from the everyday world to meditate in a cave, or wanders dreamlike around a garden like Isaac Newton or Charles Darwin, or whatever. This is a heroic and inspiring type of image, which has some relevance to what can happen during the research process. A lot of the time, the creative process of arriving at a new understanding may be facilitated by a period of immersion in the topic, which can be greatly aided by withdrawing from everyday demands. But it is also an incomplete image. The question being investigated by the seeker after truth is never just their own personal question – it is always one that has been asked before, in some shape or form, which has then been passed on to the seeker. Even on a journey of discovery someone will be cooking the meals or, on the end of the line when the time comes to phone a friend. And at the end of that journey, the truth that has been uncovered will require an audience.

This point is worth emphasising because the way that counselling and psychotherapy research has been organised has had a tendency to promote an individualistic model of inquiry. Most published research studies will have been conducted by students, and there is pressure on students to be able to demonstrate that what they hand in is their own individual work. There is no university regulation that prohibits a student from doing their research as part of a team. But it is generally regarded as safer and clearer, for assessment purposes, if the project has transparently been a solo effort.

On the whole, successful scientific research is carried out by teams – in labs, research institutes and clinics. Probably the single most influential programme of research in the field of counselling comprised the output of the team that was led by Carl Rogers from the mid-1940s to the mid-1960s (McLeod, 2003). Although nowadays this body of research is generally attributed to Rogers, even brief scrutiny of books such as Rogers and Dymond (1954) or Rogers et al. (1967) reveals that at least 20 active researchers were involved at any one time. Closer examination of these texts, and the flow of ideas within that group, makes it possible to see that many of the major breakthroughs and insights in fact originated in the work of lesser known members of the group.

Historically, research teams have been based in a single geographical location, to make it possible to engage in regular conversation. In recent times, the internet has made it possible for researchers to collaborate even when they are located many thousands of miles from each other. Even in these situations, however, international research teams will usually find ways to organise face-to-face meetings on a regular basis.

From the point of view of a person who may be taking a lead role in a research study, for example a student undertaking a dissertation project, other people can take on a variety of supplementary roles:

- Source of research skills and knowledge (tutor, supervisor, mentor, consultant).
- Provider of emotional support.
- Dialogue and challenge around theoretical ideas and analysis of data.
- Provider of complementary skills – no one individual is good at everything – one member of a team may generate creative possibilities, another one is well organised and gets things done on time, another one binds the group together, etc.
- Member of a research network.

In addition to these functions within a research team, counselling and psychotherapy research almost always requires collaboration with people and groups within the community, such as clinic managers who enable access to clients, and therapists or clients who are willing to be interviewed or complete questionnaires. An important external point of contact for any research study is its relationship with the relevant ethics committee; developing an understanding of ethics committee requirements and procedures is essential to the success of any project.

The collective nature of research can be regarded as a source of potential enjoyment and personal development. Research relationships offer opportunities to spend time with people you like, or who stimulate personal growth and learning.

Exercise 1.8   Who is in your research team?

Who are the people available to you in relation to your research endeavours, or who might be available? How satisfying and supportive is your contact with these individuals? In what ways might the collaborative dimension of your research be enhanced? If you are at the stage of planning a research study, who can you recruit to your team?

Principle 8: Social context is always a key factor in any research on therapy

Counselling and psychotherapy are forms of help that focus on individual and personal dimensions of experience. Often, therapy will explore the ways in which family and community processes have shaped the beliefs and choices of a client. But therapy is not primarily an instrument of social change. Nevertheless, one of the defining characteristics of practically useful therapy research is that it takes account of social context. The reason for this is that while research seeks to identify general therapeutic interventions, strategies and concepts, in practice these ideas are always applied within a specific social, organisational and cultural context. For example, a great deal of research has shown that therapy tends to have a better outcome if a strong alliance between therapist and client has been established by around the third session (Muran and Barber, 2010). This is a useful idea, because it draws therapist attention to a particular aspect of therapy that needs to take priority right at the start. At the same time, studies on the therapeutic alliance are of limited value to practitioners unless they also describe the context within which a study has taken place. For example, the therapeutic alliance may be different in court-mandated clients, or bureaucratically-organised managed care systems, compared to clients seen in private practice settings. The type of relationship a person has with a professional expert is likely to differ across culture and social class. There are historical differences in therapeutic relationships – for example, contemporary clients have access to much more information about therapy, and possibly have clearer expectations, compared to clients seen by Freud or Rogers. The context includes the therapist. Some therapists are trained to be highly attuned to relationship factors, while other therapists have been trained in ways that may lead them to be less relationally-oriented.

The example of research into the therapeutic alliance illustrates some of the ways in which it can be hard, or even impossible, for practitioners to evaluate the implications of research findings for their own personal practice, in the absence of information about the context within which the research was carried out. In general, therapy research studies typically provide only limited data on the cultural and organisational context.

There is also a broader sense in which an appreciation of social context has an influence on therapy research. Shifts in approaches to therapy that are used in a society largely arise as a result of social change. For example, during the eighteenth century there was a shift from religiously-oriented to secular frameworks for emotional support. In the early and mid-twentieth century, psychoanalytic ideas and practices were transformed through exposure to American cultural values. From the 1970s, brief therapy and managed care emerged as a means of accommodating the requirements of large-scale healthcare systems. At around the same time, feminist, multicultural and gay-affirmative models of therapy were a response to political change in western democracies in the direction of equality of opportunity and social inclusion. A powerful analysis of these developments can be found in Cushman (1990, 1992, 1995). Another valuable perspective can be found in the writing of Jerome Frank (1973) who studied psychotherapeutic practices at various times in history and in a variety of cultures. His conclusion was that it was possible to identify common factors, such as the provision of healing relationships and rituals that instilled hope, even when the ways in which these elements were delivered varied a great deal according to the social context.

Exercise 1.9   Developing an awareness of the social context of research

Here are two 'thought experiments' that are relevant to the development of an awareness of the significance of social context in therapy research. First, as you read research papers, take a few moments to reflect on the extent to which the findings reported by the authors might be linked to the specific group of clients and therapists that were studied, the organisational context in which data were collected, and the time and place when the study was carried out. To get a handle on these issues, it can be useful to try to imagine how clients, therapists, etc. from different social groups or at different points in the past, might have responded to the research tasks (e.g., questionnaires, interviews) used in the study. A second reflective experiment involves taking some time to make a list of cultural factors within your own research. How might you collect information on these factors and report that information in publications in a way that would be helpful for readers? To what extent, and in what ways, would paying attention to such factors diminish or deepen your understanding of the topic you were investigating?

Principle 9: The research training environment plays a crucial role

Although several thousand research studies on counselling and psychotherapy have been published over the past decades, is seems clear that there exists a substantial gap between research and practice (Cohen et al., 1986; Morrow-Bradley and Elliott, 1986). For the most part, therapy practitioners do not regard the findings of research studies as being relevant to their work, and are reluctant to take part in research. One of the reasons for this is that the research inputs that counselling and psychotherapy students receive as part of their primary training are a major turn-off, and leave most of them with a negative attitude to research in all its forms. A team of researchers, led by Charles Gelso at the University of Maryland, has carried out a series of studies into the characteristics of facilitative and non-facilitative research environments in university postgraduate degrees in counselling and clinical psychology in North America (Gelso et al., 2013). Their conclusion, on the basis of this evidence, was that there exists a set of essential characteristics associated with research training environments that can prove effective in encouraging an interest in research and capacity use research to inform practice:

1. Members of academic faculty function as models of appropriate scientific behaviour and attitudes.

2. Scientific activity is positively reinforced in the environment, both formally and informally.

3. Students are involved in research early in their training, and in a minimally threat-ening way.

4. The environment emphasises science as a partly social-interpersonal experience.

5. It is emphasised in training that all research studies are limited and flawed in one way or another.

6. Varied approaches to research are taught and valued.

7. The importance of students looking inward for research ideas and questions is emphasised when they are developmentally ready for this responsibility.

8. Students are shown how science and practice are interconnected.

9. Statistics teaching is made relevant to applied research; and emphasis is given to the logic of a research design as well as statistics.

10. Students are taught during the latter part of their programme how research may be conducted in practice settings.

11. Each student is able to develop a relationship with their research supervisor that is characterised by creating a rapport, being an apprentice to the supervisor, and identifying with that supervisor as a role model.

All of these elements of a productive research training environment make sense to me, based on my experiences as both a student and teacher. One further element that I would want to add is this:

12. Encouragement and an opportunity to work collaboratively on research tasks with fellow students.

The importance of these 12 themes is backed up by the findings of a study by Duffy et al. (2013), who interviewed research-active counselling psychologists about their views on what had been helpful in their research careers.

Gelso et al. (2013) carried out their research in North America, and their findings inevitably reflect the experience of tutors and students on courses where the majority of participants held psychology degrees. In other countries, a significant proportion of counselling and psychotherapy trainees will come from non-psychology backgrounds, and there will be differences in the relative weighting given to research as against clinical practice and personal development. Nevertheless, it is likely that there are some general lessons that can be derived from the work done by Gelso et al. (2013). Essentially, what they are saying is that if trainee therapists are to appreciate the value of research, they need to be taught by tutors who model how this is done. Gelso et al. (2013) are in effect recommending a form of apprenticeship learning, where practical research tasks are tied in to what a student can handle at each stage, and the students join in with research being carried out by their tutors or supervisors before being expected to come up with their own ideas. Throughout training, research is not treated as an academic requirement that is separate from clinical practice, but as a means of enhancing that practice.

The development of facilitative research environments within university and college training programmes is not just a matter of enabling and inspiring students to do good research and then continue to use research to inform practice throughout their careers. These environments are also essential for research-active academic staff, by giving access to a steady stream of students who are able to contribute to the research being done by the tutor and then can take that line of inquiry forward in creative ways. Finally, such environments function as a resource for therapy practitioners and managers of therapy services and clinics, through providing flexible, low-cost or no-cost opportunities for research collaboration.

Conclusions

This set of principles is intended to function as a series of points of reference for anyone carrying out research in therapy. The following chapters provide guidelines and information on general research skills, such as using qualitative and quantitative methods, and then show how these skills can be applied to create different types of research product. Throughout all of these chapters, it will be helpful to refer back to basic principles, by reflecting on various questions: for example, ask yourself 'How does using this research method, or recruiting participants from this population, look when considered in light of the principle of generating practical knowledge, using my own reflexive knowledge, and so on?' These principles can be viewed as equipping novice researchers to reflect critically and constructively on the many decision points that can arise throughout the life of a research project.

Suggestions for further reading

The research principles outlined in this chapter reflect my own experience as a researcher, research supervisor, and consumer of research. I make no claim that these principles are comprehensive or complete, or are right for everyone. In the end, it is vital to be able to identify one's own personal principles. A sense of the underlying personal experiences and values that have shaped the work of well-known contemporary figures in the field of therapy research can be found in the following edited books:

Castonguay, L.G., Muran, J.C., Angus, L., et al. (eds) (2010) *Bringing Psychotherapy Research to Life: Understanding Change through the Work of Leading Clinical Researchers.* Washington, DC: American Psychological Association.

Hoshmand, L. and Martin, J. (eds) (1994) *Method Choice and Inquiry Process: Lessons from Programmatic Research in Therapeutic Practice.* New York: Teachers' Press.

Soldz, S. and McCullough, L. (eds) (2000) *Reconciling Empirical Knowledge and Clinical Experience: The Art and Science of Psychotherapy.* Washington, DC: American Psychological Association.

Companion website material

The companion website (http://study.sagepub.com/mcleod) for this book provides access to a range of papers in which leading researchers reflect on the values and principles that have influenced their work:

Busch, R., Strong, T. and Lock, A. (2011) Making sense of epistemological conflict in the evaluation of narrative therapy and evidence-based psychotherapy, *Refereed Proceedings of Doing Psychology: Manawatu Doctoral Research Symposium,* 2011: 49–56.

Duffy, R.D., Torrey, C.L., Bott, E.M. et al. (2013) Time management, passion, and collabora-
    tion: a qualitative study of highly research productive counseling psychologists, *The
    Counseling Psychologist*, 41: 881–917.
Gray, K. and Wegner, D.M. (2013) Six guidelines for interesting research, *Perspectives on
    Psychological Science*, 8: 549–53.
Mackrill, T. (2009) Constructing client agency in psychotherapy research, *Journal of
    Humanistic Psychology*, 49: 193–206.
Rogers, C.R. (1965) Some questions and challenges facing a humanistic psychology, *Journal
    of Humanistic Psychology*, 5: 1–5.
Strong, T. (2010) Collaboration, generativity, rigor, and imagination: Four words to focus and
    animate our practice-oriented inquiries, *Human Systems: Journal of Therapy, Consultation
    and Training*, 21: 380–96.

2

Reading the Literature: Placing Research in Context

Introduction

A key activity, in the opening stages of doing a research study, consists of becoming familiar with previous research on the topic in which you are interested. The aim of this chapter is to provide guidance on how to read the literature in as productive a manner as possible. For anyone who is using this book to inform their preparation for undertaking a research study for the first time, it is recommended that this chapter should be read in tandem with the next, which focuses on how to decide on a research question. It does not make a lot of sense to read the research literature in the absence of at least some notion of the intended research topic or question. Equally, it is not possible to develop a research question in the absence of an appreciation of the types of research, and types of research question, that have gone before.

Why is it important to be familiar with the literature?

There are three main reasons why thorough and careful reading of the research literature represents an essential element in any research study:

1. *Not re-inventing the wheel.* No matter how esoteric your research topic seems to be, it is almost certain that someone has studied it (or something like it) before. It is always best to find whatever previous research has been done, and build on this, rather than designing a study completely from scratch.
2. *Ensuring that your research has the maximum impact.* Practical, research-based knowledge consists of findings from a network or web of interlocking research studies. This is because no one research study can ever be rigorous enough to yield reliable knowledge, taken in isolation. The existence of a rich literature of interconnected studies ensures that the findings of each study are supported by findings from other studies, and the limitations of any particular study are counterbalanced by corresponding strengths elsewhere in the literature. As a consequence, if readers cannot see how your research is embedded within the literature, they are likely to ignore it.
3. *Ensuring that your research meets the required standard.* It is hard to achieve reliable, valid and ethically sound knowledge, in any field of inquiry. Researchers are always looking for ways to do research better. Current research is always informed by an on-going cycle of critical debate and methodological innovation. If your research does not take account of this ever-shifting 'quality threshold' there is a risk that it may be viewed as lacking in credibility.

These factors, taken together, demonstrate why the experience of doing research always needs to involve a willingness to become immersed in the relevant literature. However, it is also vital to be realistic. It is not possible for undergraduate and Master's-level researchers to gain a comprehensive understanding of the literature in their area of inquiry, because of the limited amount of time available to them. By contrast, there is a general expectation that a doctoral candidate will, at the point of submitting their thesis/dissertation, be a world expert on their chosen topic. Developing an in-depth knowledge of the literature represents an aspect of the inquiry process where it is extremely helpful to be able to function as an apprentice, and be guided through the relevant literature by a research supervisor or mentor who already possesses a close familiarity with that particular body of writing.

Suggested preliminary reading

Cooper, M. (2008) *Essential Research Findings in Counselling and Psychotherapy: The Facts are Friendly.* London: Sage. Provides an overview of the therapy research literature and what it contains.

McLeod, J. (2013) *An Introduction to Research in Counselling and Psychotherapy.* London: Sage. Chapter 4 ('Finding your way around the research literature') offers an introduction to how the therapy research literature is organised. The first half of Chapter 5 also describes where the task of literature reviewing fits into the overall process of conducting a research study.

Finding and organising the literature: practical skills and strategies

Carrying out a literature review is a practical skill. As with any other practical skill, practice is necessary to improve performance. A first attempt to conduct a research review is typically associated with frustration and wasted time. More experienced researchers can complete reviews much more quickly. There are five main areas of skill that need to be developed: *searching, organising, reading research papers, quality evaluation* and *time-management.*

Searching skills consist of a set of competencies associated with the task of identifying relevant items of literature. The first step is to be able to generate appropriate search terms. A search term is a word or phrase that serves as a 'tag' or label for the topic being reviewed. The task of a reviewer involves scanning the literature looking for these tags. A lot of the time, research in a particular area of interest may have been described using a range of tags. For example, I have been interested in the topic of what clients want from therapy. Research in this area has used many different terms or concepts: attitudes, expectations, beliefs, preferences, credibility of therapy, insider knowledge. In order to find interesting studies, I need to keep a lookout for all of these terms in the titles, abstracts and keywords lists of articles. The next step in searching involves deciding on where to look: online databases such as PsycInfo or Medline, general databases such as Google Scholar, and reference lists of published book and articles. How far to take this? Sometimes it can be helpful to contact leading researchers, to ask them if there are any relevant studies they know about that have not yet been published.

Organising skills consist of a set of competencies that are applied to the job of keeping track of the information that is generated by the search process. There are bibliographic tools, such as EndNote and Papyrus, that are able to copy on-line reference details into the personal database of the researcher, where they can be categorised and commented upon. Alternatively, it is possible to construct a similar system just using WORD files. A decision needs to be made on whether a record is to be kept of how many items were generated using each search term, and the basis on which some were rejected and others were retained for detailed scrutiny.

Decisions also need to be made about the extent to which it is sufficient to read the abstract of a study, or whether a more in-depth appraisal of the entire document is required (and whether this is better done using a paper copy rather than on-screen). One way or another, anyone carrying out a literature review needs to develop a robust and effective filing system.

Reading skills are important, as a core skill in all of this concerns the ability to read a research paper in an efficient manner. For anyone who has not been trained in psychology or one of the sciences, the structure of a typical quantitative research paper can seem strange, confusing and mysterious. For individuals who do have a background in science or psychology, the structure and language of many qualitative research articles can be equally opaque. After a while, most readers become familiar with the way that research papers are written, and can quite rapidly extract the information they need from any paper that they come across. But to begin with, this can prove to be a slow process.

Quality evaluation skills always play a part in the review process. When drawing conclusions from the research literature, it is essential to find some way of differentiating between studies that provide strong and credible evidence, and studies that are less convincing. One way of doing this is to include only studies published in journals that use a peer review procedure. Another way is to evaluate or screen each potentially relevant study by using a rating scale for methodological quality. A further strategy involves including everything that is found, but incorporating this into the review, a commentary on the methodological strengths and weaknesses of each item.

Time-management skills are often a factor in literature reviewing, for a variety of reasons. Quite often, an article or book may be identified as relevant to the review, but may need to be ordered through a library, thus leading to a delay. Careful and critical reading of research articles is time-consuming. Also, reading one article may generate new ideas about further directions that the review might take, leading to a renewed search cycle. All of this may be happening right at the start of a project, when as a researcher you will be under pressure of time to meet a deadline for submitting your proposal. For these reasons, it is important to plan carefully around when and how a review is to be carried out. For example, it can be useful to devote an intensive block of time to a review as early as possible, as a means of getting 'into' the literature and accumulating key articles or sending off for them. This makes it possible for the next available blocks of time to consist of more relaxed reading of items as they come in, culminating in a final intensive block of time when everything comes together into an actual review document.

There are many sources of training and support available to researchers, in relation to these areas of skill. University library staff tend to possess high levels of expertise around search skills and organising skills, and may offer training workshops and/or tutorial help on an individual or small group basis. There are also websites that offer information on quality evaluation procedures, as well as many review articles that include information on the quality evaluation approach that was adopted and the rationale behind it. Research training courses and research supervisors are good places to look for ideas about reading research papers and time management. For practitioners, practice research networks should be able to offer support in all of these areas.

Exercise 2.1   What are the key words in your area of interest?

Allow yourself at least 30 minutes to reflect in a creative way on all of the possible concepts and terms that might be relevant to your chosen research topic or question. Think about the ways in which the topic might be understood within different theoretical frameworks, and the specific terminology that may have been used within these paradigms. Also think about the way that the topic has been defined and understood within different areas of practice or professional communities. Once you have generated a list or 'mind-map' of key words, identify the terms that are likely to have been most widely used in the literature, and which would offer the best start-points for your literature search.

What you are looking for

Reviewing the literature is not a matter of wandering around a body of knowledge, in the hope that some conclusions will emerge through a process of osmosis. To gain maximum advantage from time spent reading the literature, you will need to be clear about what you are looking for.

To some extent, reviewing the literature is similar to fishing with a net. Rather than just using a net that catches one type of fish, it will be helpful to build a net that enables you to pay attention to, and make notes on, several aspects of the literature that may be of potential significance:

How is this topic conceptualised and theorised?

What are the main debates or controversies within this area of inquiry?

What are the various methodologies and research instruments and tools (e.g., specific questionnaires or interview schedules) that have been deployed within this area of knowledge?

What are the ethical issues associated with this area of inquiry? How have these issues been addressed?

Are there distinct 'lines of inquiry' or sequences of studies that can be identified? Or: to what extent is this area of knowledge fragmented, with studies making few references to other studies?

What do we know now, in terms of conclusions that can be made with confidence?

To what extent, and in what ways, are these conclusions conditional on, or associated with, specific populations (e.g., true for people in one culture) or specific methodologies (e.g., different findings emerge from qualitative and quantitative studies, or from the use of different quantitative questionnaires)?

What is missing from the literature?

What do we need to know next (i.e., what do authors identify as necessary directions for further research)?

Trawling for all of these types of information makes it possible to generate a nuanced and critical review. Perhaps, in the end, what you are really interested in is a basic 'findings' question such as 'How effective is CBT for depression?' or 'What is the role of empathy in the process of therapy?' An appreciation of the ways in which 'findings' (i.e., the conclusions of research studies) are linked to the populations studied, methodological approaches adopted, theoretical models used by researchers, and so on, makes a review much more interesting and more useful in practical terms.

An alternative metaphor for the review process is to see this as hunting for treasure. There are three types of treasure to look out for. The first type consists of glittering and wonderful studies that stand out from the rest. Such studies may not necessarily exist within a particular topic area, but if they do they deserve to be showcased within the review that is being compiled. The second type of treasure is a variant on the first type, namely hidden treasure. Sometimes, within studies, there will be nuggets of information that may not have been recognised by the authors as particularly glittering, but whose value shines out when seen in the context of a wider review. The third type of treasure consists of personal epiphany studies. Sometimes it is possible to find studies that immediately strike a chord, in terms of what the researcher hopes to achieve in the research. The researcher may not necessarily wish to replicate a particular study (although this may be a good thing to do) – it may just be that there is an aspect of the design or methodology of the study, or the way that the samples were recruited, that represents a vital piece of the jigsaw. Another type of personal treasure consists of finding studies that are most similar to the study that you as a researcher intend to carry out. When the time comes to write up your study, or defend it in a viva, one of the key questions that you will need to answer will be this: 'What does your research build on, or represent the next step on from, in terms of how it connects up with previous research?' The point here is that a review of the literature is, at least in part, a search for studies or bits of studies that can function as templates or exemplars.

Exercise 2.2   Developing skills around critical analysis of research papers

Find some colleagues who are interested in reading research papers. Set up some face-to-face or on-line meetings where you can share your critiques of the strengths and limitations of specific published studies. If possible, invite some experienced and expert researchers to critique the same articles. Ask your research supervisor if you can collaborate around review-ing articles that have been submitted to journals – if you can do this, you will get to see the (anonymous) reports submitted by other reviewers, which is a fascinating experience.

Issues and challenges

There are many issues and challenges that frequently arise in relation to the task of reviewing the therapy research literature. Here are some of the most frequently voiced ones.

Too much literature. Sometimes, a literature search rapidly generates several hundred items that are potentially relevant. For example, a review of 'the effective-ness of psychotherapy for depression' or the 'the relative effectiveness of psychotherapy vs. medication for depression' would produce several hundred hits, including a large number of empirical studies. This situation can be overwhelming and scary for novice researchers. There are, however, several straightforward strate-gies for dealing with this eventuality. One approach is to start by looking for existing reviews. If a lot of research has been carried out on a topic, then it is highly likely that someone, or several different research teams, will have already subjected it to a systematic review. It may then be sufficient to conduct a 'review of reviews'. Alternatively it may make sense to anchor your own review in the most recent pub-lished review, or the most rigorous review, and add on any examples of studies conducted since the cut-off date of the published review. Another strategy is to nar-row the focus of the review. For example, a search for studies of the effectiveness of therapy for depression will generate a large number of items, whereas a search for studies of the effectiveness of *psychodynamic* therapy for depression will generate a somewhat smaller number of items. Narrowing the review may be a good choice in any case, because the study being planned by a researcher will inevitably consist of a specific form of therapy offered to a specific client group.

Not enough literature. Another scary scenario for novice researchers arises if the review turns up nothing, or next to nothing. For example, my guess is that even the most thorough search for studies of the significance of tummy-rumbling in therapy would produce no more than four studies e.g., King, 2011; Sussman, 2001). It is possible that these studies could provide a sufficient platform for further research. However, it would not be a substantial platform. In this instance, it may make sense to expand the review, to include other similar phenomena. There may be studies on other bodily events in therapy sessions, such as the client feeling sick or getting a headache. There is certainly a literature on the broader topic of non-verbal communication in therapy. Another strategy is to search within studies. It may be that tummy-rumbling is mentioned in passing in some studies of the client's experience of therapy, or in some case studies. Finding such evidence, when a concept is not flagged up in the abstract of a study, takes a lot of time and effort. In the end, it may be that all that can be done will be to offer a practical or theoretical rationale for investigating a neglected topic, and make sure that the study is described as 'exploratory' in nature.

Literature reviews in qualitative studies. Sometimes, people conducting qualitative research studies can encounter difficulties in relation to the task of contextualising their proposal, or their study as a whole, in previous research. There are two main ways in which this problem can arise. First, some leading figures within the phenomenology and grounded theory traditions of qualitative research would advise that a researcher should abstain from reading the literature in advance of collecting the data (e.g., interviewing participants) and analysing that data. What they are concerned about is that immersion in the literature will mean that the researcher will have too many preconceived ideas, and as a result will not be sufficiently open and sensitive to the experiences of participants. This is a perfectly reasonable position to take. However, this creates problems for anyone (i.e., most researchers) who needs to submit a proposal before they can get permission to start their study. It also fails to take account of the fact that, when research is carried out by a practitioner, such as a counsellor or psychotherapy, the researcher has already been trained and socialised into a particular set of assumptions about what happens in therapy, and, by implication, what they will find in their research. The solution to this dilemma, one that is increasingly being adopted by qualitative researchers, is to complete a preliminary literature review, but then to put in place a set of procedures that aim to promote researcher reflexivity. These procedures may include keeping a research diary, working with colleagues or an auditor who will challenge the researcher's assumptions, and encouraging research participants to be involved in the design, data collection, analysis and reporting of the study. The idea here is that reading the literature may have a positive influence in helping to sensitise the researcher to what might be found, but that there are strategies that can be implemented to make sure that other things will be found as well. The second problem that some qualitative researchers have with literature reviews is that, in general, qualitative studies are 'discovery-oriented' – that is to say, you do not know what you are going to find until you have actually embarked on the study. The problem here is that the research may generate themes and findings that were absent in the studies that were reviewed in the literature review carried out at the start of the project. This can be a tough call. A qualitative study that produces new insights is probably an exceptional piece of work, and these insights deserve to be fully explored in any publications that are produced. On the other hand, by the time these insights have crystallised, the researcher may have run out of time and will not be able to do much more reading. Probably the best answer to this is to produce a paper or thesis that is mainly contextualised within the original literature review, but also mentions the new idea or theme as an emergent or tentative area that will be pursued in a later article. This buys some time to assemble the background literature that is required. Some qualitative researchers, in this situation, will try to explain in their primary thesis or article why a change of direction was necessary. This is hard to pull off effectively – there is a risk that the researcher may come across as muddled ('I should have thought of this idea at the start and it took me by surprise') rather than as someone who has in fact been highly creative and resourceful.

It is a mistake to regard any of the issues and challenges that can arise during the process of conducting a literature review as personal failings, or to fall into the trap of believing that there is one correct solution that the researcher can arrive at through personal diligence. These are problems that are part of the intrinsic messiness of the research process. In most circumstances, there will be many ways that the issue can be satisfactorily resolved. Investment in dialogue, where different people can share and discuss the pros and cons of the various possible ways forward, is the preferred route.

Exercise 2.3   Getting inside key studies

What are the two or three essential studies that you have unearthed during your search? Read these studies carefully, and on more than one occasion. Try to get 'inside' each study. What are these studies telling you, about how to go about investigating your chosen research topic? What are they saying to you, about what *not* to do?

Writing the review

There is no single correct way to write a literature review. The lengths and style of a review will depend on its purpose (e.g., a section in a research proposal, the introduction to a research paper, a chapter in a thesis or dissertation). There are also free-standing published review articles, discussed in Chapter 10). It is essential, therefore, to follow the requirements that are stipulated for the particular type of review that is required, and to take advice from mentors and supervisors. Writing a research literature review that is comprehensive, thoughtful and easy to follow, is a demanding academic task. This is because the writer needs to analyse and present complex information, while at the same time evaluating the quality of that information. Both of these aspects of review-writing present challenges for novice researchers. Usually, inexperienced researchers will find it much easier to compile an actual research paper or report than to write a literature review. This is because a research paper is structured around clearly-understood sections (introduction, methods, results, etc.), and there is a sense in which the author just needs to fill in the blanks in the framework. Reviews of the research literature tend to work best when complex information is presented in a linear, step-by-step manner, leading to clear conclusions. Literature reviews tend to get into trouble when the author tries to say everything all at the same time. It is essential to keep in mind, when writing a review 'intro' for a research paper or proposal, that the most important section is the section where the review looks at studies that are the immediate precursors to the actual study that is being proposed or reported. This is the bit that really needs to be clearly described and carefully argued, because it is the only section of a review where there is space to go into detail. The earlier sections of a review, that describe the general background and history of research into the topic, are always necessarily somewhat condensed and generalised.

Conclusions

For anyone undertaking a therapy research study for the first time, placing their research in the context of the research literature is a vital and challenging task. It is essential to be realistic about what can be achieved. There is a massive amount of therapy research that is published every year, and it is hard to find an initial foothold in what can seem like a daunting and impenetrable mountain of knowledge. The message of this chapter is that reviewing the literature is a skill, which gets easier with practice. The intention of the chapter has been to suggest some starting points and strategies. Further discussion of the literature review process can be found in Chapter 10, around the possibility of going beyond the kind of literature reviewing that is required during the planning of an investigation, and attempting to compile a publishable review article or report.

Suggestions for further reading

The ideas and strategies introduced in this chapter are explored in more detail in the following:

Aveyard, H. (2010) *Doing a Literature Review in Health and Social Care: A Practical Guide.* Maidenhead: Open University Press.
Greenhalgh, T. (2010) *How to Read a Paper: The Basics of Evidence-based Medicine* (4th edn). Chichester: Wiley.
Jesson, J., Matheson, L. and Lacey, F.M. (2011) *Doing Your Literature Review: Traditional and Systematic Techniques.* London: Sage.

Companion website material

The companion website (http://study.sagepub.com/mcleod) facilitates exploration of the counselling and psychotherapy research literature through links to the web pages of influential researchers and research groups.

3

Developing Your Research Question

Introduction

Research is guided by questions. The aim of research is to be able to answer questions and generate new questions that open up previously taken-for-granted areas
of experience. So where do such questions come from? Some counselling and psychotherapy research is stimulated by 'burning questions' that arise from practical
experience. But many other would-be researchers, particularly those faced with the
demand to choose a research topic that will have to be pursued for a college or
university degree, will become blocked and uncertain at this point. There are so
many potential topics from which to select. Considerations of relevance, importance, practicability, legitimacy and interest value flood in, making the choice even
harder. In yet other situations, the research question is given or handed over – the
researcher is recruited to work within an already existing programme of research,
and has relatively little scope to influence the direction that the study will take.

Formulating a research question (or set of questions) represents a key step in the
research process, because it involves moving from a general topic to a specific,
focused investigation of some aspect of that topic. If you are doing research, people
will ask you what you are doing research *on*. They may also ask what you are
looking at. These images imply the existence of a research topic that is something
'out there' in the external world. A research *topic* usually refers to a broad area of
interest, within which many questions can be asked. By contrast, a research question is like a searchlight that illuminates parts of this area of interest, or like a tool
for dissecting it or digging into it. Areas of interest are expressed in book titles and
chapter titles. The titles of research studies are quite different. If you have a
research question that reads like the title of a book or a chapter in a book, chances
are that it is not yet sufficiently focused, concrete and specific to operate successfully as a research question.

The aim of this chapter is to offer some ideas about how to arrive at an interesting, relevant and feasible research question. We begin by thinking about where
research topics come from, and how to choose a topic. The next section of the
chapter introduces some strategies for refining and focusing the topic into a set of
specific and researchable questions. The chapter concludes by exploring the language of research questions, and ways that different research methodologies are
associated with different types of question.

For anyone who is using this book to inform their preparation for undertaking
a research study for the first time, it is recommended that this chapter should be

read alongside Chapter 2, which focuses on using the research literature. It is not possible to develop a research question in the absence of an appreciation of the types of research, and types of research question, that have gone before. Equally, it does not make a lot of sense to read the research literature in the absence of at least some notion of the intended research topic or question.

This chapter is somewhat longer than others in the book. This is because it explores a key aspect of doing research: namely, learning to 'think like a researcher'. It is one thing to be interested in an area of theory or practice, from the position of a consumer of research. It is quite another thing to be a producer of research. The focus here is, at one level, on the steps that are involved in choosing and refining a research topic and question. At a deeper level, however, what is being talked about is a more fundamental shift in identity.

Deciding on a research topic

There are many sources of research ideas, and many counselling and psychotherapy research studies that need to be carried out. The choice of a research topic, from within the many possibilities that exist, is a personal matter. Before committing to a research topic, it is necessary to devote some time to exploring various possibilities.

Sources of research ideas

Possible research topics do not exist in a vacuum as abstract ideas. Rather, the meaning of any potential research idea is always embedded within a complex web of social, interpersonal and personal relationships and meanings. For anyone thinking about embarking on a research journey, unravelling these webs can be helpful in clarifying the personal pay-off of alternative research directions. It is possible to identify four main sources for research ideas.

The existing research literature. There are many research possibilities to be found within the literature. Within any specific area of research, there are on-going research programmes that cry out for the application of a particular research methodology or theory to a new population, or the replication of existing findings. It is not hard to find neglected lines of inquiry that have been opened up but not been pursued fully. Research papers often conclude by identifying areas for further research. Occasionally, leading researchers will review progress on research into a particular topic, and make suggestions regarding future research priorities. Choosing a research topic that has emerged from the research literature has the advantage of making it rather easier to justify the study, make connections to previous literature, and choose a methodology – all of these factors are already taken care of.

Policy and practice initiatives. There is a continuous stream of calls for research, and funding initiatives, that emerge from government departments and other organisations. For example, in recent years the issues associated with an ageing population have resulted in many research initiatives around the care of older people. There are also many policy and practice research project ideas generated at a local level by counselling and psychotherapy agencies and service providers. For example, annual reports from therapy agencies may indicate those agencies' desire to collect information on certain aspects of their work. Alternatively, when asked, managers may have a clear idea of what it is they need to know in order to make their organisation more effective. In addition, local agencies may have ideas about research projects that they would like to develop in response to government initiatives. Choosing a research topic that fits with national or local policy and practice initiatives is a good way to ensure organisational collaboration, and perhaps even some funding. This kind of project also easily passes the 'so what' test, as the potential social value of the study has been established by experts in the field.

Personal contact. A valuable source of research ideas comprises other people with whom one might wish to work. These individuals could be members of an existing research network or interest group, or potential research supervisors, mentors or colleagues. Selecting a research topic that is aligned with, or part of, on-going research carried out by others, may represent a particularly attractive option for new researchers, because it offers the possibility of support from others and perhaps also the chance to learn in an apprenticeship role. The disadvantage of making this kind of choice is that it may involve abandoning, or compromising, one's own personal cherished research ideas.

Personal 'burning questions'. What does the question mean to you personally? Almost all practitioner research, as well as many student research projects, are motivated by a burning interest, a need to know more about some area of experience. This source of research ideas may include topics associated with first-hand experience as a client or therapist, or second-hand observation of episodes in the life of a close family member. These root experiences may be positive ('I want to demonstrate the importance of spirituality as a factor in therapy') or negative ('I want to draw attention to the risks of a particular type of therapy'). The advantages of working with a research topic that is personally highly meaningful are that the researcher is highly motivated and may possess special insight into the topic. The disadvantages are that the researcher may find it difficult to make connections between their unique experience and the existing literature, may come across as biased, and may be too emotionally involved to complete the study successfully.

To some extent, the majority of research topics will connect in some way or another with all four of these sources. However, within any specific topic area, the relative weighting of the four sources is unlikely to be completely equal.

Exercise 3.1   Reflecting on the sources of your research ideas

Give yourself some time to write about, reflect, or discuss with a colleague, potential research topics that are associated with each of these four sources: the literature, policy and practice initiatives, people you might work with, and personal interest. Map out the pros and cons, for you, of pursuing questions that originate in different sources.

The personal meaning of the research

In big, programmatic research studies, the research question may have been laid down by someone else (a principal investigator, a government committee), with the result that it might possess only limited personal meaning for the person or people actually carrying out the research. By contrast, the kind of practitioner research or student research undertaken by readers of this book tends not to be like that. Such research is much more integrated with the life of the researcher, and so it is important to be aware of the conscious and implicit meanings that such an investigation may hold. Some of the reasons for examining the personal meaning of research include:

- avoiding potential sources of bias, for example through collecting data that 'confirm' what the researcher needs to believe;
- making the research more alive and interesting, and not getting trapped into a sense that the topic is alienating and distant;
- creating the possibility of drawing on emotional and spiritual sources of understanding, to augment cognitive/intellectual analysis of the topic;
- being clear about what you want from the research – for example, are you intending or hoping that completion of the research will open up new career opportunities (and if so, how might the choice of topic and the way that topic is investigated, make the maximum contribution to accomplishing that goal)?;
- from a psychotherapeutic perspective, creating the conditions for using 'countertransference' reactions to the research in a positive or constructive way: all researchers have feelings about the work they do; therapy researchers possess the skills and awareness to begin to understand what these feelings might mean;
- acting in accordance with a view of scientific inquiry which questions the role of the detached scientific 'observer', and holds instead that knowledge is intrinsically linked to personal interests and values.

Becoming aware of the personal meaning of research can be a painful process. In my own work, for example, I know that the research I have done into experiential groups, and into storytelling in therapy, has been closely tied to areas in which I have a strong personal need to learn. It is as if there has been a personal gap that research has helped to fill. That research has been personally enabling but also disturbing. In carrying it out I have been sensitive to the danger that exploring personally meaningful issues solely through research could lead in the direction of an over-intellectualised kind of pseudo-resolution that could cut off what are much more important emotional and interpersonal dimensions of who I am, or can be, in relation to these areas of my life. Research as a way of knowing needs to operate alongside other ways of knowing, such as practical action or therapy. Other dangers include inarticulacy (learning about the research topic at a feeling level, but having difficulty putting it into words), and being personally 'thrown' by what the research uncovers.

One of the consequences of examining the personal meaning of a research topic may be a decision *not* to pursue that topic. It could turn out that opening up a set of issues by subjecting them to research inquiry could lead to so much personal material being generated that it might be difficult to complete the project in the time allocated. For example, this can happen when someone researches an issue that is linked to a problematic life episode. One student was drawn to studying the experience of people who had been hospitalised during psychological breakdown. His interest in this question was derived from a similar experience he had undergone in his adolescence. As the research progressed, he found that more and more memories of this painful episode in his life were intruding into the research process. He decided to change topics and carry out his research on a different question.

The personal meaning of a research topic may be bound up with the meaning of doing research itself. For some people, carrying out a research study for a Master's degree or doctorate may have great personal significance, in defiantly demonstrating their intellectual abilities: 'At last I'll show them that I am just as good/clever as my brother/sister, etc.'. Other researchers may have a strong sense of responsibility toward the subjects of the research, a desire to use that research to help people in need, perhaps by using the findings to justify services and resources for those clients. Still others may be driven by a wish to be a heroic innovator, to make new discoveries (Freud was one of these). All of these factors can have an effect on the ultimate form that the research question takes.

Exercise 3.2   Exploring the personal meaning of potential research topics

What is the personal meaning of each potential research topic that you are considering? What are the points of connection between the topic and your life as a whole? To what extent might these points of connection make a positive contribution to the experience of doing the study, and to what extent might they be a hindrance?

Identifying the audience

One strategy for narrowing down the field and converging on a specific research topic is to think ahead to the end of the study and ask yourself 'Who is this for? Who is the intended audience for my research?' There are basically four audiences for counselling and psychotherapy research: the person doing the research; other counsellors, managers and policy makers; the general public; and other researchers. The interests of these different audiences are not by any means the same, although they will to some extent overlap. By contrast, research that is intended to have an impact on counsellors' practice will be likely to rely on case reports, and include detailed descriptive material on clients and interventions. Policy-oriented studies require data that can be used to address issues of cost-benefit and cost-effectiveness. Articles for the general public need to include vivid examples and case histories. Research aiming to advance the literature must be explicitly linked to issues, theories and methods already identified as important in previously published work. The anticipated audience or 'market' for a piece of research can be seen to have a crucial influence on the way a study is carried out, the type of methods that are used, and the form in which this is written up.

Once a researcher has selected his or her audience or audiences, it will be helpful to look at the kinds of research reports that have been published for that group. If the intended audience is identifiable and accessible (e.g., other therapists in a professional association, the management executive of an agency, key contributors to the research literature), it can be productive to go and ask them about the kind of study they would like to see carried out. It is worth noting, with some regret, that at the present moment it is difficult to envisage *clients* as consumers of research, except in so far as clients or would-be clients will read popular articles in newspapers and magazines.

A key factor in the choice of audience is the function that the research is intended to have in the personal or professional development or broader 'life projects' of the person carrying it out. The choice of research question is an issue that can usefully be worked on in personal therapy, or explored with supportive friends or colleagues. It is essential to be aware, for example, of the implications of tackling an investigation into a question that is very personal. With highly personal studies, a researcher may find it difficult to gain enough distance from his or her own individual experience to be able to grasp the bigger picture implied in the experiences of others. Also, it may be hard to write up autobiographical material that still evokes strong, raw feelings. There are other literary forms, such as novels, autobiographies or poetry, that are more appropriate in allowing a voice to the person. On the other hand, a research study that does not connect with any personal experience runs the danger of becoming dry and lacking in motivation and sparkle. If a research project is to be located within the context of the career development of the person carrying it out, then it is necessary to look at what this will entail in terms of how the findings might be presented to managers and interview panels, and to shape the study accordingly.

Exercise 3.3   Choosing a research topic: consulting other people

The preceding sections of this chapter have offered some ideas about where to look for research topics, and perspectives on factors to take into account when deciding on whether a particular topic is right for you at this stage of your life. In addition to thinking it through on your own, it will also be valuable to discuss these options with other people who know you well, or with whom you are involved in research roles (e.g., fellow students, academic advisers, research mentors and supervisors, etc.).

Deconstructing the topic: formulating researchable questions

Okay, so now you have decided on a topic. At this point you will need to identify some researchable questions that relate to the topic. It is worthwhile remembering here that not all questions are researchable. Very often, people new to research will generate questions that would happily supply a lifetime of endeavour for a lavishly funded research unit. The trick in finding a good research question is to narrow and sharpen the focus of inquiry so that it becomes a question that can be answered within the resources that are available, but without ending up with a study that is so dry and technical that the original meaning and value of the study, the big issues that inform the question, are lost. There are certainly questions which I personally have laid aside because I could not figure out *how* to research them. There are other research questions which just take time; it can be years before one feels able to say something on a topic, or even to know what are the meaningful questions that might be asked about it. As Flick (2011: 53) has written, 'research questions are like a door to the research field under study'. This image of a door is of course an important metaphor in therapy. Opening a door is good, but so is finding the handle, or even believing that such a door exists.

This section of the chapter offers some strategies for *deconstructing* your topic and the many different possible research questions that are contained within it. In any study, it is unlikely that there will be just one question. Part of the work of designing a research study is to identify the many questions that could be asked about a topic, and then to unfold or unpack the most promising of the questions into their constituent sub-questions. Usually, the original 'big' question that motivates a piece of research is too all-encompassing to be answered within a single study. It is only by deconstructing the question that it is possible to find a version of it that can be addressed meaningfully within the time and resources available.

When engaged in a process of deconstructing your research question, it can be helpful to adopt, at least temporarily, an attitude that 'anything is possible'. Of course, everything is not possible. At some point, your research ideas will need to match up with the reality of how much time you have, your research skills, what your supervisor wants you to do, your access to participants, and so on. But if you can develop a deep appreciation of the potential meaning and significance of your question, using these deconstruction techniques, you will then be in a better position to make the most of the practical opportunities that are available to you.

Start writing

It is never too early to start writing. Wolcott (1990) recommends that at the beginning of a study a researcher should write down as much as possible of the final report. This allows him or her to get a sense of what they already know, and what they need to know. It is also a way of being able to externalise personal biases so that these can be tackled out in the open rather than operating at an unconscious level. Keeping a research diary or journal is helpful as a means of recording hunches and ideas, and as an aid to reflecting on the personal meaning of the research.

Use your imagination

One of the things that you are trying to do, when deconstructing a research topic, is to generate a list of as many aspects as possible of the topic that could potentially be of interest. This task calls for imagination and creativity. Visual thinking techniques such as brainstorming and mind-mapping tend to increase awareness of the number of meanings that can be associated with a core concept. Useful suggestions on how to use these methods can be found in Buzan (2009) and Lupton (2011).

Try out alternative theoretical perspectives

A valuable means of developing a rich understanding of the research possibilities of a topic is to explore it from different theoretical perspectives or view it through alternative theoretical 'lenses'. For example, a researcher may be interested in the topic of how client preferences for various therapy interventions can have an impact on the drop-out from therapy (on the assumption that clients who are offered a therapy experience that seems alien or strange to them will just quit). A valuable activity, early in the research planning process, might include thinking about how the concept of 'preference' might be understood in relation to various theoretical models. For example, psychodynamic theory would draw attention to unconscious aspects of preferences, and perhaps also the role of defence mechanisms (e.g., some preferences might arise from a wish for insight and intimacy, while other preferences may be driven by avoiding difficult or painful emotional content). Cognitive-behavioural theory might regard preferences as reflections of beliefs or cognitive schema. Humanistic theorists would assume that preferences might reflect, at least in part, the sense that a person has about the possibility for growth and actualisation in their life. Narrative and postmodern therapy theories would focus on the existence of cultural narratives and discourses around mental health and healing, and perhaps also highlight ways in which those discourses differ according to gender, ethnicity and social class. This example illustrates some of the ways in which using theoretical perspectives can open up new understandings of a topic, which in turn can form the basis for a wide range of research questions.

It may well be the case that, if you are beginning research for the first time, your questions may be highly practical ones, inspired by your experience as a practitioner. However, even if that research is focused on a very practical issue, theoretical constructs can have an invaluable *sensitising* function: they can tell you where to look but not what to find. Theoretical ideas may also help you reflect more deeply on a topic, and go beyond your immediate assumptions. Finally, an awareness of alternative theoretical perspectives may enable you to take a more questioning and critical, and ultimately more profitable, use of your review of the literature. Quite often, when reviewing previous studies, there may seem to be 'something not quite right' about the way that a researcher has approached a topic. The temptation here can be to attribute this unease to methodological weaknesses in the study ('Was the sample representative? Were the data analysed properly?'). More often, however, the difficulty lies in the way that a researcher has *conceptualised* the topic of inquiry. By gaining proficiency in considering alternative theoretical perspectives it becomes possible to uncover conceptual contradictions in published research.

Think about the relevance of meta-theory

The concept of 'meta-theory' refers to broad sets of ideas that transcend therapy theory, but that nevertheless influence the ways in which we think about therapy, as well as the way we practise it. Examples of 'meta-theories' that may be relevant to an understanding of a therapy research question might include feminism, democracy, social justice, and multiculturalism. It can be useful to take account of these perspectives even when undertaking research into fairly 'technical' aspects of therapy. For instance, there has been a lot of research on the therapeutic alliance, much of it using questionnaires that are completed by the client and therapist. Imagine that you are thinking about designing a new therapeutic alliance measure, perhaps for use with a particular client group. Feminist and multicultural meta-theories open up ways of thinking about the therapeutic relationship that are not reflected in current questionnaires, at least not in an explicit manner. A feminist perspective invites consideration of the relevance of concepts such as connection, mutuality and empowerment. A multicultural perspective invites consideration of what it might mean to make sense of the therapeutic alliance through a 'collectivist' lens.

Try out alternative methodological perspectives

A further strategy for generating fresh ideas about the potential meaning of a research question, is to imagine how that topic or question might be investigated using different research methodologies. Any methodology that is selected has the effect of 'constructing' a topic in a particular way. For example, measuring a phenomenon by using a questionnaire requires precisely defining the attributes of that entity. By contrast, carrying out interviews opens up the possibility that new attributes might be uncovered. In research on depression, for instance, the questionnaires are constructed around psychiatric symptom lists. By contrast, interviewing a person about their depression leads to an understanding that can include attributes that are not included in diagnostic categories, or are unique to a specific person or group. Using yet another methodology, such as a case study approach, opens up other possibilities. A case study of therapy for depression has the potential to high-light the way in which the meaning of depression changes over time for an individual.

Take advantage of images and metaphors

The way we understand things, including the use of scientific theories and methods, is heavily influenced by the use of metaphor. Paying attention to metaphors and images that arise in discussion of a research topic, or appear in the published litera-ture on that topic, provides a valuable means of developing a more comprehensive appreciation of the meaning of that topic. One of the most important areas for therapy research in recent years has explored the impact on therapy of the use of client feedback and tracking procedures, such as inviting the client to complete a brief outcome measure at the start of each session. In this context, 'feedback' and 'tracking' are technical terms that are also metaphors. 'Feeding' is a universal human function that can be understood at many levels. 'Feedback' is a term derived from systems theory, and may evoke an image of a closed system. For some people it will also evoke images of guitar feedback in rock music, or experiences of management-speak. Historically, 'tracking' is a metaphor that refers to the actions of a hunter or stalker, or more recently to the functioning of parcel delivery companies. A 'track' implies a route that has already been established by people who have passed that way before. All of these meanings, and others, are implied when these terms are used in therapy research, and each of them opens up a further way of making sense of the topic. In relation to research on 'feedback' and 'tracking' systems in therapy, it can be seen that deconstructing the meaning of these images or metaphors draws attention to an assumption that the person doing the tracking or deciphering the feedback is active and purposeful, while the person being tracked is not. For some researchers who have been interested in these therapy practices, this has led to a search for an alternative metaphor, such as the idea that these episodes might be regarded as 'rituals' or opportunities to use 'conversational tools'.

Unpack the meaning of key words

Metaphors and images are particular types of words that occur when talking about research ideas. There are many other types of language-use that are also worth our attention: reflecting on the meaning of metaphors and images is only the start. For example, there are some key terms that are widely used in the therapy literature, which can be understood in many different ways. Examples include: self, outcome, process, change. The occurrence of any one of these terms in a research planning discussion should trigger a pause for reflection. The concept of 'self', for example, is understood in many different ways by therapy theorists, and in yet other ways by ordinary people. If the term 'self' is used in a research study, it is essential to be clear about which of these meanings are intended, otherwise readers will most likely just interpret the word in terms of their own preferred meaning, whatever that might be. The process of deconstructing a topic or question by looking at the *key words* within it, can be illustrated through two examples.

Example 1: 'How effective is an information leaflet in changing attitudes towards stress counselling in police officers?'

This is a research question that might be asked by a counsellor working in a police force who was finding that the uptake of services was low. The key words in this question are: 'effective', 'information leaflet', 'change', 'attitudes' and 'police officers'. All of these words or concepts can be opened up to further reflection. For example, what is meant here by 'effective'? 'Influential', 'persuasive', 'useful' or 'cost-effective' are other terms that might replace 'effective', and introduce slightly different meanings and research possibilities. Another angle on effectiveness is to think about who *defines* effectiveness. Is effectiveness to be estimated by clients, other officers, senior officers or counsellors? The term 'attitude' can also carry many meanings. It could be interpreted in terms of image, fantasy, expectation, behaviour (e.g., attendance at counselling), or beliefs (e.g., accurate knowledge about what a stress counsellor does). Even the term 'police officers' can be opened up. Does this mean *all* police officers, or only stressed officers, or particular ranks or age groups? Each of these alternative readings of key words would lead in the direction of different types of research study. A definition of 'attitude' in terms of what can be measured by an attitude questionnaire might result in a study in which 100 officers complete the questionnaire before reading the information leaflet, and then again one month later. A definition of attitude in terms of behaviour might involve looking at take-up rates for counselling for the year before, and the year following distribution of a leaflet across the entire force. A more psychodynamic approach to attitude might define in terms of unconscious fantasy, and lead to a research design in which a small number of officers were interviewed in depth around their responses to a leaflet.

Example 2: 'What is the impact of counsellor self-disclosure on the therapeutic relationship?'

There are three key concepts here: 'counsellor self-disclosure', 'impact' and 'therapeutic relationship'. All three would repay close inspection, but for reasons of space only 'counsellor self-disclosure' will be examined in detail. The concept of self-disclosure has been interpreted very differently by researchers in this field. For some, it has been understood to refer to the communication of factual biographical information (e.g., where the counsellor lives, whether he/she is married, etc.). It can also be interpreted in terms of the communication of here-and-now feelings (e.g., 'I feel disappointed about our progress together') or intentions (e.g., 'My belief is that it would be more helpful to spend this session talking about the loss, without look-ing at your work situation'). Some researchers have also explored self-disclosure through its opposite ('things not said') and have assessed the impact of what the counsellor holds back. Self-disclosure can also be planned, versus spontaneous, can vary in timing (early versus late in a session), and can refer to different domains of information about the self (emotional, autobiographical, sexual, religious). Self-disclosure can follow the client (e.g., the client mentions their religious affiliation, and then the counsellor follows) or can be initiatory. Many more facets of self-dis-closure can be imagined. The effect of paying this kind of close attention to the meaning of a key term has the result that a researcher who begins with an intention to study an experience such as counsellor self-disclosure, finds that he or she is faced with choices about which aspect of the topic to follow up. Some of these aspects are not interesting or relevant and some are, and in this way the researcher converges (eventually) on the precise question that is right for them.

Build a model

It can often be useful, at this stage in a study, to attempt to create a model of the topic being investigated. A good model provides a visual depiction of the relation-ships between concepts (qualitative research) or variables (quantitative research). The model must be more than a mere listing of concepts/variables, but should indi-cate the possible cause-and-effect linkages, feedback loops, sequences and processes that might exist. A useful heuristic device that can facilitate model construction in any branch of the social sciences is to ask 'What are the stages in the development of this phenomenon?' Any human or social activity develops and changes over time. As a rule of thumb, a usable model will have less than seven elements. More than this number can make a model very difficult to comprehend. The mechanics of model construction are facilitated by using large pieces of paper, coloured pens, and a generally playful attitude.

Constructing a model can help a researcher to be explicit about what needs to be observed, and may enable decisions to be made about which areas or variables are of crucial importance (central to the model) and which can be omitted from the study. Perhaps most important of all, constructing a model enforces progression from a static to a process conception of the phenomena being investigated. Finally, the existence of a preliminary model will assist the researcher in communicating with a supervisor or with people who might be interested in supporting or sponsor-ing the study.

One of the fundamental aspects of any research topic in counselling is that under-standing will inevitably involve making sense of how a variety of different factors interrelate. Cause-and-effect linkages are not easy to identify in counselling, because events tend to have multiple causes or antecedents and in turn produce multiple effects. A valuable means of making sense of the complexity of a topic or phenome-non can be to construct a model. Building a model is a good way of becoming sensitised to the various dimensions of a question, and as a result being better able to focus in on the facets of the question that are most important, are most open to research, or have/have not been studied before. Figure 3.1 gives an example of a tentative model that was constructed in order to tease out some of the factors that might be relevant to exploring the question 'How effective is time-limited counselling in the workplace?' Using a model-building approach, it is possible to see very quickly that there are far too many factors to be included in a single piece of practitioner research. Indeed, there are probably too many factors to even be taken on board in a government-funded major research initiative on the issue (in the highly unlikely event of such an initiative being set up). Anyone researching this topic therefore needs to make a choice about which factors are most important or relevant to them, or which can realistically be included, given the time and resources available. Finally, building a model should ideally be seen as a kind of 'thought experiment' which can in itself lead to new discoveries.

As the model of workplace counselling in Box 3.1 expanded and became more differentiated, it became possible to *see* new questions. For instance, the model points toward a sub-set of questions related to gender: do men and women differ in their use of counselling, just as they differ in their use of other coping strategies? Are there gender differences in outcome – do men and women have different criteria for what counts as 'successful' counselling? To what extent do these differences depend on the 'gendered' nature of the work (e.g., nursing versus the fire service), or on the organisational culture? Do men and women have different perceptions of in-house and external counselling services? Does the provision of male or female counsellors make a difference?

Once a research idea is 'externalised', and modelled through being pictured on a piece of paper, it becomes possible to look at each element of the model and ask further questions about it. In this instance, it became apparent that virtually all the 'building blocks' of the model concealed interesting questions about potential gender differences. There are, of course, many other sub-questions implicit in the model. The point is that model-building is a way of generating more specific questions.

Making the question more specific

Most of the time, new researchers will start off with questions that are too broad and general. The act of looking closely at key words can be one way of achieving a clearer focus for a study. Another way can be merely to think about how the question can be made more specific. This involves narrowing down the time, place, person and method. A useful principle to keep in mind is the advice to 'think big, and act small': in other words, be informed and inspired by profound ideas and grand aims, but make sure that you make a valid contribution to knowledge by focusing on specific events and processes that can be observed reliably.

The process of 'thinking big and acting small' can be illustrated through the use of an example: '*How effective is counselling for patients referred by their GP in a Primary Health Care setting?*' This question has in fact been the focus for a number

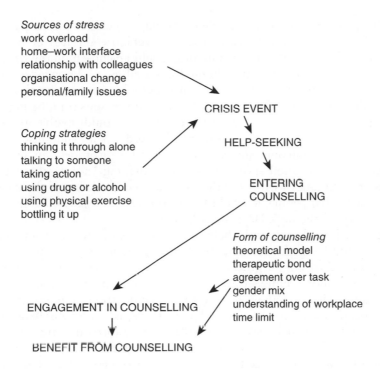

Sources of stress
work overload
home–work interface
relationship with colleagues
organisational change
personal/family issues

CRISIS EVENT

Coping strategies
thinking it through alone
talking to someone
taking action
using drugs or alcohol
using physical exercise
bottling it up

HELP-SEEKING

ENTERING
COUNSELLING

Form of counselling
theoretical model
therapeutic bond
agreement over task
gender mix
understanding of workplace
time limit

ENGAGEMENT IN COUNSELLING

BENEFIT FROM COUNSELLING

Figure 3.1   How effective is time-limited counselling in the workplace?

of studies, and one of the criticisms that has been made of these studies is that, on the whole, they have not been specific enough. Studies of the effectiveness of vaguely defined 'counselling' with heterogeneous groups of primary care patients inevitably lead to results that are difficult to interpret, since the outcome of the counselling will in all probability be highly influenced by such factors as the mix of patients referred (e.g., how seriously disturbed or needy they are), the experience of the counsellor, the quality of the GP-counsellor collaboration, and so on. It is easy to see that this is an area where the more specific the research is, the more likely that it will produce useful results.

There are several strategies that can be used to increase specificity. Narrowing *time* parameters might involve such decisions as: looking only at clients seen over a six-month period; using only clients that have received at least three sessions; using only counsellors who have received two years of training and have been in post for at least one year. Narrowing *place* parameters could be achieved by selecting the clinics to be used (e.g., urban, rural, group practices, single-handed practices) or choosing areas in which there were either a range of other counselling services available or where the GP counsellor represented the only therapy service on offer. Making *person* more specific entails considering the various central participants in the study: clients, counsellors, GPs. The study could be restricted to clients from particular diagnostic groups, such as anxious, bereaved, depressed, relationship problems. Alternatively, clients could be included on the basis of other factors such as age, gender, previous use of psychiatric services or psychotropic drugs, or attitude to counselling. Counsellors could be chosen on the basis of theoretical orientation, training in time-limited counselling, or knowledge of medical procedures. GPs might be used to represent those who are positive about counselling versus those who are critical, or on the basis of previous training in psychiatry. Making the study more specific in terms of *method* could involve general methodological choices (for example, designing the study as a randomised controlled trial, a naturalistic outcome study, a survey of GP attitudes, an ethnographic inquiry, etc.). Also, method specificity includes making choices about the actual technique or techniques used for gathering data. For instance, if the client group comprised depressed people, it would be appropriate to assess outcomes using an instrument such as the Beck Depression Inventory.

The point here is that it can be helpful to think creatively about how your piece of research could be made more specific. Some of the ideas you come up with will certainly be off-beam, but the process of opening up your set of options should make it possible to be more confident about the final version of the question that you decide to adopt. Thinking about how to make the question more specific may well stimulate you to search the literature. For instance, in the counselling in General Practice example discussed above, if it made sense to focus the study on depressed patients, it would be useful to review some of the literature on the advantages and disadvantages of alternative questionnaire measures of depression, to see which one would be most appropriate for counselling clients in a General Practice setting.

Deconstructing your research question: a practical exercise

The aim of this exercise is to give you a chance to explore various dimensions of your research topic or question through a combination of personal reflection and collaborating with others. The guidelines below describe one possible way of conducting this exercise – other options are possible, depending on time and the availability of colleagues.

Take a sheet of flipchart paper and some pens and crayons, and spend at least 30 minutes creating your 'topic map'. Allow yourself to develop your map in any way that seems right for you. Use words, images and metaphors to express yourself as fully as you can.

Here are some suggestions for creating a topic map:

- In the centre of the page, give the topic a brief title.
- In the top right-hand quadrant of the page put: what are your aims and goals? what is the study for? who are your audiences for the study?

- In the top left-hand quadrant put: key words, images and metaphors associated with the topic. Deconstruct the topic idea into as many elements as you can.
- In the bottom left-hand quadrant put: the personal meaning of the study for you, the personal experiences that led you to choose this topic.
- In the bottom right-hand quadrant put: how will the study be done? what possible methods might you use? who would you need to collaborate with?

Once you have completed your map, join up in a circle of chairs with a group of colleagues. Take 10 minutes to describe your map and talk through it, to explain your thinking about the topic. It is okay to decide not to share some parts of what you have drawn – it is your decision to disclose as much or as little as you want. For those in the group who are receiving this information, it is important to just listen and give the speaker some space. It is also important for the speaker to get a chance to reflect on what he or she has created.

Once the speaker has presented his or her ideas, members of the group have 20 minutes to ask questions. It is valuable if one person takes on the role of recorder in order to make notes of the questions, and the person's responses to the questions – this then helps the presenter to keep a record of the ideas and themes that emerge.

The role of questioners is to respond spontaneously to the researcher's ideas, in a way that expresses curiosity and interest. Examples of questions and statements that may be useful are:

- What makes you interested in this research topic?
- How do you define … ?
- What do you mean by … ?
- Can you give an example of … ?
- What other words might you use to describe that concept?
- What your ideas trigger in me is …
- My attention is drawn to …
- The main images or metaphors you use when you talk about this topic are …
- Other images or metaphors that come to mind are …
- Have you considered …. ?
- It might be useful to read …
- How are you using theory to help you to make sense of this question?
- What do you expect to find?
- How would you feel if your study showed the opposite of what you expect?

The aim is not to enter into a sustained discussion around any one of these questions. That can come later. The aim instead is to open up possibilities, to help the researcher to glimpse aspects of his or her idea that were not immediately apparent. The presenter has the option of closing down the exercise at any point, if they feel they have had enough.

Arriving at something you can work with

The earlier sections of this chapter have suggested various ways of deciding on a possible research topic or question, and then looking at that question from all possible angles in order to develop as complete an understanding as possible about what the question might mean, and how it could be tackled. In the end, however, it is necessary to arrive at a clear and final statement of your research question. You will need to arrive at something you can work with, and which works for you. Your research question is the key point of contact with the research literature. The question reflects your understanding of a desirable and justifiable next step in the research literature, that builds on what has gone before. The research question is also a kind of promissory note: this is what my study will deliver. Most forms of research product, such as journal articles, are organised around a research question, and tell the reader why that question is important, how it was addressed in terms of evidence (method), and ultimately how it was answered (the results of the study).

The closing section of this chapter considers the issue of how to phrase a research question, and offers some practical suggestions for how to formulate and use research questions. The key message, as we approach the end of this chapter is this: be guided by the literature, and do not try to invent your own research language.

Different types of question

There are different types of research question. Sometimes questions may be intentionally open and loosely boundaried, as in qualitative research. Examples of this type of question would be 'What is the client's experience of a therapy session?' or 'What is the experience of being really understood?'. These are open, exploratory questions. In other research situations, for example in most quantitative research, questions will be formulated as precise hypotheses of the type: 'Is behavioural counselling more effective than client-centred counselling for students with study skills problems?' This is a more precise question, which seeks to confirm the truth (or otherwise) of a proposition, rather than opening up an area for exploration.

There are many different research 'action words', such as 'explore', 'describe', 'analyse' and 'predict', that have subtly different meanings. For example, a researcher might be interested in therapist empathy and how it facilitates client change. Consider the following research questions:

- 'Do levels of therapist empathy *predict* client outcomes in early sessions of client-centred therapy for depression?'
- 'Are levels of therapist empathy *associated with* client outcomes in early sessions of client-centred therapy for depression?'
- 'Do clients *perceive* therapist empathy as contributing to outcomes in early sessions of client-centred therapy for depression?'

- 'How do clients *experience* therapist empathy as contributing to outcomes in early sessions of client-centred therapy for depression?'

Each of these questions refers to the same basic idea, but each leads to a fundamentally different research design. The first question ('predict') requires some sort of experimental design, in which the causal impact of empathy can be controlled and measured. By contrast, the final question ('experience') is consistent with the use of open-ended qualitative interviews. Using interviews to investigate a 'predict' question does not work, nor would using a controlled study to investigate an 'explore' question.

Further discussion around how to develop research questions in qualitative studies, can be found in Agee (2009) and McCaslin and Scott (2003), as well as in many qualitative research textbooks. It can be useful to contrast these sources with the approach taken by Riva et al. (2012), who describe the PICOT framework for formulating research questions in quantitative RCT studies of therapy outcome (P – Population; I – Intervention; C – Comparison or reference group to compare with the treatment intervention; O – Outcome; T – Time duration of data collection).

Using exemplar studies

One of the strong recommendations made in Chapters 1 and 2 was that the best way to acquire research skills, and to conduct a successful first publishable study, is to adopt the role of apprentice. While not abandoning his or her own creativity and sense of curiosity, an apprentice is willing to learn from those with more experience. Apprenticeship learning is not classroom-based (or book-based, or on-line learning package-based) but involves personal contact with a teacher, organised around the making of things. In Chapter 2 it was suggested that one of the key tasks, when searching the literature, is to identify 'exemplar' studies, that might function as templates or guides to investigations that 'fit the bill' in terms of what a novice researcher might want to carry out for him- or herself. It is also possible that a research supervisor, mentor or consultant may be able to supply their own exemplar studies for consideration. An exemplar study may not necessarily be a study of the specific topic that the researcher intends to pursue. For example, a researcher who is interested in clients' experiences of bereavement counselling may have difficulty in locating good-quality studies of that particular topic, but might discover that the Morris (2005) qualitative study of client experiences of psychodynamic therapy describes a methodological approach that they can adapt for their own purposes. In this context, a 'methodological approach' might encompass such aspects as how the study was written, the way that ethical issues were dealt with, the way that interviews were organised, the interview questions, the way the data were analysed, the way the researcher reflexively described their own involvement, and so on. Alternatively, it may be that a novice researcher will find some suitable methodological elements in one study, and other bits elsewhere.

Each of these exemplar/template studies will include examples of how research questions are phrased and handled in a study of the type that the researcher intends to carry out. It is therefore extremely useful to pay particular attention, when arriving at a final formulation of a research question, to the relevant sections of these model studies. If the research is being carried out for the award of a Master's degree or a doctorate, it will also be helpful to look at previous dissertations to find out if there is a university 'house style' that needs to be followed. Many PhD theses are published on-line on university websites, so it is also possible to look at how research questions have been formulated by successful candidates elsewhere. When reading dissertations and theses, it is vital to remember that different research genres (e.g., qualitative *vs* quantitative) are associated with different forms of question.

Practical realities

There are some further practical considerations that are worth bearing in mind when arriving at a final formulation of a research question:

- A research proposal will always require a clear statement of the research question (or set of questions).
- Typically, somewhere in a research proposal there will be a requirement that the research question is explained at three levels: (i) the aim of the research; (ii) the main question; and (iii) sub-questions. For example: (i) aim: to examine the effectiveness of CBT for depression in a community setting; (ii) main question: is short-term CBT for clients seen in a low-cost community counselling clinic as more effective than treatment as usual (TAU) from their GP?; (iii) specific questions: (a) is reduction in depression scores, measured by the Beck Depression Inventory, more likely to occur in patients who receive CBT, compared to those who receive TAU?; (b) are clients who receive CBT more likely to report reliable and clinically significant change at the termination of therapy and three-month follow-up? (c) what proportion of clients drop out of treatment? (d) is the level of severity of the depression associated with the outcome?
- Traditional or conventional Masters and PhD dissertations and theses (i.e., long research reports that are not written in an immediately publishable form) will usually include a statement of the research questions at the end of the literature review chapter, or the start of the method chapter. These questions may be re-presented at the start of the discussion chapter, as a means of structuring the discussion of findings in terms of how the original questions have been answered. A dissertation or thesis will also usually include a more general statement of aims in the abstract and in an introductory chapter.
- In research proposals, statements of research aims such as 'to review the literature' or 'to contribute to better treatment' are not needed – these can be assumed as general goals for any project.
- Published papers do not always make use of the term 'research questions', but instead may make use of terms such as 'aim', 'objective', 'purpose' or 'intention'. Different journals tend to be associated with different forms of words in this respect.

- In general, the aims and questions in published quantitative studies are stated in a more explicit way, while the same sections in qualitative papers are less explicit. It is helpful to develop an appreciation of both styles.
- The aims of a study, and research questions, need to be consistent with, and implicit in, the title of the study.
- In a published research article, the abstract, at the start, needs to include a succinct statement of the aim of the study.
- It is not unusual, particularly in large or complex studies, for some questions to turn out to be unanswerable (for instance, if some data were lost, or a questionnaire or interview schedule turned out not to make sense to participants). In addition, occasionally it turns out that the original way a question was phrased could be improved. In these situations, researchers will proceed on the basis of what makes most sense in the circumstances. Sometimes it will make sense to readjust the questions retrospectively. In other situations, the fact that the initial question did not work out is an interesting finding in itself, and needs to be reported.

Conclusions

In this book, research is understood as an activity that contributes to the development of a *collective* knowledge base. In the field of counselling and psychotherapy, potential consumers of research encompass therapists, therapy educators and trainers, the managers and administrators of therapy clinics, agencies, clients, potential clients, policy-makers, the general public, and academic theorists and researchers both within the field of counselling and psychotherapy as well as in cognate disciplines such as psychology, sociology, management studies, nursing or social work. Each of these audiences has different interests, and looks for different things in what it reads (and in fact reads quite different kinds of publications). At some point, all researchers are faced with the challenge of conveying the results of their work to different audiences. It is inevitable that many members of these audiences will be somewhat shaky regarding the technical aspects of a study. The aspect of a study that has to be communicated clearly and convincingly to readers from all backgrounds is the research question. In the end an interesting question, which has a plausible rationale, and which evokes curiosity and interest in the mind of a reader or listener, lies at the heart of all good research.

Suggestions for further reading

Most generic research methods textbooks will include a chapter on developing and formulating research questions.

The approach taken in the present chapter reflects the spirit of inquiry conveyed in:

Strong, T. (2010) Collaboration, generativity, rigor, and imagination: four words to focus and animate our practice-oriented inquiries. *Human Systems: Journal of Therapy, Consultation and Training,* 21: 380–96 (available on the companion website: https://study.sagepub.com/mcleod).

Companion website material

Other relevant items within this section of the website include:

McCaslin, M.L. and Scott, K.W. (2003) The five-question method for framing a qualitative research study. *The Qualitative Report,* 8: 447–61.
Riva, J., Malik, K.M.P., Burnie, S.J. et al. (2012) What is your research question? An introduction to the PICOT format for clinicians. *Journal of the Canadian Chiropractic Association,* 56: 167–71.

4

The Research Proposal

Introduction

This chapter explains what is involved in writing a research proposal, and the part that a proposal plays in the life-cycle of a research project. Different versions of research proposals are sometimes described as research protocols or plans, depending on the context. The primary purpose of a research proposal is to describe and justify what it is that the researcher intends to do. The proposal can be viewed as a 'plan of action' or a 'blueprint'.

Why do you need to write a research proposal?

There are two main functions of a research proposal. The first function is to force a researcher or research team to decide what the research is intended to achieve, and how it will be carried out. In this sense, constructing a proposal follows on from identifying a topic and narrowing that topic down to a set of research questions.

A research plan is similar to any other design task, in that it requires different kinds of information and activity to be brought together. When designing a house, an architect needs to achieve a balance between the wishes of the client, the cost envelope, the materials and workforce that are available, and government building regulations. All of this needs to fit into a sequence of activities – the roof needs to be on before the wiring can be installed. Similarly, a researcher or research team must achieve a balance between a range of factors. Constructing a research plan operates as a reality check for a researcher, which may lead to some rethinking about research priorities.

The second function of a research proposal, plan or protocol is that it serves as the basis for a contract between the researcher (or team of researchers) and the other people who may be involved. These people may include:

- providers of funding for the study;
- academic committees whose role is to decide whether, once completed, the study is in principle appropriate for the award of a degree;
- the academic supervisor(s) of the study;
- ethics committees or Institutional Review Boards who give ethical approval for the study to go ahead;
- managers of agencies that are being asked to provide access to informants;
- primary informants/participants, such as members of the public, therapists and therapy clients;
- colleagues who may be asked to help with aspects of data collection and analysis.

These different audiences have different interests and requirements. For example, primary participants in a study are not likely to want to read through a lengthy proposal. Institutional audiences, such as funding agencies, university project approval panels and ethics committees, will almost always require a proposal to be written in accordance with their specific requirements regarding length, subheadings and referencing. It is therefore sensible to think in terms of a general proposal document that can be edited and reshaped for a variety of purposes.

In relation to the process of submitting a proposal to external gatekeepers, it is crucial to develop an understanding of what that agency or committee is looking for, in terms of both the content and style of the proposal. It is not uncommon for a research project to falter or stall at the proposal stage, either because the proposal is turned down by a committee, or because of a failure to resolve issues that are raised by the committee. It is important for researchers to retain a sense of perspective around the interpersonal dynamics of this process. The researcher is usually operating from a place of passionate personal interest. By contrast, a funding agency, ethics committee or similar group will usually be struggling to process a backlog of applications. Its members are unlikely to have a personal stake or interest in any particular project that is submitted – their interest is in dealing with the paperwork with the minimum amount of fuss, consistent with maintaining standards.

Because a proposal is a complex document, it is extremely difficult to get it right first time. It is sensible to allow time for draft proposals to be read by supervisors, peers and other interested parties, and for subsequent revisions to be recirculated for comment. Even when a final version of a proposal is submitted to a funding agency or ethics committee, it is common for further modifications to be required.

Exercise 4.1 The heart of your proposal

A research proposal inevitably includes a lot of detailed information. However, at the heart of a good proposal is a simple idea. Once you have developed a clear idea of what you plan to do in your research, try to explain the core idea, or heart of the proposal, to various people. With each person or group, summarise the proposal in less than two minutes, using non-technical language. Listen carefully to the questions that they then ask you – these will be indicators of how successful you have been in communicating your ideas. It can be valuable to try out this exercise with people who know nothing about your research area, as well as with those who possess expertise and experience. Ethics committees and research boards will often include 'lay' members, whose role is to determine whether proposals pass the 'common-sense, plain English' test.

What a proposal looks like

This section offers an outline of the types of information that may be included in a research proposal. It is necessary here to keep in mind that different audiences or organisations may stipulate other subheadings or domains of information. In such circumstances, it would be unwise to include domains or subheadings that have not been specifically asked for – this can be confusing and the people assessing the proposal will already have enough material to work through without having to take account of even more stuff. Research proposals will usually consist of information under the following headings:

1. *Cover sheet*. Name(s) or researcher(s), date, title of study, your postal and email address, title of the research programme/degree (if appropriate).
2. *Aims of the study*. This section briefly indicates the general aim or objective of the study. Examples of research aims are: to evaluate the effectiveness of psychodynamic psychotherapy for depression; to explore client experiences of psychodynamic psychotherapy for depression; to identify preferences for therapy methods in individuals with depression seeking therapy in a community counselling agency. The statement of research aims should not be cluttered up with any mention that the researcher aims to conduct a systematic review of the existing research literature on the topic, or derive implications for practice – these objectives or tasks can be taken for granted as representing essential elements of any research study, and are typically reported in other sections of the proposal.

3. *Review of the literature on the topic.* A full, detailed review is not required, due to space restrictions. However, a researcher does need to demonstrate that he or she has read widely enough on the topic to provide an authoritative and convincing rationale for the research, in terms of how it builds on previous studies or fills a gap in the literature. It can be particularly worthwhile to briefly describe two or three previous papers that are most directly similar and relevant to the study which is being proposed. The literature review may need to discuss not only the findings of previous research into the topic, but also the use of different research methods applied in the investigation of the topic. Ultimately, this section will be evaluated on how well the review is able to establish (a) what is currently known about the topic, and (b) why the proposed study is necessary, in terms of what it adds to previous knowledge. It is unlikely that there will be enough space in this section to allow for an exploration of theoretical issues or clinical examples. The focus needs to be very much on research that is directly relevant to the proposed study. It would be helpful to describe the search strategy and quality criteria used to identify items included in the review.

4. *Methodological issues.* There is not always a separate subheading provided for this theme, but it is worthwhile to try to weave it in somewhere. Readers/reviewers of a proposal may well respond to the research plan with a view that 'this is interesting, but it won't work because ...' A brief discussion of the main difficulties or challenges associated with the study, and how they will be addressed, can go a long way towards alleviating any anxiety that is being felt by readers and gatekeepers. Common methodological issues include: defining, observing or measuring the key phenomena, gaining access to informants, the ethical sensitivity of the topic, and the lack of previous research on the topic.

5. *Research questions or hypotheses.* What are the actual research questions or hypotheses you intend to investigate? The reader needs to be able to see, in later sections of the proposal, exactly how these questions will determine the sample, the data that are collected, how these data will be analysed, and the conclusions of the study. For example, a study that aims to evaluate the effectiveness of psychodynamic psychotherapy for depression may break down into the following questions: (a) what proportion of clients completing psychodynamic psychotherapy for depression record clinically significant and reliable levels of change on a standard depression scale, the Beck Depression Inventory?; (b) how does the success rate for this form of therapy compare with improvement rates reported in relevant benchmark studies?; and (c) to what extent are therapy outcomes related to the number of sessions, age and gender of the client, and their previous experience of therapy? These research questions will allow the reader of the proposal to gain a clear appreciation of what the study will deliver. The rationale for the questions also needs to be outlined in the literature review – for example, evidence that gender, age, length of therapy, and previous therapy, have been found to be linked to outcome.

6. *Design of the study.* Usually a brief description of the type or genre of the study – e.g., survey, grounded theory, naturalistic outcome study, etc. This section may also include a brief description of what will happen in the study, suitable for a lay reader (for example: The study will consist of a naturalistic, practice-based evaluation design). All clients applying for psychodynamic therapy for a depression at a community counselling centre will

be invited to complete a depression scale at the start of each weekly session of therapy, and at a three-month follow-up.

7. *Prior work/pilot study.* This is information about any previous research or publications by the researcher or research team, that have provided a rationale or background for the present study. For example, a counselling clinic may have been using weekly questionnaire completion for several years, and be able to point to annual reports which show that this practice has been acceptable to clients.

8. *Sample/participants.* The information you can give about your research sample: number of participants, demographic characteristics, inclusion and exclusion criteria, arrangements for recruiting participants. If access requires permission from an external agency, a letter from the manager of that agency must be provided in an appendix. Similarly, if participants are to be recruited through a poster or newspaper advertisement, this also needs to be available in an appendix. A rationale needs to be provided for the sample size. In qualitative research, it is usually acceptable to refer to sample sizes in existing published studies that made use of the same methodology. In quantitative studies, sample size is justified by a statistical power calculation or accepted practice. Procedure for dealing with attrition rates (drop-out) from the study needs to be explained, if appropriate. Sampling strategy should be explained and justified – e.g., random sample, stratified sample (for instance, certain number of people in each age band), a homogeneous *vs* a heterogeneous sample.

9. *Intervention.* If the aim of the study is to explore or evaluate some form of therapeutic intervention, then information about the therapy should be provided.

10. *Ethical procedures.* The measures that will be taken to ensure informed consent, confidentiality, security of data, avoidance of harm, etc. Copies of participant information sheets, consent forms, letters, etc., may be included in an appendix. Information should also be included about the procedure through which ethical consent is obtained, such as the length of time the participant has to decide whether to be involved, and what happens if a participant quits the study; about how the participant can complain if something goes wrong; about actions taken to ensure the safety of the researcher. For some purposes (e.g., a proposal to a funding body) it is sufficient to indicate that ethical consent has been received, or specify the ethics committee by which the proposal will be scrutinised.

11. *Equal opportunities and social inclusion.* Information about how the research is open to people with disabilities, for example participants who require wheelchair access or have reading difficulties. It may be necessary here to explain any special action taken to respect the rights and needs of children or vulnerable adults who may be taking part in the study.

12. *Procedures for data collection.* Details of the interview schedule, questionnaire, rating scales, etc., that are used in the study. Indication of when, where and how these instruments will be administered. Be clear about exactly what will happen to participants, and what they will be asked to do. Copies of questionnaires, rating scales or interview schedules must be provided in an appendix. Details should be given about the reliability and validity of all data collection tools, in terms of previous studies in which these attributes have been established. If a purpose-designed questionnaire or interview schedule is to be employed, information should be provided about how it was designed, and (if appropriate) any pilot work that has been carried out.

13. *Method of data analysis.* How the data will be analysed, explaining the statistical or qualitative methods that will be applied. Information about who will be involved in data analysis, and their roles/responsibilities.
14. *Dissemination of findings.* Will informants be offered a copy of the report – and if so, how will this be accomplished? To which journal(s) will the study be submitted? Information about other forms of dissemination – conferences, seminars, internet, etc. The rationale for the dissemination strategy. Timescale to publication.
15. *The social and/or clinical value of the study.* Account of how the findings of the study might contribute to enhanced treatment, or quality of life, for a particular client group, or how this might be of benefit to the sponsoring organisation.
16. *Background and qualifications of the researcher(s).* This section may consist solely of factual information, such as the qualifications or CV(s) of researcher(s). In some circumstances it may be appropriate to use this section to reflect on the meaning of the research for the researcher (researcher reflexivity).
17. *Training and support.* Information about research training courses that the researcher may be required or expected to attend, as well as research conferences, seminars and workshops. Description of supervision arrangements and the qualifications and experience of members of the supervisor team. If the project is not part of an academic degree, then this section may include information about any external consultants involved in the study, and the extent and nature of their engagement.
18. *Timeline/Gantt chart.* Specifies the target dates for the completion of different aspects of the study.
19. *Resources.* Information about the costs of the study, including materials, travel, staff time, equipment, licenses, consultancy fees, payments to participants, etc.
20. *References.*
21. *Appendices.* Ethics and risk assessment checklists, client information sheet and consent form, questionnaires, interview schedules, etc.

What makes a good research proposal?

The criteria that are used to evaluate research proposals will depend on the terms of reference of the individual or group being consulted. Ethics committees are mainly interested in the ethical soundness of a proposal. However, some ethics committees will also make some evaluation of the scientific merit of a proposal, on the grounds that a study that has no hope of producing meaningful or valid findings is ethically problematic because it is a waste of participant time. By contrast, academic panels will tend to look for intellectual rigour, while funding bodies are often more interested in practical relevance and value for money. At the same time, there are also some more general criteria, described below, which would normally form part of any appraisal of a proposal. Within each of these criteria it is possible to identify a continuum of excellence: occasionally research proposals will turn up that describe genius-level breakthrough ideas under one or more of these headings. However, each criterion can also function as a deal-breaker. For example, a proposal that describes an ethically abusive or manipulative set of procedures will never be approved, no matter how compelling the intellectual rationale.

Does the proposal describe a relevant topic, that is being investigated at an appropriate level? Sometimes a proposal can be sound, in research terms, but not on track in terms of topic. For example, some students on counselling and psycho-therapy training programmes will submit research ideas that are more appropriate for health psychology or developmental psychology programmes. Likewise some proposals will describe projects that are too ambitious for the level of competence of the researcher, the resources that are available or the level of degree that is being sought, or are not ambitious enough.

Does the proposal give a clear account of what is intended to happen (who, where, when and how), and why? It is essential that someone reading a proposal is able to gain a clear understanding of what it will be like for a participant to be involved in the study, and the roles, tasks and responsibilities of all members of the research team. The reader needs to be able to mentally track through the unfolding process of the study, all the way from start to finish. Any gaps in the narrative, or contradictory information in different sections of the proposal, will undermine the confidence that a reader has in the viability of the project.

Other important criteria include:

Is the proposal sufficiently informed by knowledge of previous research in this area (including knowledge of alternative methods)?

Is the proposal internally consistent? Do the methods and sample enable the research question(s) to be answered?

Is the study ethically sound? Has everything possible been done to ensure that no harm comes to the participants?

To what extent will the study add significantly to previous knowledge of the topic? How creative or innovative is it?

Is the plan realistic? Have costings and a timetable been calculated so that there is a reasonable chance of completing the study on time and within budget?

Does the researcher possess the experience and skills that are required to carry out this study? Are appropriate supervision and training available, to ensure that the researcher develops appropriate skills and knowledge?

In many instances, the committee or organisation to which a proposal is being submitted would have published their own evaluation criteria. It is always worth looking closely at these documents. It is also valuable to talk to people who have experience of making proposals to these agencies. Typically, officers within committees and funding agencies are willing to respond to requests for clarification of their procedures, but are reluctant to enter into a detailed discussion of proposals that could be construed as comprising selective coaching that would disadvantage other candidates.

Suggestions for further reading

Clear and accessible guidelines for qualitative research proposals can be found in many generic qualitative research textbooks. Particularly recommended are:

Silverman, D. (2013) *Doing Qualitative Research: A Practical Handbook* (4th edn). London: Sage.
Willig, C. (2013) *Introducing Qualitative Research in Psychology* (3rd edn). Maidenhead: Open University Press.

Companion website material

It is not hard to get access to high-quality research protocols/plans for randomised controlled studies (RCTs). Increasingly, researchers using RCT methods publish their research protocols ahead of carrying out the study, as a means of being transparent about what they intend to do. These protocols can be found in several places, including two open-access journals: *Trials* and *BMC Psychiatry*. Use the search term 'protocol' in the journal search tool. Many of the studies that come up will be medical trials, but these journals have also published several psychotherapy research protocols.

Two examples of this type of proposal can be directly accessed through the companion website (https://study.sagepub.com/mcleod):

Alves, P., Sales, C. and Ashworth, M. (2013) Enhancing the patient involvement in outcomes: a study protocol of personalised outcome measurement in the treatment of substance misuse. *BMC Psychiatry*, 13: 337.
Boeschoten, R.E., Dekker, J. Uitdehaag, B. M. J. (2012) Internet-based self-help treatment for depression in multiple sclerosis: study protocol of a randomized controlled trial. *BMC Psychiatry*, 12: 137.

5
Ethical Responsibility

Introduction

Being able to deal with ethical issues, and making sure that research is conducted within a sound moral, ethical, and legal framework, are essential elements of researcher competence. The aim of this chapter is to provide an overview of the kinds of ethical issues that arise in research on counselling and psychotherapy, and how these issues can be addressed.

Why is ethical responsibility important?

Ethical responsibility lies at the heart of any research. There are several reasons why it is necessary to take ethical issues seriously:

- There is a broad social consensus, backed up by law, around the freedoms and rights of individuals as regards the research process, in terms of factors such as voluntary participation, informed consent, avoidance of harm, and confidentiality of information. This consensus is reflected in the insistence on the part of universities and other research institutions that all research projects need to undergo ethical approval prior to the commencement of data collection, and the fact that research journals will only publish studies that have been ethically approved.
- Researchers have a responsibility to the research community to act in an ethically appropriate manner – if members of the public get the impression that researchers exploit or deceive participants, then it will become much harder to recruit participants, or to argue for public funding for research.
- Researchers who are not secure in relation to the ethical probity of their work may feel anxious and guilty, and ambivalent about publishing their findings.
- Research participants who feel safe and who trust the researcher are more likely to respond to research questions in an open and honest manner. In therapy research, access to clients or patients is controlled by professional gatekeepers such as agency or clinic managers, and therapy practitioners, who are always cautious and wary in respect of any possibility that clients will be harmed or confidentiality will be compromised.

These considerations, taken together, mean that it is vital for therapy researchers to develop skills and knowledge in relation to ethical dimensions of the research process.

What do you need to know?

There are basically four levels or layers of knowledge that are required, in respect of research ethics:

1. *An understanding of basic ethical principles.* Within the broad arena of social research, and studies of health and social care, there is general agreement on a set of core ethical principles: *beneficence* (acting to enhance client wellbeing); *nonmaleficence* (avoiding doing harm to clients); *autonomy* (respecting the right of the person to take responsibility for him- or herself); and *fidelity* (treating everyone in a fair and just manner) (see Kitchener, 1984). All therapy researchers should already be familiar with these principles, in the context of their primary training as therapists. However, it is necessary to extend this clinical knowledge of ethical issues by reflecting on the implications of ethical principles for the research process.

2. *Routine procedures for implementing ethical principles within research studies.* There are a number of standard methods through which ethical aspects of research are typically handled: information leaflets for participants, informed consent forms, strategies for dealing with participant distress, and procedures for ensuring data security. These techniques form part of the design of a study, and are included within the research proposal.
3. *Strategies for responding to ethical dilemmas that arise during the research process.* Even when robust ethical measures are in place, such as consent procedures, it may be necessary for a researcher to deal with ethically-sensitive situations during the process of recruitment, data collection and data analysis.
4. *Strategies for dealing with ethical issues associated with sensitive research topics and groups of participants.* There exists a category of ethically sensitive research topics that are associated with a higher level of risk. Researchers working in these areas need to be familiar with specific ethical debates and solutions around their topic, and possess sufficient experience and confidence to be able to handle whatever comes up.

These areas of ethical knowledge and competence can be viewed as existing on a continuum or dimension. It is important to recognise that this dimension does not merely refer to increasing cognitive and theoretical knowledge, but also takes account of what Carroll and Shaw (2012) describe as 'ethical maturity' based on personal experience and a capacity to reflect on practice. For example, it is not sensible for a novice researcher to undertake research that is highly ethically sensitive, such as interviews with vulnerable participants. Such projects may be ethically viable and defensible, but are better carried out by researchers who have more experience of how to respond effectively to any ethical dilemmas that may arise.

There is a further aspect of what a researcher needs to know about ethics: *knowing how to consult.* Ethical good practice does not arise from the application of a set of rules that can be learned or worked out by an individual researcher in isolation. This is because the ethical rules or principles may be in conflict with each other or lack clarity. For example, how much information do research participants need in order to guarantee that informed consent has taken place? How do you know that they have understood the information that has been provided? Deciding on how best to proceed, in relation to ethical issues, requires a willingness to engage in a dialogue with others: research colleagues and supervisors; professional gatekeepers; ethics committee members; advocates for groups of clients.

Preparatory reading

Introductory overviews of ethical principles that need to be taken into account when undertaking therapy research, can be found in:

Cornforth, S. (2011) 'Ethics for research and publication', in K. Crocket, M. Agee and S. Cornforth (eds), *Ethics in Practice: A Guide for Counsellors*. Wellington, NZ: Dunmore.
McLeod, J. (2013) *An Introduction to Research in Counselling and Psychotherapy*. London: Sage. (See Chapter 5.)

It is also worthwhile reading the research ethics codes of major therapy organisations such as the British Association for Counselling and Psychotherapy, the British Psychological Society, and the American Psychological Association. These documents are usually available on-line.

Exercise 5.1   Using your existing knowledge of ethical issues

Take a few minutes to reflect on your knowledge and experience of ethical issues, in relation to your practice as a therapist. Make notes about the key themes and events that have been most important for you in relation to this aspect of your practice. Having carried out this piece of self-reflection, move on to consider the implications for your research project, of each item that you have included in your notes. Then, consider the nature of any ethical issues that might arise in your research, that are not informed by your pre-existing ethical understanding. It can be useful to carry out this exercise with a group of colleagues, as a means of developing a more comprehensive appreciation of the connections between practice ethics and research ethics.

Gaining ethical approval

There is a standard set of hurdles that any research project needs to negotiate, in order to gain approval from the relevant ethics committee, Institutional Review Board (IRB) or organisational management committee. The basic steps involve:

- carrying out an audit of the potential risks to participants;
- designing a participant information leaflet that explains what the study is about, what the person will be asked to do, what will happen if they decline or withdraw, what will happen to the data, and what to do if they wish to make a complaint;
- designing a form that the participant can sign to indicate that they agree to take part (or otherwise);
- constructing a set of procedures for ensuring data security;
- working out how the various ethical procedures fit together, perhaps using a flow diagram. For example, it is necessary to give participants enough time to think about their decision to take part, an opportunity to ask questions, and possibly also the option to review their decision at various stages. It is also necessary to be clear about who handles the data, and how long these will be stored.

The process of gaining ethical approval usually consists of sending a package of information, including consent forms and leaflets, along with a version of the research proposal, to an ethics committee or other suitable mode of external consultancy. The task of the ethics committee is to look at the project from the point of view of the participant. The committee may then make recommendations or require alterations, to make sure that the interests of participants are being looked after to the maximum extent. For a researcher or research team, this is usually a helpful and illuminating process. It is very hard for those on the 'inside' of a project (the researchers) to ever fully appreciate what the project is like from the perspective of an 'outsider' (the participants). It is the job of the research committee to supply that critical outsider perspective. In projects that are particularly ethically sensitive, it is good practice for the researcher or research team to consult with potential participants, or those who can speak for them, from the earliest stages of the research planning process.

When working out these procedures, it is important to keep in mind that in some studies the therapist will be a participant (for instance, if his or her performance is being evaluated). Also, it is possible that third party individuals, such as family members, may be affected by the research, and may need to be consulted.

Responding to ethical issues once research is underway

There are many ethical dilemmas and choice points that can arise once participant recruitment and data collection have commenced, no matter how much thought and care have gone into the formulation of the ethical procedures that are being applied. These dilemmas represent decisions that need to be made by the researcher, in respect of situations that could not be precisely anticipated in advance. Examples of such situations include the following:

- A client in a therapy outcome study has completed a lengthy assessment before commencing therapy. By the third session, it becomes clear that he was never really interested in receiving therapy, but believed that being seen to seek therapy would convince his estranged wife to come back to him. Is it ethically acceptable to drop him from the sample?
- A client has completed therapy and is being interviewed about her experience. Towards the end of the interview she starts to get very upset. What should the interviewer do?
- A client is being interviewed about her experiences in therapy over the past decade. She starts to talk about an episode of therapy that the interviewer regards as having been exploitative and abusive.
- Employees in a large organisation are asked to complete a stress questionnaire, to evaluate the potential need to introduce a counselling service. One of them writes in the margin that he is feeling suicidal.
- In a randomised trial, clients are randomly allocated to either CBT or psychodynamic therapy at the end of a screening interview. The researcher has spent over an hour listening to a person who desperately needs therapy, but who has had a previous negative experience of CBT. On opening the random number file, the researcher sees that this individual should be allocated to CBT.

- A PhD student carries out an autoethnographic study in which he carefully documents and analyses his personal experience of sexual abuse in childhood. The thesis is then made generally available through the university on-line archive. His mother reads this and gets very upset, even though she knew what his research was about, and had signed a consent form.

These scenarios represent what Guillemin and Gillam (2004: 262) have described as 'ethically important moments' in the research process. Useful guidelines on how to apply ethical principles in order to arrive at the best response to these situations can be found in Danchev and Ross (2014) and Haverkamp (2005). These research ethics dilemmas are similar, in many respects, to the kinds of ethical challenges that arise in counselling and psychotherapy practice. The ethical decision-making strategies that therapists already possess, arising from basic training, are therefore highly relevant.

However, these scenarios can also be viewed as calling for a different kind of ethical response. The common thread that joins together most of the ethical dilemmas that arise during the process of doing a research study is the notion of the researcher-participant *relationship*. These dilemmas are difficult to deal with because what is happening is that there is a conflict between general ethical principles, such as autonomy and avoidance of harm, and the in-the-moment connection that the researcher has with the research participant. This connection encompasses a set of relational values, such as care, mutuality, respect and dialogue. A concern to do justice to these values has led contemporary ethicists in the direction of developing a distinctive form of *relational ethics* (Gabriel and Casemore, 2009), informed by feminist and multicultural perspectives, and the writings of the postmodern philosopher Emmanuel Levinas.

A relational ethical perspective has been particularly influential within the field of qualitative research. Qualitative inquiry can be characterised as requiring a high degree of personal involvement on the part of the researcher, and in many instances the richness of qualitative research data depends on the establishment of a strong researcher-participant relationship. Quite often, in qualitative research, participants may be asked to talk in detail about painful experiences. Examples and further discussion, of the ways in which qualitative researchers have grappled with these issues, can be found in Ellis (2007), Etherington (2007), Guillemin and Gillam (2004), Haverkamp (2005), Josselson (1996), Miller et al. (2012), Shaw (2008), Thompson and Russo (2012), Tolich (2010) and Van den Hoonard (2002). At the present time, there does not appear to be an agreed set of ethical principles or rules that has emerged from this literature. However, there does seem to be a broad consensus that: the quality of both the research relationship and researcher reflexivity needs to be taken seriously; a researcher needs to have access to a supervisor or other colleagues who are willing and able to help them talk through any ethical issues that arise; and ethical difficulties can be minimised if research participants are treated as co-participants and explicitly involved in the decision-making process.

Exercise 5.2 Conversations about ethical issues in research

Who do you talk to about ethical issues associated with your research? What topics are covered in these conversations? How often do these conversations occur? Are these conversations sufficient to give you a secure sense of the ethical grounding of your research activities? What could you do to establish more satisfactory ethical conversations?

Specific ethical issues associated with therapy research

It is not helpful to imagine that psychotherapy is a special area of human experience that requires its own ethical rules. Such an attitude has resulted in some therapists adopting a position that research on what happens during the therapy hour is impossible. In my view this stance is elitist, undermines open dialogue, and makes the profession look foolish. It also ignores the fact that research colleagues in other disciplines and occupational groups also have experience of dealing with similar ethical issues. However, even if there is nothing ethically unique about therapy research, there are some important ethical issues that are particularly highlighted in therapy research: the influence of the therapist, the impact on the therapy process, and the use of randomised trials.

One of the basic therapeutic processes that occurs in psychotherapy is that the client forms a particular type of relationship with their therapist. This relationship can consist of many disparate elements, including an emotional bond, trust, love and anger, the sharing of sensitive information, and dependency. Even though it may be that in some, or even most, cases the client retains a capacity for autonomy, it is also clear that a temporary loss of autonomy is something that may occur in therapy – it goes with the territory. What this means, in respect of ethical decision making, is that any involvement by the therapist is problematic. This is because the decisions of a client who is at that moment caught up in a transferential relationship with their therapist may be shaped by a wish to please that therapist. It is therefore important, when designing a study, to make sure that, as far as possible, the participant consent-taking process incorporates a strong degree of externality, or (even better) is wholly separate from the therapist. This does not mean that therapists should not be involved in research on their own clients. This is ethically possible, but requires careful planning, and the participation of individuals who are able to act as independent advocates for the client. The area of therapy research where this issue is most acute, is in the field of case study research. Strategies for doing ethically sound case study research, and examples of what can go wrong, can be found in McLeod (2010a).

Another area of ethical complexity that is associated with therapy research concerns the impact of research on the therapy process. In medical research, there are many situations where research can be carried out on data that are routinely collected as part of treatment, such as blood tests or heart monitoring. In these situations, the fact that research is being carried out has no impact on treatment at all. The growing popularity of 'practice-based' research in counselling and psychotherapy (see Barkham et al., 2010, and Chapter 12 of the present book) is partly due to this factor. However, most counselling and psychotherapy research involves some degree of alteration or intrusion to 'treatment as usual'. This intrusion may not necessarily have a negative impact. There is a lot of evidence that, up to a point, clients find personal meaning and benefit in taking part in research activities such as filling in questionnaires or being interviewed. Clients report that these activities help them to reflect, help them to monitor their progress, and give them a sense of making a contribution to the greater good. These positive reports raise the question of whether, in some cases, it may be ethically wrong to deny clients these potential benefits by excluding them from research. But it is also indisputable that there are some occasions when research activities may have a negative impact on therapy. Clients can be asked about this. But, for example, if 90% of clients report that completing a questionnaire was a positive or neutral experience, and 10% say that it upset them, then does that make it ethically acceptable? Would 98% *vs* 2% be acceptable? One answer to the possibility of negative impact is to mention this in the information that is provided at the start of a study, prior to consent forms being signed. The problem here is that it can be hard to explain what the risks are, and harder still to know whether a client can really appreciate or understand the nature or likelihood of these risks, based on a brief paragraph embedded within an otherwise positive information sheet.

A third area of ethical difficulty in therapy research is associated with the use of randomised controlled/clinical trials (RCTs). The main advantage of this methodology, from a scientific perspective, is that it makes it possible to test causal hypotheses. In an RCT, clients are randomly assigned to two (or more) treatment conditions. If the clients assigned to Condition A have better therapeutic outcomes than those in Condition B, then there are good grounds for concluding that the effect is due to the treatment – because all other potential causal factors have been balanced out by the randomisation process. There are several ethical problems associated with this form of research. There is good evidence that many clients have preferences for the sort of therapy that they believe will work for them, and that receiving a preferred treatment leads to better outcomes. In an RCT, there is a risk that a client will be allocated to a non-preferred treatment. While it is possible to take account of preferences in the design of an RCT, this is not straightforward, and significantly increases the cost of the study (because larger samples are required). An associated risk is that gatekeepers will manipulate the randomisation process to ensure that needs clients receive the therapy that seems best for them. It could be argued that people do not need to take part in a clinical trial if they are worried about receiving a type of therapy they do not want. However, it is hard to gain access to good quality therapy in many localities, so there may be pressure on the person to go for whatever they can get. It is also the case that participants may not find a way, on the basis of the information available, to know whether the therapies that are being trialled map on to their preferences.

Other ethical issues arise in RCTs in respect of the therapies that are being compared. There are scientific and practical advantages in comparing a new model of therapy with either 'treatment as usual' (whatever that might be in a particular setting), a placebo condition (for instance, weekly supportive conversations with no active therapeutic intervention), or a waiting list condition. In any of these situations, research participants may be allocated to an option that the researchers know to be less beneficial. This can also happen when two 'active' therapies are compared. For example, if CBT and psychodynamic therapies are compared, it is probable that the lead researcher will personally regard one of these approaches as less effective. This information is not disclosed to the participant. Classic RCTs carried out in the field of medicine were conducted on an assumption of 'equipoise', where the researcher genuinely believed that both treatment options had their merits, and was genuinely interested in finding out which one was more effective. In therapy RCTs, by contrast, equipoise is very hard to achieve.

Yet another ethical issue in RCTs of counselling and psychotherapy is that typically the therapist is required to follow a treatment manual which specifies the interventions that can be offered, and the length of the therapy. In other words, professional discretion is severely limited. This is also another situation in which scientific rigour (i.e., knowing that a specific intervention is being delivered) may conflict with the best interests of the client.

It is important to acknowledge that the ethical dilemmas outlined in this section are not deal-breakers. Even a brief look at the therapy research literature will reveal many published studies in which therapists were involved in collecting data, the research had an influence on the therapy process, and clients were randomised to different forms of manualised intervention. What is concealed by these studies is the number of potentially valuable projects that were abandoned because these ethical issues could not be resolved, or the hours of negotiation and the compromises that shaped the design of the studies that were eventually carried out. These are serious ethical issues. Yes, they are resolvable, but only with a willingness to look long and hard at what research participants are being asked to do, and to be open to external consultation around a collaborative search for acceptable ethical solutions.

Advanced ethical issues

The ethical issues and procedures described in this chapter refer to the types of ethical consideration that are associated with mainstream research, where it is possible to build a robust ethics procedure around an informed consent process in which it is reasonable to expect that participants will have a good-enough understanding of what is involved. Beyond this mainstream, there is an area of research that is sometimes characterised as ethically 'sensitive'. Examples of ethically sensitive research include studies that involve children or vulnerable adults (who may not be able to understand the consent process), people from different or 'minority' cultural backgrounds (who may have quite different ethical values), and participants in case study research (who are particularly at risk of being identifiable in research reports). Again, it is clear that research has been conducted into these groups. But it is essential, for anyone intending to carry out such research, to undertake a careful study of the specific ethical dilemmas and procedures that may be relevant. Further discussion of this topic can be found in Liamputtong (2007). A good example of the use of collaborative research approaches to overcome this type of ethical issue, in this instance in respect of research with people with dementia, is available in Wilkinson (2001).

Research into ethical issues

Most of the literature on research ethics is written from a philosophical perspective, and consists of rational argument interspersed with occasional case examples. However, there has been a fair amount of research into how research participants feel about ethical procedures. For example, Biddle et al. (2013) interviewed people who were suicidal, about their experience of taking part in a research study of their suicidal tendencies. Other studies have explored the extent to which participants understand informed consent procedures (e.g., Flory and Emanuel, 2004). The findings of such research can represent a valuable resource for researchers, in clarifying ethical issues and even in helping to persuade gatekeepers and research supervisors around types of ethical action that should or should not be pursued.

Conclusions

This chapter has provided an overview and introduction to the main ethical issues associated with research in counselling and psychotherapy, and the ways in which these issues can be addressed. To a large extent, knowledge and skills in relation to ethical issues can be regarded as a rather neglected area of the research literature. Typically, ethical issues receive scant attention in research articles. Most researchers are keen to get on with the actual research, and are reluctant to write or read about ethics. What this means, in practice, is that ethical know-how tends to be located in organisations. In a university or healthcare system, the research ethics committee, the people who sit on it, and those who submit research projects to it, function as an informal repository of ethical knowledge. The extent and complexity of this knowledge are rarely apparent in any written documents. Instead, ethical knowledge takes the form of a set of shared understandings around what is possible, often connected to specific examples of research proposals that presented particularly thorny ethical dilemmas. It is important to realise that ethics books and chapters serve only as means of learning the language of research ethics, as a means of being able to enter into the conversation. It is only then, by talking to other people, that it is possible to decide what needs to be done.

Suggested further reading

Further exploration of the issues outlined in the present chapter can be found in:

Danchev, D. and Ross, A. (2014) *Research Ethics for Counsellors, Nurses and Social Workers.* London: Sage.
Sieber, J.E. and Tolich, M.B. (2013) *Planning Ethically Responsible Research* (2nd edn). Thousand Oaks, CA: Sage.

Companion website material

The companion website (https://study.sagepub.com/mcleod) includes a set of informed consent documents used in a study carried out by the author.

The site also provides access to classic articles on a wide range of key issues in research ethics:

Ellis, C. (2007) Telling secrets, revealing lives. Relational ethics in research with intimate others. *Qualitative Inquiry*, 13: 3–29.
Etherington, K. (2007) Ethical research in reflexive relationships. *Qualitative Inquiry*, 13: 599–616.
Guillemin, M. and Gillam, L. (2004) Ethics, reflexivity and 'ethically important moments' in research. *Qualitative Inquiry*, 10: 261–80.
Kitchener, K.S. (1984) Intuition, critical evaluation and ethical principles: the foundation for ethical decisions in counseling psychology. *Counseling Psychologist*, 12: 43–55.
Lambert, S.F. (2011) Ethical and legal issues in addictions outcome research. *Counseling Outcome Research and Evaluation*, 2: 25–36.
Lindsey, R.T. (1984) Informed consent and deception in psychotherapy research: an ethical analysis. *The Counseling Psychologist*, 12: 79–89.
Shaw, I. (2008) Ethics and the practice of qualitative research. *Qualitative Social Work*, 7: 400–14.

6

Criteria for Evaluating the Quality of a Research Study

Introduction

There are several ways in which an understanding of the criteria for evaluating research studies can be helpful to someone who is planning to embark on their own research project. An appreciation of what to look for in a research paper makes the process of conducting a literature review more interesting, as well as making it possible to arrive at well-argued and balanced conclusions regarding the field of research that is being reviewed. Being guided by a sense of what makes for quality and excellence in research, is also relevant during the research planning and proposal-writing process, as a means of identifying appropriate standards. A thorough knowledge of criteria of research quality is vital at the stage of writing up the findings of a study, and submitting a paper for journal publication. Finally, familiarity with quality criteria makes it possible to play a role within the research community, as a reviewer of proposals and journal submissions, and adviser to students and colleagues.

In this chapter, the issue of quality criteria for evaluating research is approached in a step-by-step manner. First, there is a discussion of some general quality criteria that are influential within the field of science and the humanities. The focus then turns to specific criteria that are associated with various types of research. When reading this chapter, it is important to keep in mind that there exist significant differences in opinion around what counts as good research work.

The ideas that are presented in the following sections, around evaluating research, are best understood in the context of reading research articles. It may be useful to refer to the discussion of the structure of a typical research paper that is provided on pages 222–24. It may also be useful to think about how the evaluative criteria outlined in this chapter can be applied to research articles in the process of conducting a literature review (Chapter 10).

Preparatory reading

McLeod, J. (2013) *An Introduction to Research in Counselling and Psychotherapy*. London: Sage.
Chapter 3 explores the philosophical perspectives around the nature of knowledge and science that form the background to current thinking about research quality.

Exercise 6.1 Exploring your own quality criteria

Identify some therapy research studies (or studies in other fields) that have been meaningful and inspiring for you. Then identify other studies that have left you feeling bored, annoyed or frustrated. What are the key attributes that you associate with each group of studies? What have you learned from this exercise, about the quality criteria that are most important to you?

General criteria for evaluating research

Research, as it is understood within contemporary culture, consists of a process of knowledge-building through collective critical debate. Philosophers and sociologists of science have made a great deal of progress, over the past hundred years, in developing an understanding of what this means in practice (see McLeod, 2013b, Chapter 3, for an introduction to that literature). Essentially, scientific research can be regarded as a core aspect of modern democratic societies, in which everything is up for discussion. That is why secretiveness and the corruption of scientific transparency, such as the distortion of science for political purposes in Nazi Germany and Stalinist Russia, or the abuse of science for commercial purposes by drug companies who conceal negative results, are such a serious problem – they strike at the heart of democratic society.

Critical debate needs a shared language. In relation to research, that language consists of a complex structure of ideas, values and principles that refer to what counts as acceptable and useful knowledge, and serves as a means for rejecting certain knowledge claims as unreliable or wrong. What lies behind this is a big question: what is true? Taken far enough, this question will always dissolve – ultimately, we can never know what is true. But groups of people who live together need to be able to operate on the basis of an agreed set of principles for deciding whether a statement is true or false.

Within the field of counselling and psychotherapy research, as well as elsewhere in the natural and social sciences, it is possible to identify some general quality criteria or 'truth tests' that are applicable to all research. These general evaluative criteria can be divided into five broad categories: adequacy of theoretical basis, logical coherence, communicability, replicability, and moral integrity. In practice, these dimensions are often interconnected: if a study does not tell a credible theoretical study, it is unlikely to hang together as a piece of writing, and as a result will be hard to follow.

Adequacy of theoretical basis is an evaluative criterion that reflects the importance of theory in any form of systematic inquiry. Careful and accurate observation and description of phenomena are hugely important, but it is only when we are able to make connections between disparate observations, by using concepts and theories, that we will be able to develop a form of knowledge that makes a difference to our lives. Howard (1985) has defined some of the characteristics of useful and productive theories: predictive accuracy, internal coherence, external consistency, unifying power, fertility and simplicity. Every piece of research is informed, to a greater or lesser extent, by theory. The research questions that are asked, the way that a phenomenon is conceptualised, the implications that are drawn from findings – all of these key aspects of the research process are shaped by the explicit or implicit theoretical understanding of the researcher.

Logical coherence refers to the extent to which each element of a study is connected to each other element. Does the literature review provide a credible rationale for the research question? Does the methodology represent an appropriate means for collecting data that are relevant to the research question? Are the conclusions justified in terms of the evidence? Most studies are reported in some variant of APA style, which requires the author to adhere to a logically coherent framework, and makes it easier for readers to detect logical slippage.

Communicability is a key criterion because any piece of research consists of a complex set of procedures that rests upon an even more complex set of assumptions and theories. It is therefore not an easy matter to communicate research findings in a clear and concise manner. Lack of clarity makes it impossible for a reader or consumer of research to judge whether the conclusions of a study are valid or reliable. Communicability is a major issue in research on counselling and psychotherapy because researchers may get caught between trying to write for other researchers, who are interested in the technical details of methodology, and also for clinicians, who do not want technical detail but want to know about who the clients are, what the therapist did, and other practical matters. In addition, the world of therapy encompasses many different theoretical languages. So, for example, a psychoanalytic researcher may be able to write in a way that makes complete sense to other psychoanalysts, but is unintelligible to CBT colleagues (and vice versa).

Replicability refers to the possibility that a study could be repeated, by another researcher or research team and in a different setting. The principle of replicability is integral to the whole notion of science: a result that can only be obtained by one researcher or research team might as well be considered as magic or alchemy. The replicability criterion means that a reader of a research article should be provided with sufficient detail regarding what happened to participants, and how the data were collected, to be able to be in a position, in principle, to carry out the study for him- or herself. This does not mean that every methodological detail needs to be included in the actual article. For example, it would take too much space to include a copy of every questionnaire that was used. However, enough information should be provided for the reader to be able to obtain a copy of the questionnaire (or any other aspect of the study) if necessary. The issue of replicability also draws attention to the question of whether different researchers get the same results. There are many instances within the counselling and psychotherapy research literature (and in other fields) where very promising results were reported for a new technique, only for later researchers to fail to obtain the same level of positive findings. The likely explanation for this phenomenon is that early adopters, or inventors, of a technique are highly enthusiastic about the intervention, which conveys positive expectations to participants. By contrast, subsequent researchers may be more skeptical. A final issue associated with the concept of replicability, particularly associated with qualitative studies, concerns the clarity with which findings are reported. Researcher A interviews some clients and describes the emerging themes in a somewhat poetic and evocative manner (which may be interesting and stimulating to read). Researcher B then uses the same interview schedule with a comparable group of clients, and produces a set of themes that are expressed in a more prosaic manner. In this kind of situation, it can be hard to determine whether the findings of study B corroborate the results of study A, or not.

Moral integrity is an evaluative dimension that is probably not given sufficient attention within the research literature. The obvious approach is to assess the ethical soundness of a study. For readers of research, the question of ethical soundness is rarely an issue, because any glaring ethical issues will have been dealt with by the ethics committee or IRB that assessed the original research proposal. In addition, journal reviews and editors will not publish a study if they have any doubts about its ethical probity. Occasionally, examples of scientific fraud will arise, where results are manufactured or tampered with, but this is also rare (or is rarely reported). However, there also exists a more subtle level of moral integrity, relating to the good faith of the researcher. Is the researcher trying to put a 'spin' on the findings, in order to provide evidence for his or her theory or therapy approach? In the most extreme cases, some studies function as public relations or promotional activities in support of brands of therapy. Does a study, or a programme of research, systematically exclude certain groups of people? More broadly, it can be useful to ask: in whose interest was this research carried out? From the opposite perspective, if a study has been conducted with a high degree of moral integrity, does that mean it is worthy of attention even if the methodology is flawed?

The application of these criteria is seldom clear-cut. Although there is evidence that there is a broad level of agreement around the importance of these criteria among experienced researchers (Gottfredson, 1978), there exist legitimate differences in how these criteria are interpreted, and how these can be applied in relation to specific studies. The construction of knowledge consists of a process of critical debate, in which these criteria (as well as more specific criteria, described below) are discussed in relation to specific studies, until an acceptable level of consensus is reached.

Criteria associated with particular genres of research

The field of counselling and psychotherapy research can be divided, for the most part, into studies that look for patterns in numbers (quantitative methods) and those that look for patterns in words and stories (qualitative methods). In Chapter 1, it was argued that each of these approaches is necessary in therapy research, and that therapy researchers need to be comfortable and competent in both of them. However, it is important to recognise that qualitative and quantitative methodologies generate different types of 'knowing' that are associated with different quality criteria. For example, in general, quantitative research produces more reliable findings if there is a large sample of participants. By contrast, qualitative research yields more interesting findings with a small or moderate number of participants (for example 3–20) and tends to produce somewhat superficial findings if the sample is too large. In addition, there are clear-cut statistical techniques for evaluating the reliability and validity of measures, such as questionnaires, whereas reliability and validity in qualitative research are more a matter of informed judgement. Further discussion of these criteria can be found in Chapter 7 (quantitative research) and Chapter 8 (qualitative research) and in later chapters in which particular qualitative and quantitative projects are described.

The existence of different evaluation criteria associated with qualitative and quantitative methods creates special difficulties for anyone seeking to undertake *mixed methods* research, in which qualitative and quantitative techniques are combined. Detailed consideration of mixed methods is not within the scope of the present book, which is primarily aimed at novice researchers. Most types of mixed methods research do not represent sensible choices for a new researcher, because they require competence in two approaches, as well as an understanding of the issues involved in combining them. Further discussion of these issues can be found in Bergman (2008), Hanson et al. (2005) and Plano Clark and Creswell (2008). However, later chapters in this book describe strategies for combining qualitative and quantitative data that are relatively straightforward, and within the scope of a novice researcher. In Chapter 9 within the section on developing a new scale or measure, a sequential use of qualitative and quantitative approaches is outlined. The researcher wishing to develop a new measure starts off by collecting information on how people experience the construct being targeted, through qualitative interviews of focus groups. The statements, themes and categories generated by these qualitative techniques are then shaped into questionnaire items, which are subjected to statistical validation. In Chapter 13 on conducting a systematic case study project, it is suggested that a rich data set should be collected on the case, consisting of both qualitative and quantitative information. This data set as a whole is then subjected to interpretive or 'hermeneutic' analysis.

Specific technical criteria

At an even more detailed level, there exists a wide range of specific technical criteria associated with the use of different research techniques. For example, there are generally recognised conventions, defined by the American Psychological Association (APA), in relation to the reporting of statistical analyses (see for example, Cooper, 2010). In qualitative research, there are accepted ways for reporting on the proportion of participants who mentioned a particular theme, and for displaying material data from transcribed conversations. These conventions are highlighted in later chapters that describe specific research approaches. It is also valuable to look closely at how data are presented in published journal articles. In addition to presentational criteria, there are also criteria that relate to correct or incorrect use of particular statistical and qualitative techniques. Learning about these technical criteria plays a central part in being trained in how to use these techniques. General evaluative criteria, discussed in an earlier section of this chapter, are largely philosophical in nature and open for debate and differing interpretation. By contrast, specific technical criteria are more cut and dried – what you have done is either right or wrong.

Using rating scales

In some situations, it will be useful to be able to apply a standard set of criteria to the assessment of research papers. For example, when conducting a literature review on a topic where a lot of research has been carried out, it may be necessary to impose a quality threshold, and only consider papers that reflect a higher level of methodological rigour. In such situations, the team conducting the literature review will normally employ a rating scale, in order that they can quantify the degree of adequacy of various aspects of the study, and compare their judgements. Examples of research quality rating scales can be found in Deeks et al. (2003) and Downs and Black (1998). It is worthwhile to get into the habit of taking note of the quality evaluation ratings scales and other procedures used by authors of systematic litera- ture review reports. Although these rating scales are primarily designed as tools for assisting the review process, they also represent valuable tools for learning. There are many different criteria that can be applied when assessing the quality of research, and many different ways of interpreting these criteria. What a rating scale does is simplify all of this into a set of maybe 10–12 summary statements.

Conclusions

This chapter has explored the various kinds of evaluative criteria that can be applied when assessing the merit of research studies and research publications. Sometimes, it can happen that the more a person reads about methodology, the more critical they become of the research that is carried out. This tendency can even give rise to a form of nihilism or deep scepticism about research, in which all research is irre- deemably flawed. In my view, this is a trap. My own position is that any research that has been carried out with integrity, and from a position of genuine curiosity, will usually have something interesting to offer. It is essential to be able to affirm the value and contribution of a study, while at the same time recognising its limitations. All research has its limitations.

One of the key skills involved in evaluating research is to be willing to look for detail. A study may be generally sound, while containing one or two weaknesses. Similarly, a study may be fundamentally ill-conceived, but nevertheless contain some useable ideas or nuggets of information. Attention to detail may lead to the interest- ing discovery that the conclusions that the author derives from a study may not represent the only way of interpreting the results, or even the best way.

A valuable means of learning about how to arrive at a balanced appraisal of the strengths and weaknesses of a research study, is to act as a reviewer for research journals. Journal editors are generally delighted to add to their list of potential reviewers, and may offer support to novice reviewers, such as being paired up with a more experienced reviewer. Some journals encourage research supervisors to invite their students to be co-reviewers. Even in the absence of these kinds of support, the usual review process incorporates a built-in learning mechanism. Once the editor has received the requisite number of reviews (typically three), he or she will write to the author with copies of all the reviews, plus an overall judgement letter. The reviewers are copied in on this, which allows each of them to see how the others have evaluated the paper. Reviewers may also have an opportunity, if they are inter- ested, to follow the paper through to publication (or rejection) by being copied in on further correspondence around revisions to the paper.

Suggestions for further reading

An invaluable source for any therapy researcher or practitioner wishing to develop critical skills, is:

Girden, E.R. and Kabacoff, R.I. (2010) *Evaluating Research Articles from Start to Finish* (3rd edn). Thousand Oaks, CA: Sage.

Further exploration of the issues discussed in the present chapter, can be found in:

Barker, C. and Pistrang, N. (2005) Quality criteria under methodological pluralism: implications for conducting and evaluating research, *American Journal of Community Psychology*, 35: 201–12.

Companion website material

The companion website (https://study.sagepub.com/mcleod) provides access to two highly influential quality guidelines:

Deeks, J.J., Dinnes, J., D'Amico, R. et al. (2003) Evaluating non-randomised, intervention studies. *Health Technology Assessment*, 7(27).

Spencer, L., Ritchie, J., Lewis, J. et al. (2003) *Quality in Qualitative Evaluation: a framework for assessing research evidence*. Government Chief Social Researcher's Office. Occasional Paper Series no. 2.

7

Using Quantitative Methods

Introduction

Historically, research in counselling and psychotherapy, along with research in psychology, social science and the health sciences, has largely consisted of quantitative studies. The use of measurement to carry out comparisons between different groups or interventions, or to identify patterns and causal linkages, has proved to be an essential tool in the development of research-based knowledge. The present chapter provides an overview of the role of quantitative methods in therapy research, what novice researchers need to know in order to make use of such methods, and how statistical skills can be acquired.

Why is it important to know about quantitative methods?

There is a substantial degree of resistance to quantitative methods within the counselling and psychotherapy professional community. Part of this resistance arises from a view that the transformation of the therapy experience involves losing the real meaning of what happens in therapy. Those who espouse this position would argue that quantitative methods have only a very limited relevance to the advancement of practical knowledge about therapy, and that we would be better served by pursuing other forms of inquiry, such as qualitative research, clinical case studies and philosophical critique. Another source of rejection of quantitative methods is that at least some people who are drawn to therapy as a profession, and are effective therapists, have great difficulty in making sense of numbers. It may be that their thinking and reasoning processes, and learning style, are more verbal, kinaesthetic or visual than logico-linear-numerical. Or it may be that their educational pathway has by-passed the learning of mathematical concepts. A further form of avoidance of statistical knowledge is associated by individuals who are heavily involved in qualitative research, and have been able to construct a rich evidence base for their practice without needing to take account of quantitative research.

I would strongly encourage all readers who are resistant to quantitative methods to reconsider their position. Avoidance of studies that use quantitative methods means cutting oneself off from around 90% of the therapy research literature. It also means cutting oneself off from dialogue and debates with groups of colleagues who carry out quantitative research and use it to inform their practice. Within the field of contemporary research in counselling and psychotherapy, there is a broad consensus that qualitative and quantitative methodologies represent distinct and complementary approaches to inquiry, and that both are necessary. It is therefore important for each approach to be required to engage with the other. For example, the argument against the 'quantification of everything' needs to be made, but is more convincing if it is grounded in an informed understanding of what it is that is being criticised. In fact, within the research community, the most powerful arguments against statistical methods come from those who possess a sophisticated knowledge of mathematics (see for example, Michell, 1999, 2000).

Exercise 7.1   Your attitude to quantification

How do you feel about the practice of measuring aspects of therapy? Does it fill you with excitement, around the possibility of developing a more rigorous evidence base? Or do you have more ambivalent or even negative feelings and images around this kind of approach? It can be valuable, in relation to your development as a researcher, to explore the origins and basis for these attitudes. Where do these attitudes and beliefs come from? What were the critical events and relationships that shaped the way you think about numbers? Once you have mapped your own stance in relation to quantification, it can be instructive to engage in dialogue with individuals whose position on quantification is different from your own. What can you learn from them? What can they learn from you? To what extent does the attempt to engage in dialogue lead to a modification of your position?

What do I need to know?

It is possible to identify three levels of statistical knowledge: reading-level knowledge, novice user, and advanced user. It is important for all counselling and psychotherapy practitioners to possess sufficient understanding of statistical concepts to be able to read and make sense of quantitative research papers. This is not a particularly difficult hurdle to negotiate, because in any quantitative research paper, any tables of numbers, or passages describing statistical techniques and results, will always be accompanied by a non-technical narrative account of the same information. To be able to read a quantitative paper, therefore, it is only necessary to be familiar with basic statistical terminology (such as 'mean' and 'standard deviation'), along with a grasp of what the researcher is trying to achieve by carrying out a statistical analysis (e.g., look at whether one group of clients has better therapy outcomes than another group). The possession of a basic reading-level competence does not allow the reader to evaluate whether the right statistical techniques have been applied, or whether the appropriate conclusions have been drawn. This is not a major problem, because any published article should have been carefully reviewed by independent referees who know about these things. Developing reading-level competence in quantitative methods requires a willingness to read and reflect on the ideas that are discussed in introductory chapters such as in McLeod (2013b, Chapter 6) or Cooper (2008, Chapter 1). The most important step in the development of this level of competence is to read quantitative papers, if necessary looking up the meaning of terms that are unfamiliar, and to persevere. It will also be helpful to be able to talk to colleagues who are a few steps further down that road. Sometimes, it will be less helpful to talk to advanced experts in statistical methods, because they know too much and find it hard to get on the same wavelength as statistical beginners.

Being able to use statistical techniques in a piece of research requires training and/or collaboration. This can take the form of being taught by someone who is competent in the statistical method that is being used in the study. That kind of apprenticeship training is probably the best way to learn, because it is tailored to the learner and goes at the learner's pace. However, it is somewhat time-consuming for the teacher. As a result, the option in most universities is to sign up for a statistics class that offers structured, step-by-step training, accompanied by assessment of learning, support, and feedback. All universities and most colleges offer statistics training, usually at all levels from introductory to advanced, and are generally happy to enrol students in these classes even when they are not registered for a specific degree.

Typically, a statistics class will be organised around a specific textbook, which will be used by all students. There are many excellent statistics textbooks on the market. Within the present chapter, frequent reference will be made to the statistics textbook by Andy Field (2013). This book is particularly recommended because it is widely used, and therefore likely to be available in a local library. It is written with a fair amount of humour, and supported by a well-planned and comprehensive website. The website includes particularly useful video demonstrations of key statistical skills. It is important to understand that Field (2013), along with other statistics textbooks, does not spend much time agonising over whether quantification is justifiable, or try to persuade the reader that statistics are a good thing.

The level of statistical knowledge required in order to attempt a first quantitative counselling/psychotherapy study, is covered in Chapters 1–7, 9, 11 and 18 of Field (2013).

An alternative strategy, for anyone thinking about carrying out a quantitative study, is to join a research team that includes a stats specialist, or find someone who will do the stats for you. This is a perfectly legitimate solution which is widely used in many areas of medical research. University-affiliated teaching hospitals will normally employ statisticians whose job it will be to take responsibility for analysing quantitative data collected in medical studies.

Advanced users of statistical methods are people who are particularly interested in statistical techniques, and who have undergone training in methods such as regression, complex analysis of variance, factor analysis and multilevel linear modelling. These approaches are discussed in Chapters 8, 10, 12–17, and 19–20 of Field (2013). There are also many even more advanced statistical techniques that go beyond the topics covered by Field (2013). Advanced statistical methods are often found in papers written by students who have undergone doctoral-level training in clinical or counselling psychology, which has traditionally placed a strong emphasis on these skills.

The present chapter refers to SPSS, a leading statistics package which is available in most universities and health services, and to the SPSS guide by Field (2013), which is widely used, includes an invaluable glossary of terms, is well supported by on-line teaching material, and is hopefully less intimidating to counsellors and psychotherapists than alternative texts. However, it must be acknowledged here that the licence to use SPSS is fairly costly, and as a result a number of open source/free statistics packages have become available. The most popular of these is probably GNU-PSPP, but several similar tools can be found on the internet.

Suggested preparatory reading

Field, A. (2013) *Discovering Statistics using IBM SPSS Statistics* (4th edn). London: Sage. (See Chapters 1 and 2.)

McLeod, J. (2013) *An Introduction to Research in Counselling and Psychotherapy*. London: Sage. (See Chapter 6.)

What practical skills do I need to develop?

Training in quantitative methods and statistics always involves a considerable amount of 'hands-on' experience in relation to the intricacies of entering data into SPSS or an equivalent statistics package. Learning how to make sense of the various menus and options that are available, and the outputs that they produce, also requires concrete practice guided by someone who is familiar with these topics. These hands-on practical aspects of using quantitative methods are not covered in the present book. Readers are advised to consult Field (2013) and the accompanying website, for a taste of what is involved in this kind of learning, before enrolling on a course or finding a tutor or mentor. However, there are also vital conceptual skills that need to be acquired. To do good quantitative research involves 'thinking like a quantitative researcher'. Some of the main principles of a quantitative mind-set are outlined in the following sections. To anyone who has been trained in a scientific discipline, these principles will seem utterly obvious. However, many counsellors and psychotherapists have backgrounds in the arts and humanities, and can find it hard to connect with the logic of quantitative inquiry.

Thinking like a quantitative researcher. Quantitative research methods form part of a broader movement within science, sometimes described as 'positivism'. The image of scientific knowledge that emerged in Europe in the seventeenth century regarded nature as obeying cause-and-effect laws. The task of science was to uncover these laws. Mathematics – the 'queen of sciences' – provided a universally-applicable language within which the logical structure of scientific laws could be expressed. Ultimately, everything could be represented in numbers. This philosophical and cultural shift encompassed a rejection of religious beliefs. No longer was everything driven by a prime cause (God's will). Instead, the world operated like a machine. The notion of a 'positive science' referred to the assumption that the mechanical, cause-and-effect laws that were so readily applicable in fields such as physics and optics, could also be applicable in domains of social life, such as economics, sociology and psychology. As a reflection of these underlying beliefs about science, quantitative researchers do not see the world in terms of personal choice and intention. The world is made up of 'factors' that have an 'impact' on each other, or that can be used to 'predict' other factors. So, for example, therapy outcome predicts later use of medical care. Quality of therapeutic alliance predicts therapy outcome. Fulfilment of therapy preferences predicts therapeutic alliance. Previous experience of therapy predicts therapy preferences. Everything is caused by something else. The job of the researcher is to contribute to the development of a reliable matrix of cause-and-effect linkages. Eventually, when that matrix is constructed, it is then possible to predict and control what happens in the world, with a high degree of confidence.

Hypothesis testing. There are two ways in which cause-and-effect matrices can be constructed. One way is to measure a lot of variables or factors, and then look at the patterns that emerge. This is the basis of statistical techniques such as correlation, factor analysis and regression. There are many valuable studies that have followed this general strategy and have produced practically useful results. However, there are some notable logical limitations associated with this approach. Co-variance (things clustering together in a pattern) does not necessarily imply causality. For example, imagine that client satisfaction data are available from questionnaires completed at the end of counselling. It is then possible to analyse many potential correlations and patterns in that data set. It may emerge that (a) female counsellors receive higher satisfaction ratings than male counsellors, and (b) that there is no difference in the satisfaction ratings received by more experienced counsellors, and trainee counsellors. These are interesting findings. However, it is not reasonable to argue, on the basis of these results, that counsellor gender influences client satisfaction, while therapist experience-level has no effect. Both of these linkages could be the result of at least one (and maybe several) other causal factors, such as the assessment and case allocation system used in the counselling service. It may be that the more hostile or potentially violent cases are allocated to male counsellors, and the more straightforward (i.e., higher likelihood of success) cases are allocated to trainees. A better way to investigate such causal linkages, leading to more confidence about results, is to design a study in which specific factors are controlled, and then followed up over time. This is usually called a 'quasi-experimental' study or a 'randomised controlled trial'. To test the hypothesis that gender of counsellor has an effect, clients would need to be randomly allocated to either male or female counsellors. To test the hypothesis that experience-level had an effect (or had no effect), clients would need to be randomly allocated to a group of experienced therapists, or a group of trainees. The key point here is that 'thinking like a quantitative researcher' involves looking at research as a process of hypothesis testing. On the whole, statistical tests have been developed to allow researchers to test hypotheses. A quantitative study therefore should, if possible, be driven by a hypothesis or hypotheses. (By contrast, most qualitative studies are driven by curiosity – for example, the intention to explore, in as open a manner as possible, the experiences of a group of clients.) In a quantitative study, the heavy lifting takes place at the start, in the form of identifying a hypothesis and then devising a set of procedures through which that hypothesis can be subjected to a fair test. This aspect of quantitative research has significant implications – the researcher needs to demonstrate, before any data are collected, that their hypothesis is warranted in terms of a combination of previous research and theory.

Probabilistic thinking. A further key aspect of 'thinking like a quantitative researcher' involves embracing the concept of *probability.* In some areas of science, it is possible to determine cause-and-effect relationships with a high degree of certainty – for example, the boiling point of water at a certain atmospheric pressure. The situation in psychology, social science, and therapy research is quite different. In these domains, the researcher is dealing with complex real-world phenomena, in which each factor or variable is subjected to multiple sources of causal influence. Also, the phenomena that are being investigated are not amenable to precise measurement – it is not possible to measure 'depression' with anything approaching the same level of precision as 'length'. As a consequence, the results of therapy research studies can never be reported in the form of simple formulae (x causes y under condition z), but instead need to be reported in probabilistic terms (there is a high/low probability that x causes y under condition z). In quantitative studies of therapy, this is reported in terms of the 'p' (probability) value, or confidence limits, of findings. As a rule, a finding is generally considered as credible if it can be shown that it occurs less than one time in twenty ($p < .05$) by chance. (The probability level/confidence limit that is considered acceptable will depend on the type of study that has been carried out – more highly controlled studies allow stricter probability/confidence levels.) A key implication of this facet of quantitative research is that it demonstrates the importance of identifying the research hypothesis from the outset. In a 'fishing expedition' investigation, in which the researcher measures a range of variables and then looks for patterns, it is likely that several statistically significant findings will emerge, purely by chance. It is then usually possible to produce a plausible interpretation of why this pattern of results is meaningful. However, in statistical terms, this is defined as a 'Type 1' error – appearing to detect an effect when in fact no real effect has occurred. Being clear about the primary hypotheses that are being tested represents a crucial means of avoiding Type 1 errors – the researcher concentrates their attention on the data relating to that hypothesis, and regards any other, unanticipated patterns as being of secondary importance. Alternatively, in a study where quantitative data have been collected on a wide range of factors (e.g., in a survey or audit), it is sensible to restrict the analysis as far as possible to providing a descriptive account of what was found, along with a report on any patterns or trends that have merged very clearly in the data, and avoid any temptation to over-analyse.

Exercise 7.2   Thinking like a quantitative researcher

To what extent do you make use of hypothesis testing and probabilistic thinking that occur in your practice as a therapist, or in other areas of your life? What have you learned about these ways of thinking, in the context of non-research situations, that could be relevant to your work as a researcher?

Designing and planning a study so that statistical data are meaningful: statistical power/sample size. The way that a statistical technique operates is that it identifies a 'signal' in a mass of background 'noise'. The assumption is always that a pattern of results will consist of a certain proportion of random error (noise) along with some real effects (signal). In order to increase the likelihood that the signal will be detected, it is necessary to increase the power of the transmitter (size of the sample) or the sensitivity of the detector (accuracy of measurement). Sample size is therefore of paramount importance in quantitative research. The concept of *statistical power* refers to the interplay between the validity and reliability of measures, the predicted effect size of findings, and the sample size that will be necessary in order to achieve a sufficient level of statistical probability/confidence. There are several free, open-access statistical power calculators available on the internet. The concept of statistical power is explained in more detail in Field (2013: 69–90) and other statistics text-books. To gain an understanding of how statistical power operates in research, it is necessary to pay attention to the sample sizes in published studies, as a rough guide to the kind of sample size that is required to carry out different types of investigation. It can be very frustrating to complete a study that is 'under-powered': a great deal of time and effort may have been expended on setting up the study and collecting data, only to find that the results are statistically inconclusive because the sample size was insufficient.

Choosing the appropriate stats technique. There exists a massive statistical 'toolkit' that is available for quantitative researchers – different statistical techniques that have been developed for different tasks. A key skill for any quantitative researcher involves selecting the appropriate statistics technique for the specific study and data-set that have been compiled. All statistics textbooks provide guidelines and criteria for the use of different techniques. In practice, most researchers acquire this kind of knowledge in apprenticeship mode, through guidance from research mentors and supervisors, or being part of a research team. In some situations it may be possible to call on the expertise of statisticians employed within an organisation. It is always valuable to pay attention to the statistical techniques used in recent published studies, as a way of learning about current good practice: guidelines provided in statistics textbooks tend to reflect general principles, rather than specific technical solutions and adaptations that have emerged within particular disciplines of professional communities. In relation to publishing the findings of quantitative studies, it is not unusual for journal reviewers to require further statistical analysis to be carried out. This is because these reviewers are people who represent cutting-edge thinking around statistical methodology. In most circumstances, running an additional statistical procedure is not a difficult thing to do.

Handling data. In any quantitative study, there is a lot to think about in respect of the process of collecting data. Usually, paper or on-line questionnaires and rating scales will be completed by a large number of people. It is necessary to work out robust and ethically-sensitive procedures for making sure that all of this information is collected in a standard fashion, and entered onto a database. For many researchers, SPSS (Field, 2013) functions as a flexible database that enables many different kinds of data analysis. However, in some situations it may be preferable to use a simpler database, such as Excel spreadsheet. Companies who publish widely-used outcome measures, such as CORE or TOPS (see Chapter 9) may also supply custom-designed database systems. It is important to think in advance about whether the chosen database will be sufficient for the amount and type of data that will be collected, will be secure, and will allow the kind of analysis that the researcher plans to carry out. It is also important to give consideration to the amount of time it will take to enter data, and who will undertake this task. Once the data are entered, they will need to be checked for errors. Decisions need to be made about how to handle missing data. Most ethics committees will require a researcher to clarify the length of time that the database will be maintained, and what will happen to the data at the end of that period. None of these tasks are particularly difficult, but they do require attention to detail.

Carrying out statistical analysis. A detailed account of how to carry out statistical analysis is beyond the scope of the present book. In a quantitative study, there is not much point in running a full analysis of the data until all of the information has been collected. In fact, in some types of study, such as RCTs, it is considered poor practice to analyse early returns, because this could act as a source of bias. For example, if a researcher finds that his or her preferred therapy is not producing good results, he or she may subtly manipulate the remaining stage of the study to remedy this situation, perhaps by subverting the randomisation procedure to ensure that more difficult clients are allocated to the comparison therapy condition. The exception to the general principle of not looking at the data until the end, occurs if a study involves risk and side-effects. For example, in an RCT some participants may use their questionnaire responses to indicate suicidal tendencies, or early results may reveal that one of the therapy conditions is associated with an unacceptably high level of drop-outs. It is good practice, in such studies, to build in some minimal monitoring of information as it comes in, to safeguard against risk and harm. The good news about quantitative research is that once all the data have been entered onto a database, the ensuing statistical analysis can be carried out quite quickly. Typically, data can be analysed and the results section of a thesis or research article can be finalised within one or two days of concentrated effort.

Reporting quantitative findings. Quantitative researchers have developed very effective ways of presenting complex data and findings in succinct and accessible ways. As always, it is helpful to look at how this is accomplished in published studies. Usually, statistical data are presented in tables, accompanied by a brief descriptive account in the main text. Published articles provide templates for options around how to format and organise tables of results. Most therapy journals adhere to the American Psychological Association (APA) guidelines around how to report quantitative findings (Cooper, 2010). Other sources of guidance on writing quantitative papers include Belcher (2009), Hartley (2008) and Murray (2009).

Examples of quantitative studies

In order to get a feel for the possibilities of quantitative research in counselling and psychotherapy, it is useful to look at examples. The studies summarised in this section consist of investigations in which the researchers have used statistical techniques that are easy to understand and well within the scope of novice researchers.

Mapping the life experiences and psychological issues of adult children of alcoholics (Mackrill et al., 2012). This study was carried out in Denmark, in a specialist counselling service for the adult children of alcoholics. Over an 18-month period, all new clients who contacted the service were asked to complete a questionnaire that included items on the extent and severity of the alcohol abuse patterns, and their previous attempts to seek help. Clients were also asked to complete standard questionnaire measures of general psychological symptoms, depression and social functioning. These questionnaires were administered on a computer in the agency offices, and took around 45 minutes to complete. Computerised administration of the measures meant that the information that was collected went straight into a database that had been designed for the study. Mackrill et al. (2012) presented their findings in the form of descriptive statistics which mapped the proportion of clients who had undergone different experiences, and the proportions reporting different levels of symptom severity. The implications of these findings for counsellors working with this client group were discussed. This study provides a good example of how quantitative data can be collected within a therapy service in a cost-effective manner, and how a straightforward descriptive account of those data can identify patterns that are relevant for practice.

A naturalistic, practice-based study of successful therapy for depression, panic, and anxiety without panic (Morrison et al., 2003). The aim of this study was to collect information on how therapy works in everyday practice. The authors of the study believed that large-scale randomised trials, which provided the research base for 'empirically-validated treatment' policies in the USA, were based on samples of clients who were systematically different from the clients seen by the majority of therapists in their everyday work. The study used a purpose-designed survey questionnaire, which was mailed to 1,000 experienced therapists who had registered their willingness to be involved in a practice research network. Replies were received from 270 of these practitioners. The questionnaire, which took around 30 minutes to complete, included items on therapeutic orientation, years of experience and work setting. The main section of the questionnaire asked participants to answer questions on their last completed therapy with three clients who respectively had clinically significant levels of symptoms of depression, panic, and anxiety without panic. For each of these clients they provided information on length of treatment, other problems in addition to the main target complaint (comorbidity), time required for clinically significant change to occur, and some other questions about the personality of the client. In the research article that emerged from this study, Morrison, Bradley and Westen (2003) used descriptive statistics to provide a report on key findings such as treatment length, and used t-tests to compare treatment length between clients with no comorbidity, and those with comorbid additional problems. A more complex statistical technique (factor analysis) was used to analyse patterns in the personality data. The main findings of the study were that (a) a high proportion of clients in everyday practice reported complex, comorbid patterns of symptoms; (b) treatment duration in everyday practice was much longer (in the range 50–200 weeks) than in randomised trials; and (c) the type of client recruited in RCT studies comprised around 20% of the clients in this naturalistic study. This study shows how a relatively simple data collection strategy (relatively brief mailed questionnaires) can produce findings that can have a major impact on policy debates, without needing to use advanced statistical techniques. Although factor analysis (a moderately advanced statistical method) was used in part of the analysis, the main findings of this study were based on descriptive statistics and t-tests.

Long-term follow-up of the impact of cognitive-behavioural therapy for anxiety (Durham et al., 2003). In this study, an attempt was made to collect information from patients who had received CBT or other therapies for anxiety, in the context of two randomised trials that had taken place between 8–14 years previously. A researcher tracked down patients using their medical records, and was able to meet up with about half of those who had originally entered the study. At this long-term follow-up meeting, patients were interviewed about their symptoms, and asked about any subsequent treatment they had received. They also completed the same questionnaires that there had been during the original study. Most of the data analysis carried out by Durham et al. (2003) consisted of descriptive statistical presentations of findings related to symptom scores and diagnoses, and t-tests and chi-square tests to compare the statistical significance of differences in outcome for patients who had received CBT versus those who had received other therapies. Chi-square analyses were also used to explore the extent to which the sample of patients who took part in follow-up interviews differed, in terms of factors such as age, gender, previous treatment and other factors, in comparison to those who had not been contactable. The only advanced statistical technique that was employed consisted of a method for checking whether the absence of these missing cases could have made a difference to the over-all conclusions of the study (it did not). The findings of this study were that, on the whole, the improvements that were recorded immediately at the end of treatment were maintained by patients. There was a slight tendency for a more positive effect associated with CBT, compared to other treatments. At the same time, these improve-ments, while welcome, did not mean that those who had received CBT (or other therapies) were symptom-free. More than half still had a diagnosable anxiety disor-der, despite having received further therapy since the original study, with 30–40% being significantly disabled by their condition. For any reader who is relatively new to therapy research, the Durham et al. (2003) article can seem quite daunting – there are a lot of numbers to work through. However, careful reading makes it clear that the authors are merely doing justice to the data: having made a massive effort to locate these patients and hear their stories, they had a responsibility to look at the data from all possible perspectives.

These three studies have been selected because they illustrate what can be achieved using non-advanced statistical techniques. I would argue that each of these studies has made a notable contribution to the counselling and psychotherapy research literature. The contribution that they made arises not from complex statistical analysis, but from well-designed, focused research that investigated a meaningful question. In many quantitative studies, sophisticated statistical analysis is used to identify patterns in large data sets, but without being guided by a clear and practically-relevant research goal. These studies will always find something, and will almost always be publishable because of the respect and authority that are afforded to statistical expertise. But the three studies reviewed in this section took a different approach. The researchers in these studies set up situations in which they were able to collect intrinsically interest-ing information. They then used the minimum level of statistical analysis that was necessary to describe what they had found, and verify the extent to which the differ-ences between groups were statistically significant.

Suggestions for further reading

Comer, J.S. and Kendall, P.C. (2013) 'Methodology, design, and evaluation in psychotherapy research', in M.J. Lambert (ed.), *Bergin and Garfield's Handbook of Psychotherapy and Behavior Change* (6th edn). New York: Wiley.

Discusses the logical basis of quantitative research in counselling and psychotherapy, and the types of research design that are used.

Kazdin, E.E. (ed.) (2003) *Methodological Issues and Strategies in Clinical Research.* Washington, DC: American Psychological Association.
Explores specific statistical issues in depth. Each chapter is written by a leading quantitative researcher.

Cumming, G. (2014) The new statistics: why and how, *Psychological Science,* 25: 7–29.
In recent years, there has been a gradual movement within the field of applied statistics, in the direction of an approach that takes more account of the practical implications of findings. This short paper outlines some of the key principles that lie behind this shift.

Companion website material

The companion website (https://study.sagepub.com/mcleod) includes a set of papers that explore specific topics in quantitative methods:

Erford, B.T., Savin-Murphy, J.A. and Butler, C. (2010) Conducting a meta analysis of counseling outcome research: twelve steps and practical procedures. *Counseling Outcome Research and Evaluation,* 1: 19–43.
Leech, N.L., Onwuegbuzie, A.J. and O'Conner, R. (2011) Assessing internal consistency in counseling research. *Counseling Outcome Research and Evaluation,* 2: 115–25.
Parent, M.C. (2013) Handling item-level missing data: simpler is just as good. *Counseling Psychologist,* 41: 568–600.
Sink, C. and Mvududu, M.H. (2010) Statistical power, sampling, and Effect Sizes: three keys to research relevancy. *Counseling Outcome Research and Evaluation,* 1: 1–18.
Whiston, S.C. and Campbell, W.L. (2010) Randomized Clinical Trials in counseling: an introduction. *Counseling Outcome Research and Evaluation,* 1: 8–18.
Worthington, R.L. and Whittaker, T.A. (2006) Scale development research: a content analysis and recommendations for best practices. *Counseling Psychologist,* 34: 806–38.

8

Using Qualitative Methods

Introduction

In recent years, around 10–20% of research studies on counselling and psycho-therapy topics have made use of qualitative methods. The aim of qualitative research is to describe, explore and analyse the ways that people create meaning in their lives. Qualitative research provides a different perspective to quantitative research. For example, quantitative methods can be used to show that 60% of clients who receive a particular form of therapy report a substantial shift in levels of symptoms of depression. However, the meaning of their therapy, for clients who have undergone that type of intervention, may be quite different. It may be that some of those whose symptoms were reduced, were dissatisfied with the therapy they received. Or some of those whose symptoms remained high were able to point to other ways in which the experience of therapy was meaningful and helpful. It is not that the quantitative evidence is correct and the qualitative evidence is false (or vice versa). These are complementary perspectives. Both of them are necessary if counselling and psychotherapy practice is to be research-informed in any meaningful sense.

The aim of this chapter is to provide an overview of qualitative research, in terms of the various qualitative methodologies that have been developed and the skills and knowledge that are required in order to make use of them. The present chapter leads into Chapters 11, 13 and 14, which introduce specific types of qualitative research project that are suitable for novice researchers.

Why is it important to know about qualitative methods?

Qualitative methods play an increasingly significant role within the counselling and psychotherapy research literature. To be a research-informed practitioner, it is necessary to understand what qualitative research can and cannot do, and to be able to arrive at a balanced appraisal of the value of qualitative studies that are published. Researchers who specialise in quantitative methods still need to know about qualitative methodologies, because at least some of the relevant literature on their topic of interest will be based on qualitative approaches. Both researchers and practitioners seeking to gain an understanding of the development of research in a particular topic need to be able to appreciate the interplay between qualitative and quantitative methodologies over the course of a programme of research. For example, some programmes of research begin with qualitative research that generates themes and hypotheses that are then tested using quantitative techniques.

What do I need to know?

In order to make effective use of qualitative approaches to research, it is important to appreciate that there exist a variety of qualitative traditions, which reflect different research aims and philosophical positions. The territory of qualitative research is a bit of a jungle, so it is essential to go in there with a map. Once inside that territory, there are two key issues that need to be confronted. All qualitative research needs to take account, one way or another, of the subjectivity, personal involvement and reflexivity of the researcher. And all qualitative research needs to be based on a clear understanding of the validity criteria that can be applied to the work that is being done. Finally, there are some practical skills that qualitative researchers need to possess. These aspects of qualitative research competence are discussed in the following sections.

The territory of qualitative research

It is possible to identify a wide range of qualitative methodologies, in the sense of distinctive ways of doing qualitative research that consist of bundles of philosophical assumptions, types of questions that are asked, techniques for collecting and analysing data, and ways of disseminating findings. The most straightforward means of gaining an appreciation of the complexity of contemporary qualitative research is to consult the authoritative *Handbook of Qualitative Research* (Denzin and Lincoln, 2005). It can be quite hard for new researchers to find their bearings and navigate their way round this landscape. There are three main approaches that have been adopted by those who have attempted to find some meaning and order in all of this. The first strategy is to take the view that different qualitative methodologies reflect different underlying philosophical positions. On the whole, this is the stance taken by most of the contributors in Denzin and Lincoln (2005). My own belief is that, while it is essential to possess an understanding of the philosophical grounding of qualitative research, in the end it is not possible to define any of the basic philosophical traditions that are brought into this debate (such as social constructionism, critical realism, and post-structuralism) in a sufficiently clear and unambiguous manner. Also, these philosophical traditions have been adapted and used selectively by qualitative researchers, so that their influence on research practice is somewhat attenuated rather than being clear-cut.

An alternative approach to organising the territory of qualitative research is to look at the applicability of particular qualitative methods to particular research questions. This strategy works quite well in relation to the field of qualitative research in counselling and psychotherapy (McLeod, 2013b), because therapy research is ultimately anchored in a fairly narrow set of practical questions. For example, methods such as grounded theory and Interpretative Phenomenological Analysis (IPA) (see Chapter 11) are ideally suited to exploring the meaning of therapy as experienced by clients. On the other hand, Conversation Analysis (CA) is ideally suited to exploring the way that language is used in therapy interaction, but does not function at all well as a method for exploring the experiences of clients.

A third option is to adopt a historical perspective on qualitative research. A simplified version of the history of qualitative research makes it possible to make sense of why each research approach developed at a particular stage. The earliest qualitative research took place in the discipline of social anthropology, where researchers used ethnographic participant observation to study the culture and way of life of people in far-off places. In the mid-twentieth century, the growth of sociology meant that there was an interest in studying subcultures and specific groups of people within European and North American societies. In order to carry out this research in a cost-effective manner, and because they already possessed some understanding of the people who were being studied, researchers developed a 'cut-down' version of ethnography, involving the use of intensive interviews. This kind of research, in the form of grounded theory and its variants (see Chapter 11) became popular and influential, for example within health research, as a means of giving a voice to marginalised groups of people.

As this type of interview-based qualitative research began to be used more extensively, it became apparent to some researchers that it did not take sufficient account of some important methodological issues. One group of researchers, in ethnomethodology, discourse analysis, narrative analysis and conversation analysis, argued that it was necessary to take a closer look at the way that experience and interaction were constructed through shared use of language. Another group of researchers began to be interested in the extent to which the subjective or personal experience of a researcher might actually represent a useable source of data (autoethnography, heuristic inquiry). Finally, some researchers focused on the political and social role of research, and developed ways of doing research that were more explicitly linked to action and social change (collaborative inquiry, feminist research, queer theory).

So this is where we are today. Ethnography still exists and thrives, as do interview-based methods such as grounded theory. Over recent decades, these approaches have been supplemented by other methods that have highlighted discursive, reflexive and social action perspectives. For reasons of space, this is a somewhat over-simplified historical account. And, of course, as in any area of social life, alternative historical accounts are always available. It is hard to do qualitative research without possessing some level of understanding of why the method that one is using is appropriate, and why alternative approaches may be viewed as less appropriate. A historical perspective offers a potentially valuable means of beginning to develop an overview of this field of study.

Exercise 8.1 Being interested in stories

How interested are you in stories? All forms of qualitative research are based on a process of either collecting stories, or looking at the ways in which stories are constructed. What are the strengths and limitations of stories, as a means of learning about what happens in therapy? In what ways does your own involvement in narrative (as a storyteller, and as a consumer of narratives) shape and influence your attitude to qualitative research?

Thinking like a qualitative researcher

There is a distinctive way of thinking that tends to be found in people who specialise in carrying out qualitative research. To some extent, this can be summed up as a 'discovery-oriented' mind-set. For the most part, qualitative research does not aim to test hypotheses or assess the validity of existing theories. Instead, qualitative research tends to be about *exploring* the meaning of different kinds of experience or ways of interacting with others. The aim is to develop understanding. The concept of understanding refers to a state of knowing in which the person already possesses some degree of understanding, but at the same time has a sense that this understanding could be extended, deepened or 'thickened'. This process of developing understanding never ends – as soon as a new way of understanding has emerged, it invites curiosity about the limits of that way of seeing things.

It can be helpful to break down the concept of understanding into some of its constituent parts. Wolcott (1990) and other qualitative researchers have characterised the process of developing understanding as consisting of three stages: *description, analysis* and *interpretation*. In qualitative inquiry, there is an expectation that the researcher will describe the phenomenon being studied in detail and with memorable clarity. This is a crucial step, because conveying understanding requires that the phenomenon being studied is evoked in the mind of the reader or consumer of a study. The next step, analysis, involves identifying patterns that appear within the phenomenon being studied. This is necessary because understanding requires organisation of the topic or phenomenon, rather than just the presentation of impressions or observations. In effect, the analysis of the topic or phenomenon represents the form of understanding that has been attained by the researcher or research team. Finally, interpretation involves making connections between these findings, and the findings of other studies, and with theoretical perspectives that allow further conceptualisation of the topic. The step of interpretation can be seen as a movement of reaching out to the reader, that invites him or her to consider the value of the study as a means of deepening their pre-existing understanding of the topic.

Viewing the nature of understanding as an interplay between description, analysis and interpretation, leads to consideration of what it is that a qualitative researcher can do to promote and cultivate skills in these areas. There are two main resources that qualitative research draws on, in respect of this issue. Many qualitative researchers become interested in philosophy, in relation to what it can offer in respect of ways of making sense of the process of knowledge. Specifically, philosophical writings on phenomenology (the practice of rigorous description) and hermeneutics (the practice of rigorous interpretation) are highly relevant (McLeod, 2011). Many qualitative researchers also become interested in the act of writing, and the many ways in which meaning can be conveyed in writing. There are some respects in which qualitative research is similar to journalism and other genres of non-fiction writing. There are other respects in which qualitative research can be similar to poetry. In recent years, some qualitative researchers have begun to move beyond the text, and started to look at the ways that meaning can be conveyed through other means, such as art and drama.

Thinking like a qualitative researcher means being interested in *particular* examples or instances of a topic. For instance, to appreciate the human impact of war, it can be useful to compile statistics on death and injury rates and economic impact, read the diaries of combatants, and so on. However, gaining a more complete understanding of the meaning of war can also occur through spending time reflecting on the significance of a single painting or photograph. The principle of particularity has implications for the way that qualitative researchers think about sample sizes. On the whole, qualitative studies with large sample sizes do not work very well, because making sense of a massive amount of data has the inevitable effect of distracting the researcher from allowing the meaningfulness of particular examples or cases fully to emerge. There are many excellent qualitative studies that are based on a single case or example, or a handful of cases.

Researcher reflexivity

In qualitative inquiry, the main instrument of the research is the researcher. In quantitative research, it is possible to collect data through questionnaires or even direct measures of behaviour or physiological function, using techniques that are largely free of the interest or influence of the researcher. It is also possible to analyse quantitative data using pre-determined statistical procedures. These strategies are not available to the qualitative researcher. In qualitative research, it is inevitable that the person of the researcher will exert some kind of influence. For example, interviewee participants may be more willing to say certain things to some interviewers rather than others. When analysing interview transcripts or other forms of qualitative texts, one researcher may be sensitive to meanings that would never occur to one of his or her colleagues. As a result of these factors, the issue of researcher *reflexivity* plays a key role in all qualitative work. Reflexivity refers to the capacity of the person to reflect on his or her experience. Researcher reflexivity refers to the way that the researcher takes account of his or her personal and subjective involvement in the process of carrying out a study. Researcher reflexivity encompasses all aspects of personal identity, ranging from moment-by-moment thoughts and feelings, through to social role and status.

It is important to appreciate that the concept of reflexivity can also be used in relation to the experience of research participants. For example, a person being interviewed continually engages in a process of self-reflection as they consider what to say or not say in response to questions. A key aspect of researcher reflexivity consists of the awareness of participant reflexivity.

Although the identity of the researcher is ever-present during all stages of the research process, it is possible to identify some specific 'moments' within the conduct of qualitative research when a capacity to be reflexive is particularly relevant:

- The choice of research topic.
- Relationships with research participants and colleagues.
- Emotional responses to any aspect of the research.
- Analysing data.
- Selecting particular examples to highlight in a paper or report.

In relation to each of these aspects of a research study, it is helpful to take account of two key questions. To what extent did your personal interests and beliefs influence what you did? In what ways might these personal factors have shaped the conclusions of the study?

In practice, addressing the issue of researcher reflexivity in an effective manner requires the incorporation into the research process of specific procedures. Many qualitative researchers will keep a reflexive journal or diary, in which they will do their best to document their experiences and reflections in relation to moments when the personal meaning of the research became apparent. For example, it is usually helpful, at the start of a study, to take time to write about what one expects to find. It is also usually worthwhile to keep a note of feelings and images that were triggered by the experience of interviewing a person, or reading a transcript or other text. In addition to keeping a research journal, it is also useful to enlist other people, for example research colleagues or supervisors, in conversations about the personal meaning of the research. Other people can offer a crucial external perspective, and typically will draw the attention of the researcher to personal dimensions of the research that they had not considered, or were reluctant to admit. It is then a good idea to incorporate the product of these conversations in a journal. The value of a journal is that it then provides the researcher with a document from which they are able to quote, in subsequent articles and reports. Observations made at the time tend to be more convincing than reflections that take place months after an event. Using a journal also makes it less likely that important personal meanings are lost – sometimes these insights are ephemeral, and are hard to recall if not written down.

A further aspect of researcher reflexivity concerns the inclusion of personal and reflexive writing in dissertations, theses and articles. At the present time, there is a lack of clear consensus across the field of qualitative research as a whole, as well as within therapy research, about how such forms of writing are to be handled. For example, some journals will restrict reflexivity to a brief section within the methods part of a paper, on the identity and expectations of the researcher(s). Some journals will encourage or allow the use of 'I' and 'we'; other journals will discourage these uses. Some journals (e.g., *Qualitative Inquiry*) will actively promote innovation and experimentation in terms of forms of researcher reflexivity. Building-in reflexivity procedures from the start, such as journal writing and conversations, makes it possible for a qualitative researcher to have choices regarding reflexive writing when the time comes to publish their work.

Researcher reflexivity is not a matter of bias. Part of the ability to think like a qualitative researcher is an appreciation that this kind of research does not produce anything that could reasonably be claimed as objective truth. Instead, qualitative research generates a construction and understanding of a topic that reflect and are shaped by the identity and position of the researcher. Taking account of researcher reflexivity allows the researcher to make the most of what he or she brings to the research process. For example, previous personal experience of a topic may sensitise the researcher to the deeper significance of that topic in the lives of informants, and may make the researcher more credible and trustworthy to informants. Taking account of reflexivity also makes it possible for readers or consumers of research to make up their own minds, and interpret findings in the context of an informed knowledge of who did the study and what it was like for them to do so. From the perspective of the reader, bias warning bells will start to sound when it appears as though the findings of a study might have been shaped by unconscious and undisclosed sources of personal interest on the part of the researcher.

Further reading on reflexivity

Anyone who carries out any kind of qualitative research needs to work out their personal position around researcher reflexivity. This task necessitates doing some reading around the topic. Many qualitative researchers have found that the writings of Kim Etherington and Linda Finlay are particularly clear and meaningful, in relation to understanding reflexivity. Other useful sources include the following:

Alvesson, M. and Skoldberg, K. (2000) *Reflexive Methodology*. London: Sage.
Berg, D.N. and Smith, K.K. (eds) (1988) *The Self in Social Inquiry: Researching Methods*. London: Sage.
Etherington, K. (2004) *Becoming a Reflexive Researcher: Using Our Selves in Research*. London: Jessica Kingsley.
Finlay, L. and Gough, B. (eds) (2003) *Reflexivity: A Practical Guide for Researchers in Health and Social Sciences*. Oxford: Blackwell.
Hertz, R. (ed.) (1997) *Reflexivity and Voice*. Thousand Oaks, CA: Sage.

Exercise 8.2   Being a reflexive researcher

What does researcher reflexivity mean to you, in the context of the research that you are planning, or are already conducting? In what ways do you monitor and record the personal dimension of your involvement in research? How do you intend to use this information?

Validity issues in qualitative research

Within the mainstream quantitative research tradition, the concept of validity refers to the ultimate 'truth' of a measurement or set of research conclusions. For example, does a depression questionnaire actually measure specific symptoms of depression, or do the scores it produces merely reflect the general sense of a lack of wellbeing? Similarly, can the overall findings of research study be taken as a guide to action or are these lacking in generalisability or even erroneous? The concept of reliability refers to the extent to which similar results would be obtained in different situations by a different researcher or research team. For example, a depression questionnaire would be considered unreliable if it turned out that people gave different answers when they completed it in their own homes, compared with at a GP's surgery.

There exist well-established and widely-accepted statistical procedures for determining reliability and validity in quantitative research. In qualitative research, the situation is quite different. As discussed in the previous sections, qualitative research aims to produce a nuanced understanding of a topic, rather than 'factual truth', and the qualitative research process is influenced by the person of the researcher in several key respects. It is not possible, therefore, merely to apply quantitative concepts of reliability and validity in qualitative studies. It has been necessary, instead, to develop concepts of 'quality control' that are specific to qualitative inquiry. When discussing the value of their work, qualitative researchers tend to employ such terms as 'credibility', 'plausibility' and 'usefulness'.

Alongside these terms, qualitative researchers have identified a set of procedures for enhancing the credibility of a qualitative study. These include:

- transparency and clarity around the way in which data were analysed;
- providing examples of themes and categories;
- disclosure of relevant aspects of the identity and experience of the researcher(s);
- external auditing of data analysis.

Further discussion of these procedures can be found in McLeod (2011, 2013b). Key benchmark statements within the qualitative literature, outlining validity criteria in qualitative research, have been published by Elliott, Fischer and Rennie (1999) and Stiles (1993). It is essential for anyone planning to undertake a piece of qualitative research to become familiar with these criteria as early as possible and then incorporate them into the design of the study. Unlike in quantitative research, validity in qualitative research cannot be attained by merely following a set of procedural rules. There are few, if any, qualitative studies that implement all of the validity strategies that are discussed in the literature. Some procedures may be impossible to follow, for practical or ethical reasons. For example, it can be very helpful to have an independent expert researcher look at the whole of one's data analysis, and make comments. In practice, this is a highly time-consuming task, and it may be beyond the persuasive powers of a researcher to secure the services of an external auditor for that length of time. Similarly, it can be very helpful for research participants to comment on the analysis of their own interview, or the findings of the study as a whole. However, this kind of strategy can be ethically problematic in the absence of some facility for checking on whether participants may have become distressed in some way on reading the results of the study, and offering support.

Practical skills and time management

There are many practical skills associated with the use of qualitative methods, for example in such areas as conducting interviews, preparing transcripts of interviews, working with analysis of texts, and creating systems for managing textual data. Developing competence and confidence in these areas is a matter of learning-through-doing, preferably in the context of an apprenticeship relationship within which the novice researcher can observe how these tasks are accomplished by more experienced colleagues.

A key aspect of the practice of qualitative inquiry is a willingness to become *immersed* in the task of making sense of the data. The personal and time demands of qualitative research are rather different from those of quantitative research. Research is always hard work. The work of quantitative research can be fairly readily parcelled up into blocks of time, for example checking the accuracy of the data on one evening, running a particular stats test on another evening, and so on. By contrast, qualitative research has a tendency to take over a researcher's life. Talk to anyone who has completed a qualitative study, and they will describe occasions when they listened to interview recordings while on the running machine at the gym, while driving their car, or lazing on the beach on holiday. They will also describe scenarios in which the walls of their spare room, or all available surfaces in their dining area, were covered with post-it notes and bits of text. This kind of personal immersion is necessary because there is a point at which a qualitative researcher needs to be able to hold the totality of the material at the forefront of his or her attention, and allow the meaning of that material to be tested against his or her imagination and inner emotional life.

Exercise 8.3   Stretching exercises

A book by Janesick (2011) offers a series of 'stretching exercises' for qualitative researchers – a wide range of tasks that introduce creative ways of observing and listening that are necessary for qualitative work. Working your way through these exercises provides excellent preparation for doing a qualitative study.

Suggestions for further reading

Minichiello, V. and Kottler, J.A. (eds) (2010) *Qualitative Journeys: Student and Mentor Experiences with Research*. Thousand Oaks, CA: Sage.
This edited book consists of a series of first-person accounts on doing qualitative research for the first time. Other than actually being involved in a qualitative investigation, these chapters represent the closest that it is possible to get to a practical understanding of what it is like to engage in this kind of work.

Fischer, C.T. (ed.) (2006) *Qualitative Research Methods for Psychologists: Introduction through Empirical Examples*. New York: Academic Press.
Experienced qualitative researchers, such as Anna Madill, Susan Morrow and David Rennie, share their experience of conducting qualitative research on therapy and other areas of psychology.

An overview and introduction to qualitative research in counselling and psycho-therapy, along with many recommendations around key, must-read, exemplar studies, can be found in:

McLeod, J. (2011) Qualitative Research in Counselling and Psychotherapy (2nd edn). London: Sage.
McLeod, J. (2013) 'Qualitative research: methods and contributions', in M.J. Lambert (ed.), *Bergin and Garfield's Handbook of Psychotherapy and Behavior Change* (5th edn). New York: Wiley.

An invaluable introduction to the philosophical grounding of qualitative inquiry is available in:

Ponterotto, J.G. (2005) Qualitative research in counseling psychology: a primer on research paradigms and philosophy of science, *Journal of Counseling Psychology*, 52: 126–36.

Companion website material

The companion website (https://study.sagepub.com/mcleod) provides access to the following qualitative research resources:

Charmaz, C. (2004) Premises, principles, and practices in qualitative research: revisiting the foundations. *Qualitative Health Research*, 14: 976–93.
Finlay, L. (2013) Unfolding the phenomenological research process: iterative stages of "seeing afresh". *Journal of Humanistic Psychology*, 53: 172–201.
Hill, C.E., Thompson, B.J., Nutt-Williams, E. (1997) A guide to conducting consensual qualitative research. *Counseling Psychologist*, 25: 517–72.
Larsen, D., Flesaker, K. and Stege, R. (2008) Qualitative interviewing using Interpersonal Process Recall: investigating internal experiences during professional-client conversation. *International Journal of Qualitative Methods*, 7: 18–37.
Rennie, D.L. and Fergus, K.D. (2006) Embodied categorizing in the grounded theory method: Methodical hermeneutics in action. *Theory and Psychology*, 16: 483–503.
Woo, H. and Heo, N. (2013) A content analysis of qualitative research in select ACA journals (2005–2010). *Counseling Outcome Research and Evaluation*, 4: 13–25.

9

Basic Research Tools

Introduction

It is not easy to investigate the process and outcome of therapy, or the ways in which therapy is understood and organised within different social settings. Counselling and psychotherapy are complex activities, that take place at various levels – cognitive, physical, emotional, interpersonal – over varying periods of time. One of the primary achievements of the counselling and psychotherapy research community, over the past seventy years, has been to construct reliable tools and methods that can be used to gain access to aspects of what happens in therapy. The aim of this chapter is to provide an introduction to some of the most widely adopted therapy research tools. Within a chapter of this length, it is not possible to offer a comprehensive listing of all the scales, instruments and forms that are in circulation. The intention, rather, is to highlight the market leaders, discuss how they can be applied, and indicate some of the criteria against which their value can be assessed. Further information on many of these instruments can be found on the companion website for this book (https://study.sagepub.com/mcleod).

Why do I need to know about basic research tools?

There are several reasons for being interested in research instruments and techniques. First, these products represent the 'tools of the trade' – in order to carry out one's own personal research, it is necessary to be able to use one or more of these tools in a competent and thoughtful manner. The techniques described in this chapter all 'work', in the sense of forming the basis for successful, publishable and influential pieces of research. Appropriate deployment of any of these techniques allows a researcher to buy in to the achievements of the researcher or team who developed the method, and of subsequent researchers who have used it within published studies. For example, collecting outcome data using a particular questionnaire, such as the CORE-OM, makes it possible to compare findings with the innumerable other studies that have gathered similar data.

A second reason for learning about research tools is that it is hard to read and appreciate research papers in the absence of an understanding of the techniques that were used to collect information. Typically, in a research paper, only very brief information is provided about questionnaires or other research tools that were used. It is assumed that the reader will already be familiar with these instruments, or, if not, will be willing to go off and read about them. A third way in which an interest in research tools is important, is concerned with the necessity to take a critical and questioning approach to all knowledge claims. For example, there are many therapy studies that have examined outcome in terms of change in client scores on the Beck Depression Inventory (BDI). A full appreciation of the meaning of the results of these studies requires understanding of how the BDI is constructed, and what it can and cannot do. Closer reflection on the ways in which knowledge is constructed or 'operationalised' through the implementation of various data collection techniques can be surprisingly informative and interesting. In respect of the BDI, for instance, anyone who looks closely at how it was constructed and how it operates will realise that it captures certain aspects of depression but not others. Thinking about whether these missing aspects are important enough to make a difference to how the results of a study could be interpreted invites consideration about the very nature of depression and its treatment.

A final facet of this topic relates to the possibility of designing new research tools. In general, it is not a good idea for a novice researcher to devise their own questionnaire or rating scale. Usually, a satisfactory scale already exists in the literature. Also, developing a new tool takes a lot of time and effort, and needs to be seen as a research project in itself. Curiosity and interest around available research tools are usually sufficient to convince a novice researcher that developing a new scale is not worth the bother.

Using research tools – general principles

When using any of the techniques introduced in this chapter to collect research information that might be included in a published study, it is essential to seek approval from the client before the commencement of therapy. Issues around ethical informed consent are discussed more fully in Chapter 4. It is also important to consider practical issues associated with the use of a data collection technique, such as its acceptability to research participants and the amount of time it will take to complete.

Some of the scales and instruments discussed in this chapter are copyrighted, and can only be used with the permission of the author or the organisation that owns the copyright. Sometimes a fee will need to be paid for each questionnaire or scale that is used, or for a licence to use the instrument for a specific period of time. Occasionally, access to a scale is restricted to users who have undergone specific training. There are also many research tools that are freely available, and are accessible either through the websites of researchers or research teams/organisations, or within the text of research articles. Some researchers are willing to allow anyone to use their research instruments, but only on the basis of a personal request – this allows them to keep track of who is using the instrument, and inform those users about updates. On the whole, it is in the interests of those who develop research tools to promote and support the use of their products on as wide a scale as possible.

It is always necessary, and established good practice, to provide reference details for any research tools that are used in a study.

On the whole, once a research tool has been developed, there is an expectation that it will be used as it is, without alteration. It is important to proceed with caution in any situation where it may seem desirable to change the items, instructions or format of a research tool. With standardised, psychometric measures such as the BDI or CORE-OM, any change will mean that it is not possible to compare findings with the results of previous studies that have used the intact, 'official' version of the scale. Tampering with such a scale may even be regarded as a breach of copyright, or lead to journal reviewers rejecting an article. Other techniques, such as the Change Interview or any qualitative interview schedule, are more flexible. In these cases, the original version can be seen as a template that can be adjusted according to circumstances.

Many research tools have been translated into different languages, and data may even be available on scale reliability and validity, and norms, in a range of language communities. Translating a scale is a complex endeavour because of the ways in which the meaning of emotional and psychological terms may be subtly different in different languages.

How is it possible to decide whether a research tool is worth using? What are the criteria through which the value of research tools can be assessed? These questions can be approached from three directions: *validity, reliability*, and *heuristic value*. Deciding on the best tool to include in any particular study means finding the most appropriate balance between these factors.

Validity

The concept of validity refers to the ability of the test, questionnaire, rating scale or other type of instrument to measure the actual construct it claims to be measuring. Strictly speaking, all techniques or tools employed in research studies should be backed up by data demonstrating acceptable levels of reliability and validity. For the most widely used method, data are made available from the publishers of the instrument in the form of a test manual, or are reported in a journal article by the author of the technique. If an instrument or test has been created for use in a specific study, reliability and validity information should be provided in the report on the study.

Many tests used in counselling research have been applied in the absence of basic information about reliability and validity. A researcher utilising an instrument that has not been shown to be reliable and valid runs the risk of producing results that are meaningless or lacking in credibility.

In relation to quantitative methods, the main forms of validity include:

Face validity. The instrument, measure or test appears to measure what it claims to measure. This can be helpful in gaining acceptance for the test in some groups, but can be a hindrance if it allows respondents to guess what the test is about, and shape their answers to achieve 'impression management'.

Content validity. The items in the instrument comprehensively reflect the domain of meaning that is intended to be measured. For example, an instrument designed to assess depression will have items relating to all aspects of depression.

Criterion validity. An estimate of whether the instrument differentiates between people in the same way as other types of measures. For example, concurrent criteria for a social anxiety scale might include observations made by nurses. Predictive criteria refer to measures taken at a later time. For example, the predictive validity of a social anxiety scale might be future level of participation in a discussion group.

Construct validity. Scores on the test correlate (or otherwise) with scores on other tests in accordance with theoretical predictions. For example, measures of social and manifest anxiety should correlate more highly with each other (convergent validity) than they do with measures of depression (divergent validity).

The issue of validity is less straightforward in qualitative research, for example when open-ended interviews or diaries are used to collect research data. The question of qualitative validity is discussed on pages 99–100.

There are some rather serious issues associated with the validity of the kinds of self-report questionnaires and rating scales that are widely used in counselling and psychotherapy research. Research in social psychology has established that when people evaluate a situation or action, their judgements are heavily influenced by a general, evaluative, good-bad dimension. This has important implications for therapy research. For example, when a client completes a questionnaire that is intended to measure a specific factor such as depression, anxiety or wellbeing, it is probable that their responses will largely reflect their sense of overall distress. As a result, there tend to be high correlations between scores on specific problem areas. In other words, it is hard to differentiate between theoretically interesting dimensions of distress – what you tend to get is a picture of overall unhappiness. The other difficulty associated with the validity of self-report scales is concerned with the fact that completing a questionnaire or other instrument is a social act or performance. The person is not merely reporting on, say, how depressed they feel, but is also at the same time engaged, at some level, in a process of impression management. This dilemma is often discussed in the context of the concept of *social desirability* – when a person completes a questionnaire, is he or she describing how depressed they are, or do their responses say more about how willing they are to admit that they are depressed? Further discussion of these issues can be found in McLeod (2001). In the end, these considerations point in the direction of an acknowledgement of the importance of *methodological pluralism* (making use of different methods). Self-report measures are hugely convenient to use, and have made a massive contribution to therapy research. However, as with any other method, they also have fundamental limitations.

Reliability

The concept of reliability refers to the robustness of a test, questionnaire, rating scale or other type of instrument. A high level of reliability means that the technique produces similar results in different situations or when administered by different people or at different times. The concept of reliability is particularly associated with quantitative research tools, and the main forms of reliability which need to be established by those who have developed such tools can include:

Test-retest reliability. An assessment of the extent to which similar scores are recorded when the measure is administered to the same person or group of people on two (or more) occasions.

Alternate form reliability. The same group of people are given parallel versions of the instrument on different occasions, and their scores are compared.

Internal consistency. A reliability coefficient that estimates the extent to which different items in a test are in agreement with each other (Leech, Onwuegbuzie and O'Conner, 2011).

Inter-rater reliability. The level of agreement between different raters who have coded or categorised the same set of data.

These concepts of reliability are applicable in qualitative research, but with some caveats. For example, in an interview study, it can be very useful to conduct more than one interview with participants. However, if a person says something different in a second interview, compared to the first meeting, this may not mean that one of these statements is wrong, and the other is correct (although that may occur). It may be that the development of a stronger relationship of trust allows the informant to go deeper into their experience at the second interview. Similarly, when two researchers arrive at diverging interpretations of a segment of a transcript, it may indicate a lack of reliability (i.e., each researcher is operating from a different idea of what the research is trying to achieve) but it may equally serve as a trigger for further dialogue between the researchers, that will eventually lead to a more complete or deeper interpretation of the material.

Heuristic value

Even when a research tool possesses only marginal validity or reliability, or where reliability and validity are hard to establish, the instrument or technique may nevertheless possess a high level of *heuristic* value. The concept of 'heuristic value' refers to the capacity to generate new insights and understanding, or contribute to a process of discovery. Heuristic value can apply to the use of research tools strictly in relation to research purposes, and also to the use of tools as a means of enhancing the process of therapy. The easiest way to understand this concept is through examples.

The *Helpful Aspects of Therapy* (HAT) instrument, described in more detail later in the chapter, consists of a form that clients and/or therapists complete after the end of a therapy session, where they are invited to identify and briefly describe a helpful and hindering event or episode in the session. It is extremely difficult to determine whether these accounts are valid, in the sense of reflecting everything that was helpful (almost certainly not), or even what was most helpful (the person may not have been aware of what 'really' helped). The instrument is also somewhat unreliable, because sometimes a person may write a lot, and other times much less, and what is written may be cryptic or hard to interpret. Nevertheless, what is produced is interesting and meaningful, and in case study research (see for example Elliott et al., 2009; Smith et al., 2014) this can be triangulated against other sources of information that may be available (e.g., shifts in scores on outcome measures). In other words, as a stand-alone measure, the HAT does not work very well, but when used alongside other sources of information, its availability makes it possible to see patterns that would otherwise have been hidden from view.

The package of measures developed by Miller et al. (2005), such as the Outcome Rating Scale (ORS) and Session Rating Scale (SRS) (both described later in the chapter) are very brief, and 'visual' rather than 'textual'. As a result, they do not attain the levels of statistical validity and reliability reported by more conventional questionnaire scales such as the OQ-45. However, they are tremendously user-friendly, and work marvellously well as 'conversational tools' that help the therapist and client to collaboratively monitor the progress of therapy.

Projective techniques (described below) present the person with an ambiguous task, such as writing a story triggered by looking at an unclear image. This type of method can be used to generate a reliable and valid measure of constructs such as achievement motivation (McClelland, 1980). However, because the levels of validity and reliability associated with projective techniques do not match the standards obtained in self-report questionnaires, this approach is rarely used (Lilienfeld et al., 2000). This is a pity, because there are ways in which projective techniques have substantial heuristic value. In some research situations, it may be helpful to use a method that highlights an aspect of a phenomenon that is not accessible through a self-report questionnaire. For example, Shedler, Mayman and Manis (1993) found that some individuals who recorded low scores on a symptom questionnaire, revealed high levels of symptoms in their responses to a projective technique. This result raises important questions about the accuracy of questionnaire-based symptom measures if a client is in some sense 'in denial' in respect of his or her distress. In qualitative research, and case study research, projective tools can be used to invite and enable participants to express themselves in imaginative ways, that can then be interpreted or analysed in light of information provided by more standard means.

Because of the extent to which quantitative methodologies have dominated the field of counselling and psychotherapy research, there has been little explicit discussion or acknowledgement of the concept of the heuristic value of research tools. However, this criterion is nevertheless implicit in the design of many studies.

The following sections of the chapter provide an introduction to various types of research tool that have been used, or could be used, in therapy research.

Exercise 9.1   Learning about research tools from the inside

As you learn about new research tools, in later sections of this chapter, try to find copies of at least some of them, and try them out on yourself. Many of these measures are available on the internet. As you complete each measure, do so mindfully – be aware of the thoughts, feelings and fantasies that are triggered for you. Imagine what it would be like to complete the scale if you were a client. Look closely at the instructions and format of the measure – what implicit meanings and messages are conveyed by these aspects of the instrument?

Outcome measures

An enormous amount of effort has been expended, over many years, on the task of evaluating the outcomes of therapy. Within the research community, every decade or so, complaints arise about the proliferation of outcome measures, and the need to concentrate efforts on using an agreed 'core battery' of scales. Inevitably, this is followed by a renewed outpouring of new scales. It seems highly unlikely that an agreed core battery will ever be adopted. There are a great many theoretically interesting and practically important aspects of therapy outcome. Scale developers are continually finding ways to enhance the reliability, validity and usability of measures. There are also commercial pressures in play – there is profit to be made from outcome packages that can be sold to healthcare providers. This section focuses on describing the most widely-used outcome scales. At the present time, there is no single review or on-line resource that brings together information on all the outcome measures that are available. Useful starting points for sources of such information include Bowling (2001, 2004), Cone (2001), Ogles, Lambert and Fields (2002) and Trauer (2010). Outcome (and process) measures specifically developed in accordance with principles of psychodynamic therapy are discussed in Levy and Ablon (2009) and Levy, Ablon and Kächele (2012).

When selecting an outcome scale for use in a research study, there will be a number of factors that will need to be taken into consideration:

- Does the instrument assess an outcome factor that is relevant to the goals of the study?
- Have the reliability and validity of the scale been established?
- Do norms exist that can be used for differentiating between 'clinical' and 'non-clinical' populations or cases, and thus making it possible to engage in benchmarking comparisons and estimating the cut-off points for clinically significant and reliable change?
- Has the instrument been used in other studies with similar client groups or therapy approaches, thus allowing the results to be compared?
- Is the questionnaire acceptable to clients (e.g., clarity of questions, cultural sensitivity, length of time to complete)?
- Is the scale sensitive to change, or does it assess enduring personality characteristics that are unlikely to be effected by therapy?

Outcome assessment can be achieved through standardised questionnaire measures of symptom or problem areas such as anxiety or depression, or by using individualised personal questionnaires or target complaints scales, in which a client describes their goals for therapy in their own words. It can be valuable to use both methods together, to capture any personal or idiosyncratic dimensions of change, as well as more general problem areas. Outcome data can also be collected through interviews (see the later section).

A selection of the most widely-used self-report therapy questionnaire outcome measures is provided in the following paragraphs.

CORE-OM (Clinical Outcomes Routine Evaluation – Outcome Measure) is a 34-item, self-report questionnaire which measures general client psychological distress (Barkham et al.,

2006; Evans et al., 2000; Mellor-Clark et al., 1999). This scale was designed to yield scores on four subscales: wellbeing, symptoms, functioning and risk. However, further research suggests that these subscales do not represent distinct factors; in recent studies, only the overall score has tended to be reported. The CORE-OM questionnaire is easy to understand, and has been found to be acceptable to the majority of clients. Typically, it is administered at the beginning and end of therapy, so that change scores can be calculated. Client scores on entry into counselling can be used to examine the profile of clients seen by an agency. There are also assessment and end of therapy forms completed by the counsellor, with the result that the CORE system can operate as a comprehensive evaluation package. Versions for children and young people, and those with learning difficulties, are available. CORE materials can be downloaded from the CORE-IMS website, and copied without charge. A low-cost software package is available to facilitate data analysis. The CORE questionnaire has been widely adopted by counselling, psychotherapy and clinical psychology service providers in Britain and other countries, and translations have been carried out. A great deal of data have been collected on the progress of therapy with clients in a range of settings, enabling the 'benchmarking' of standards of effectiveness (Barkham et al., 2001; Mellor-Clark et al., 2001).

Outcome Questionnaire (OQ-45) is similar to CORE, and is widely used in the USA. The OQ comprises a 45-item scale which provides a measure of overall disturbance, as well as subscale scores of subjective distress, interpersonal relations, social role functioning, suicide, substance abuse, and workplace violence. A version of the scale for use with children and adolescents has also been produced. As with CORE, software packages and benchmarking norms are available. Further information on the OQ can be found in Lambert and Finch (1999). Access to the OQ-45 is only available by paying a licensing fee to its distributors.

Treatment Outcome Profile (TOP) is a 58-item symptom scale that generates a client profile in relation to 12 domains: sexual functioning; work functioning; violence; social functioning; panic/anxiety; substance abuse; psychosis; quality of life; sleep; suicidality; depression; mania. Versions are available for children, young people, and older people and the scale has been translated into several languages. Further information is available in Kraus and Castonguay (2010). A unique feature of this scale is that it makes it possible to analyse client outcomes in terms of broad, quasi-diagnostic categories. This can be useful for therapy services that are required to collect information on their effectiveness with different groups of clients. A further unique feature is that the scale can only be analysed by sending the data (on-line) to a central office – it is not possible for the researcher or practitioner to work out the score by him- or herself, because items are weighted according to an algorithm. Access to TOP requires the payment of a license fee.

Outcome Rating Scale (ORS) is a 4-item visual analogue scale of global psychological difficulties (Miller, Duncan and Hubble, 2005). Simple, free to use, and very acceptable to clients, this is downloadable from the internet.

Beck Depression Inventory (BDI-II) is a 21-item scale designed to assess depression (Beck et al., 1961). Each item comprises a set of four or five self-statements of increasing severity (e.g., 'I do not feel sad', 'I feel blue or sad') that can either be read out to the testee or administered as a self-rating questionnaire that the person completes on his or her own. The person selects the statement that best fits the way he or she feels at 'this moment'. The BDI is used in research as a screening and outcome measure. Beck, Steer and Garbin (1988) provide a review of developments in the validation and use of this scale.

Patient Health Questionnaire (PHQ-9) is a 9-item depression scale (Kroenke et al., 2001). Widely used in the UK, it is included in the evaluation package for the Improving Access to Psychological Therapies (IAPT) programme. It is also free to use, and downloadable from the internet.

Generalized Anxiety Disorder scale (GAD-7) is a 7-item anxiety measure (Spitzer et al., 2006). Widely used in the UK, it is included in the evaluation package for the Improving Access to Psychological Therapies (IAPT) programme. Once again it is free to use, and downloadable from the internet.

Hospital Anxiety and Depression Scale (HADS) is a 14-item scale of depression and anxiety (seven anxiety items; seven depression items) (Bjelland et al., 2002; Zigmond and Snaith, 1983). Widely used in therapy research, it is free to use, and downloadable from the internet.

General Health Questionnaire (GHQ) is available in 12, 28, 32 and 60-item versions and is a measure of general psychological stress, with (depending on the version) subscales that assess somatic symptoms, anxiety and insomnia, social dysfunction and severe depression (Goldberg and Hillier, 1979; Goldberg and Williams, 1988). The GHQ has been around for a long time, and has been used with a wide range of occupational groups and patient populations. It is perhaps better suited as a screening measure (e.g., in several studies, to determine the proportion of GP patients with psychological problems), rather than as a therapy outcome measure – the instructions are worded in a way that encourages the person to respond on the basis of longer-term issues rather than recent shifts. It has restricted access and requires the payment of a fee.

Systemic Clinical Outcome and Routine Evaluation (SCORE) is an outcome scale for evaluating the effectiveness of family therapy (Stratton et al., 2010). Available in 15, 29 or 40-item versions. Measures three dimensions of family functioning: strengths and adaptability; overwhelmed by difficulties; disrupted communication. Free to use, it is available from the principal author.

Inventory of Interpersonal Problems (IIP) is a questionnaire that assesses the patterns of interpersonal problems that are causing difficulties in a person's life (Horowitz et al., 2008; Woodward et al., 2005), and 32 or 64-item versions are available. The IIP is structured around eight sub-scales: domineering/controlling; vindictive/self-centred; cold/distant; socially inhibited; non-assertive; overly accommodating; self-sacrificing; intrusive/needy. This has been widely used in counselling and psychotherapy research studies. It requires the payment of a fee for access.

Self-Understanding of Interpersonal Patterns Scale (SUIP-R) is a 28-item scale that measures self-understanding of maladaptive interpersonal patterns (Connolly et al., 1999). Free to use, it is downloadable from the internet and explores similar territory to the IIP.

Hopkins Symptom Checklist (SCL-90) was initially developed at Johns Hopkins University. The aim of the test is to detect levels of psychiatric symptomatology. The standard 90-item version of the test has nine sub-scales: depression, anxiety, somatisation, obsessive-compulsive, interpersonal sensitivity, hostility, phobic anxiety, paranoid ideation and psychoticism. There also exist shorter versions of the test. The format of the SCL-90 presents the respondent with a list of symptoms, such as 'heart pounding or racing' or 'trembling' (both anxiety items) and the instruction to indicate the severity of these on a four-point scale ranging from 'not at all' to 'extremely'. Derogatis and Melisaratos (1983) provide further details on the operation of this test. The SCL-90 is highly regarded, but less widely used in recent years because of the substantial cost of the license.

State-Trait Anxiety Inventory (STAI) was devised by Spielberger et al. (1970) to assess anxiety both as an enduring personality characteristic or *trait*, and as a transient condition or *state*. The scale comprises 40 items, separated into two sections. The first section asks respondents to rate how they *generally* feel (trait anxiety) and the second half instructs them to answer in terms of how they feel now (state anxiety). Items consist of a statement followed by a four-point response scale. The STAI has been used to assess change in anxiety during and as a result of therapy. Access to this scale requires the purchase of a licence.

Warwick-Edinburgh Mental Well-being Scale (WEMWBS) is a 14-item measure of positive mental health (Tennant et al., 2007). Fairly recently developed, it has thus far not been widely used in counselling and psychotherapy research. It is conceptually interesting and instinctive, because it seeks to evaluate positive mental health rather than symptoms and distress.

Perceived Stress Scale (PRS) is a 10-item instrument to assess life stress (Cohen et al., 1983). There are many stress questionnaires available; this one has the advantage of being brief.

Minnesota Multiphasic Personality Inventory (MMPI) is a 566-item questionnaire developed during the 1930s to generate a personality profile focused on psychiatric or adjustment problems. The ten clinical scales included in the test provide measures of the following variables: hypochondriasis, depression, hysteria, psychopathic deviation, paranoia, psychasthenia, schizophrenia, mania, masculine-feminine interests, and social introversion-extroversion. The MMPI has often been used as a screening device to select subjects for inclusion in a study, and has also been employed in the assessment of change resulting from therapy. Shorter forms of the scale have been devised. Further information about the MMPI is available in Duckworth (1990). This scale has not been widely used in recent years because it has been shown to be less sensitive to change than other, more recent instruments such as the OQ-45.

The scales listed above are all broadly similar, in requiring participants to respond to a set of statements within the questionnaire, indicative of general symptomatology, depression, anxiety, or other dimensions of distress or wellbeing. An important strength of these instruments is that all participants are responding to exactly the same items, with the result that cross-case or cross-group comparisons can be made without difficulty. However, a drawback to such scales is that some items may not be relevant to particular individuals, and issues that are central to a person's difficulties may not be included at all. In a scale such as the CORE-OM, for example, it may be that only four or five items are directly relevant for a particular client, with all the other items functioning as 'filler'. If this occurs, it is likely that significant change may be missed, since a shift in a positive direction on only a few items may appear to not reflect a trivial amount of change. A methodological strategy that directly addresses this limitation is to use individualised measures, in which the client writes down (or the researcher writes down, following an interview) the key issues or goals for therapy. The client can then carry out ratings, week-by-week, of the degree to which these issues are still bothering them, or the degree to which goals have been attained. Individualised measures therefore have the potential to be highly sensitive to change on a case-by-case basis. In recent years, several individualised outcome measures have been devised:

- *Personal Questionnaire* (Elliott, Shapiro and Mack, 1999; Wagner and Elliott, 2001).
- *Target Complaint* rating scale (Deane et al., 1997).
- *CORE Goal Attainment Form* (details available on the CORE-IMS website).
- *Psychological Outcome Profile* (PSYCHLOPS) (Ashworth et al., 2007, 2008).
- *Measure Yourself Medical Outcome Profile* (MYMOP) (Paterson, 1996; Paterson and Britten, 2000).

Individualised measures function as a valuable supplement to standard questionnaires in many studies, because of their sensitivity to change. However, it can be difficult to compare across clients or groups because some clients may identify goals that are hard-to-impossible to attain, while others may nominate goals that are more realistic. In addition, a client's goals may change over the course of therapy. For these reasons, individualised goal/problem measures do not represent a complete solution to the issue of outcome evaluation in counselling and psychotherapy. There has been a lot of research in recent years into the nature and dynamics of client goals in therapy, and it seems likely that over time the findings of these studies will contribute to the development of a new generation of individualised outcome measures.

An issue that needs to be taken into consideration when using ultra-brief scales, such as most of the individualised measures listed above, or other widely-used scales such as the ORS, is that, in general, the more items there are in a test the more reliable and valid it is likely to be. This phenomenon can be understood by thinking about the problem of measuring anxiety. An anxiety scale with only one item (e.g., 'Do you worry a lot?') can only invite the respondent to comment on one aspect of anxiety. A scale with 20 items will enable the respondent to reflect on many different nuances of their experience of anxiety. It permits the test constructor to explore a whole range of meanings of anxiety, from panic and terror at one end to unease or disquiet at the other. Multiple item scales also help to prevent any distortion caused by the phrasing of any individual item. A major difficulty arises, however, when a researcher wishes to collect data on several variables. If each variable is assessed through a 20-item scale, in the end the respondent may be required to answer several hundred questions. In these circumstances cooperation may be threatened or the quality of the attention that the respondent gives to each item may be diminished.

A further type of outcome assessment tool, which is even more sensitive to change, is to interview the client either following the end of treatment, or at the start and finish of treatment. The *Change Interview* (Elliott et al., 2001) is a structured interview schedule, which includes a set of open-ended questions alongside some scaling items. The client is asked to identify areas of change, and then indicate on a 5-point scale the extent to which each area of change was significant, expected, and attributable to therapy.

In summary, it can be seen that there exists a wide range of methods for evaluating the effectiveness of counselling and psychotherapy. It is important to emphasise that there are many worthwhile, valid and reliable measures that could not be included in this section for reasons of space. For example, there are families of measures that have been developed to assess levels of functioning and distress (and change in distress/functioning resulting from therapy) in relation to specific problem domains such as self-harm, eating disorders, loss, sexual functioning, marital satisfaction, and many other factors.

Process measures

In most case studies, it is of interest to collect information about the general process of therapy, for example around the quality of the therapist-client relationship, or significant moments of change. In some studies, it may be necessary to assess aspects of process that are more theory-specific, such as depth of experiential processing, or levels of therapist empathic reflection. The topic of therapy process encompasses a large number of process factors that have been identified and investigated. Overviews of counselling and psychotherapy process research can be found in Barker, Pistrang and Elliott (2002), Cooper (2008), McLeod (2003) and Timulak (2008). Further information about process assessment instruments can be found in Greenberg and Pinsof (1986) and Toukmanian and Rennie (1992). Within a practitioner case study toolkit, the most useful process tools are probably some kind of measure of the strength of the therapeutic relationship or 'working alliance', such as the *Working Alliance Inventory, Helping Alliance Questionnaire* or *Barrett-Lennard Relationship Inventory*. Each of these measures has therapist and client versions, to elicit perceptions of the relationship from both perspectives. These 'relationship' scales allow statements to be made in case studies regarding how the quality of the therapeutic relationship in the case being investigated might compare with norms for clients as a whole. If administered on a regular basis (e.g., weekly or bi-weekly) these scales can also be employed to identify shifts in the relationship (e.g., 'ruptures' in the therapeutic alliance). Another process research technique that is particularly valuable is the *Helpful Aspects of Therapy* (HAT) form, which is completed after each session, and asks the client to describe the most and least helpful or significant events that took place within that session, and then rate these events on a scale of helpful/hindering. The *Session Reaction Scale* (SRS) also collects information on the extent to which the client found the session to be helpful or hindering. The *Session Evaluation Questionnaire* (SEQ) is a rating instrument that allows the client to indicate his or her sense of the overall experiential quality of the session – for example whether it felt 'deep' or 'smooth'. The HAT, SRS and SEQ can be used to assess change in the process, and to provide evidence of whether the process being experienced by the client is consistent with the theoretical approach being used by the therapist (e.g., a client receiving psychodynamic therapy would not be expected to report on the HAT form that the most helpful event in a session was when his therapist gave him some advice). These instruments are also invaluable when session recordings are being made, because they provide the researcher with information about which session recordings (and, in the case of the HAT, where in the session) may be most interesting for the purposes of transcription and further analysis. Being able to make this kind of selection can be of great practical value when studying a case in which a large number of sessions have been recorded. Widely-used process measures include:

> *Working Alliance Inventory* – a short form, 12-item scale: the client-therapist agreement around *bond, goals* and *tasks* and overall quality of alliance (Hatcher and Gillaspy, 2006).
>
> *Helpful Aspects of Therapy* (HAT) – form open-ended descriptions and ratings of most/least helpful events in session (Llewelyn, 1988).
>
> *Barrett-Lennard Relationship Inventory* (BLRI) – client and therapist forms. Subscales cover: level of regard, congruence, empathic understanding, unconditionality of regard (Barrett-Lennard, 1986).
>
> *Session Evaluation Questionnaire* (SEQ) – client and therapist forms. Subscales cover: depth, smoothness, positivity, arousal (Stiles, Gordon and Lani, 2002).
>
> *Agnew Relationship Scale* (ARM) – client and therapist forms with 5, 10 or 28 items, rated on a 7-point scale. Subscales cover: bond, confidence, partnership, openness, client initiative (Agnew-Davies et al., 1998; Cahill et al., 2012).
>
> *Session Rating Scale* (SRS) – client form. Four-item visual analogue measure of client satisfaction with the process of therapy (Duncan et al., 2003; Miller, Duncan and Hubble, 2005).

Expectation and preference scales

The type of expectations or preferences that a client has for therapy represents an increasingly important area of inquiry. Specific measures that have been developed in relationship to this topic include the *Patient Expectation* scale (PEX; Berg, Sandahl and Clinton, 2008) and the *Therapy Preferences Form* (TPF; Bowens and Cooper, 2012).

Rating scales for therapy recordings and transcripts

Transcripts of therapy session recordings are the one data source that most effectively provides readers of case studies with authentic insights into what actually happened between therapists and clients. Transcripts of sessions capture the lived complexity of the therapy encounter, and can be analysed in many different ways, depending on the aims of the investigation. It is always necessary to be sensitive to the needs of the client around making recordings of sessions, for example by asking permission each time the recorder is switched on, and letting the client know that they can switch it off at any point, or ask for the recording to be deleted. The simplest way to record therapy sessions is to use a small digital recorder. Video recordings can be valuable in terms of analysing factors such as body posture, direction of gaze and interactional synchrony. However, video cameras may be regarded by clients as more intrusive, and video data can be time-consuming to analyse as well as hard to summarise in a written report. There are various formats that can be used to transcribe audio recordings, depending on the level of detail that is required (e.g., length of pauses, ascending/descending voice tone, etc.). However, a great deal can be achieved with the simple transcription of verbal content. In terms of analysing transcript material, there is a lot to be gained from just reading the transcript (or listening to a recording), as a means of entering into the process that occurred between therapist and client, and then writing a summary statement of the topics that were discussed in each session. There will always be segments of a transcript that are highly 'quotable', as a means of illustrating key moments within the therapy. Beyond this kind of basic descriptive and exploratory use of transcript data, there exist a number of well-established guidelines for systematic analysis of transcripts, focusing on such areas as metaphor themes (Angus, 1996), depth of emotional experiencing (Klein et al., 1986), narrative processes (McLeod and Balamoutsou, 2001) and assimilation of problematic experiences (Stiles, 2002). An excellent introduction to methods of transcript analysis can be found in Lepper and Riding (2006). Some practitioners who are embarking on case study research projects worry about the amount of data, and corresponding workload, arising from the use of session recordings, for example if the therapy continues for several months. In this context, it is important to recognise that it is not always essential to listen to, or transcribe, every session. If all sessions have been recorded, it may be sufficient to analyse only those that are theoretically interesting or clinically significant (or even only to analyse segments of these sessions). Indicators of significant sessions can be found in therapist notes, HAT data, interviews with the client or therapist, or sudden shifts in scores on weekly process or outcome monitoring scales. In addition, it is always valuable to look closely at the first session – clients will usually tell their story, and anticipate the course of the therapy as a whole, in what they say during the first fifteen minutes of the first meeting with their therapist.

Some widely-used observational measures of therapy process include:

Accurate Empathy Scale – a 9-point scale, applied by trained observers to tape segments. Similar scales exist for non-possessive warmth and genuineness (Truax and Carkhuff, 1967).

Experiencing Scale (EXP) – a 7-point scale, applied by trained observers to 2–8 minute tape segments, transcripts or written materials. This scale measures depth of experiencing in client, counsellor or group (Klein et al., 1986).

Client and Therapist Vocal Quality – coding made by trained observers. Each client/therapist statement is coded. Four categories of vocal pattern: focused, externalising, limited, emotional (Rice and Kerr, 1986; Rice, 1992).

Client Perceptual Processing – trained judges rate seven categories of perceptual processing, using both transcript and audiotape (Toukmanian, 1986, 1992).

Verbal Response Modes – trained judges rate 14 categories of verbal behaviour, using transcripts of whole sessions (Hill, 1986).

Vanderbilt Psychotherapy Process Scale (VPPS) – 80 Likert-scaled items used by trained raters. Scales cover: patient exploration, therapist exploration, patient psychic distress, patient participation, patient hostility, patient dependency, therapist warmth and friendliness, and negative therapist attitude (Suh et al., 1986).

Narrative Process Coding Scheme (NPCS) – Trained judges code therapy transcripts in terms of topic shifts, and internal, external and reflexive modes of narrative processing (Angus et al., 1999).

Assimilation of Problematic Experiences Scale (APES; Stiles, 2001) – protocol for rating session transcripts for level of client assimilation of problematic experiences/suppressed 'voices'.

Innovative Moments Rating Scale (Gonçalves et al., 2011) – guidelines for identifying and analysing points in therapy when the client introduces new ideas or reports on novel actions.

There are important practical and validity issues associated with the use of these instruments. When tapes of sessions are used, it is commonplace to select segments of the tape for analysis, rather than whole sessions, to reduce the amount of time needed for the task. An essential characteristic of this type of measure is the construction of a training manual for observers, to ensure that each observer is employing the same definitions of constructs in a systematic manner. It is also necessary to check the performance of observers at regular intervals, to safeguard against 'drift' away from the procedures and criteria specified by the manual (Hill, 1991). The degree of agreement between observers is assessed by calculating an *inter-rater reliability* coefficient (Cohen, 1960; Tinsley and Weiss, 1975), which to be acceptable would normally be expected to reach 0.7 or above. As with other tests, the instrument cannot be regarded as valid unless it also demonstrates sufficient reliability.

Therapist notes and client records

There are many good quality case studies that have been published, in rigorous journals such as *Clinical Case Studies* and *Pragmatic Case Studies in Psychotherapy* (see Chapter 6), on the basis of detailed therapist notes, including near-verbatim accounts of therapy dialogue. It is important to acknowledge, however, that the therapists who produced these case studies clearly made huge efforts to record their observations of therapy in a very thorough manner. If a case study is being planned, it may be valuable to develop a structured format for writing therapist notes, to ensure that essential information is collected after every session. An example of a set of headings that might be used as a structure for therapist weekly notes can be found at the *Network for Research on Experiential Psychotherapies* site (www.experiential-researchers.org/index.html).

Client diaries

Client and therapist diaries may be used to collect information on the week-by-week experience of engagement in therapy. The diary method of data collection has been widely used in psychology and social science (see for example Alaszewski, 2006; Milligan, Bingley and Gatrell, 2005). Studies by Mackrill (2007) and Kerr, Josyula and Littenberg (2011) provide examples of some of the ways in which diaries can be used. In the Mackrill (2007) study, therapists were encouraged to use weekly diaries to reflect on their therapeutic practice and aspects of the everyday lives of their clients that emerged in sessions. Clients were asked to use weekly diaries to reflect on the significance of the psychotherapy sessions and on any changes in their everyday lives. Diary material was subjected to qualitative analysis on a case-by-case basis, to identify the ways in which therapy was shaped by the everyday life experiences of clients. In the study by Kerr, Josyula and Littenberg (2011), clients participating in mindfulness training kept daily practice logs where they noted the amount of time they spent doing various meditation techniques, and also wrote in an open-ended way (1–3 sentences) about their experiences during practice sessions. These data were subjected to both qualitative analysis, to identify themes, and systematic rating of dimensions that were theoretically relevant to the purpose of the study. Analysis of these diary entries made it possible to observe significant shifts in experience after five weeks of practice. In these studies, and other therapy research that has made use of diaries to collect data, the researchers developed their own guidelines and instructions for participants. At the present time, there are no standard diary protocols that are in general use. However, close reading of diary-based studies will provide sufficient information for any researcher to develop their own tailored protocol. A valuable review of the use of diary methods in counselling and psychotherapy research can be found in Mackrill (2008).

Exercise 9.2   Finding the right tools for you

As you explore the world of therapy measures, scales and forms, keep in mind that most researchers tend to specialise in a subset of measures that they get to know well, and that serve their own particular research purposes. The more you use a measure, the more you will understand what it can and cannot do.

Experience sampling

Experience sampling is a technique that involves participants making observations of their experience, through ratings of emotional states and behavioural activities, at regular intervals during their day-to-day lives (Csikszentmihalyi and Larson, 1987). This approach is sometimes also described as *ambulatory assessment*, or *ecological momentary assessment* (Alpers, 2009). The attraction of experience sampling is that in principle it allows access to how people actually feel and act, rather than relying on their recollection of these states. Typically, participants are reminded by some kind of pager, handheld device, digital wristwatch, or mobile phone app, when it is time to enter data into a paper-based or on-line form. At the present time, experience sampling has not been widely used in counselling and psychotherapy research. Within the field of health research, experience sampling studies have produced some fairly dramatic findings. For example, Carstensen et al. (2013) found that people tended to have more positive and stable experiences as they got older, and that those who had the most positive emotional experiences were likely to live longer. The potential application of experience sampling in counselling and psychotherapy research has been demonstrated in a study of mindfulness-based CBT, in which Geschwind et al. (2011) reported large shifts in momentary everyday emotional states, in the direction of positive experience, in good outcome clients. A review of the use of experience sampling in counselling and psychotherapy research, with a particular focus on depression studies, can be found in Telford et al. (2012).

Survey questionnaires

Another source of quantitative data in many counselling studies is the survey questionnaire. Unlike questionnaire instruments such as the MMPI or BDI which are required to have demonstrable psychometric properties and are used again and again in many pieces of research, survey questionnaires are usually designed for a specific purpose, and are used in only one investigation. It is essential for a good survey questionnaire to possess face and content validity. In other words, it must include questions on all relevant aspects of the topic, and these questions must clearly be seen to provide the information that is required. Typically, survey questionnaires are mailed out to participants, so it is essential that the instructions and covering letter are straightforward and uncomplicated to follow. Some of the other considerations in designing a survey questionnaire are as follows:

1. The layout and presentation of the questionnaire are important. It must look uncluttered and easy to fill in.
2. Begin the questionnaire with factual items (age, gender), to engage the respondent's attention, before moving to more difficult questions that may take longer to answer.
3. The wording of questions must be direct and unambiguous.
4. Keep the questionnaire as brief as possible.
5. Put a reminder and thank-you at the end to encourage return of the questionnaire.

The issues involved in designing and administering survey questionnaires are discussed fully by Robson (2011). This source also deals with issues of sampling and compliance, which are crucial in survey research.

There have been several survey investigations of aspects of counsellor attitudes and experience. For example, Macaskill and Macaskill (1992) carried out a survey in which psychotherapists in training were asked about their views on their personal therapy. Morrow-Bradley and Elliott (1986) conducted a survey of research awareness and utilisation in practising therapists. Allman et al. (1992) completed a survey of the attitudes of therapists toward clients reporting mystical experiences. Addis and Krasnow (2000) surveyed therapists about their attitudes to treatment manuals. There have been many interesting surveys of therapy clients, for example the research by Liddle (1996, 1997) into the views of gay and lesbian clients regarding the therapy they had received. It is also useful to carry out surveys of public attitudes to counselling, for example the study by West and Reynolds (1995) into attitudes to workplace counselling.

Projective techniques

Projective techniques operate in a quite different way from the other research tools reviewed in this chapter. In a projective test the participant is asked to respond to a relatively unstructured, ambiguous stimulus in an open-ended way. Typical projective techniques are the Rorschach Inkblot Test, in which the person is invited to report on what they see in each of a set of symmetrical inkblots, and the Thematic Apperception Test (TAT), where the person tells or writes imaginative stories in response to a set of pictures. Another widely used projective test, the sentence completion technique, involves writing endings to incomplete sentence stems. These and other projective instruments are described by Semeonoff (1976). The assumption underlying these techniques is that the person will project his or her characteristic way of thinking and feeling into the way he or she reacts to the open-ended projective task. For example, in a TAT story, the respondent may unconsciously invest the hero or heroine of the story with his or her own personal motives and patterns of behaviour. A person with a strong need for achievement may write stories that all make reference to winning or doing well. Conversely, a person with a strong need for sociability may write stories emphasising relationships and friendships. A key feature of projective techniques is the intention to gain access to fantasy and imagination rather than consciously processed 'socially desirable' responses.

Projective techniques have in the past been widely used within clinical and occupational psychology for such purposes as personality assessment, clinical diagnosis and appraisal of managerial potential. Projective techniques were extensively used in the early research into client-centred therapy carried out by Rogers and his colleagues at the University of Chicago (Rogers and Dymond, 1954). In recent years, however, there has been increasing scepticism over the validity of these instruments. The use of projective techniques can be criticised on two grounds. First, the responses that people make to projective stimuli tend to be affected by the situation they are in, their mood at the time of testing, and their relationship with the person administering the test. Second, the open-ended and complex nature of the response means that it can often be difficult to interpret the meaning or significance of what the person has said or written. Both these factors have led many psychologists to question the reliability and validity of projective techniques (Lilienfeld, Wood and Howard, 2000). The neglect of projective methods in counselling and psychotherapy research can be illustrated by the fact that very few therapy research papers published in recent years report the use of projective instruments.

The current lack of interest in projective techniques may be misguided. McClelland (1980) has constructed a strong case for the value of projective techniques. He argues that questionnaires evoke only the capacity of a person to respond passively to a stimulus. By contrast, the projective situation forces the person to engage in active, purposeful, problem-solving behaviour. In addition, when a person answers a questionnaire item, they are not merely reporting on what they know about their behaviour, but are drawing upon their image or concept of self. In a projective technique, the person usually has no idea of what the test is about, and answers spontaneously without reference to attitudes and self-images. Both these factors led McClelland (1980) to conclude that, in a projective test situation, the person being tested is displaying patterns of behaviour and feeling that are similar to those they exhibit in actual real-life situations. Evidence gathered by Cornelius (1983) supports this view. For example, in a review of the literature on the assessment of motivation, Cornelius found higher levels of predictive validity for projective instruments such as the TAT and lower levels for self-report questionnaires.

The implication of the work of McClelland and his colleagues is that projective techniques give access to personality structures and attitudes that are deeper and more fundamental than those highlighted by fixed response self-report questionnaires. In principle, the psychodynamically oriented and phenomenological theoretical basis underpinning projective tests would appear more consistent with much counselling and psychotherapy practice than would the trait theory that has guided the construction of more widely-adopted questionnaire instruments. In this context, it is of relevance that the psychodynamic/psychoanalytic research community is one of the few places where projective approaches are employed in research (Levy and Ablon, 2009; Levy et al., 2012).

Developing your own research instrument

The process of constructing a research measure is time consuming, and should be regarded as a project in its own right. Constructing a measure encompasses several distinct subtasks:

1. The literature must be reviewed, or an exploratory study carried out, to generate an initial definition of the construct or constructs to be assessed.

2. A large pool of items potentially relevant to this construct is assembled.
3. These items or questions are administered to as large a cross-section of people as possible.
4. These results are examined, using the statistical technique of factor analysis, with a view to reducing the item pool to the smallest possible set of questions consistent with criteria of reliability and validity.
5. The final version of the scale is put together, paying careful attention to the instructions for respondents, the layout, and the order of items.
6. Studies are carried out to evaluate the reliability and validity of the scale.
7. The scale is given to a large sample of the population, and perhaps also to special sub-groups, to generate norms for groups of respondents of different ages, gender, occupations, social class and so on.

It can be seen that measure construction and validation is a complex and costly business, which calls on a fair degree of statistical expertise, or collaboration with a colleague who possesses such knowledge (Worthington and Whittaker, 2006). It is possible to treat elements of the process as projects in their own right. A good example of how this can be done can be found in accounts of the development of the SCORE family therapy outcome measure (Cahill, O'Reilly et al., 2010; Stratton et al., 2006, 2010). These articles also provide insight into the ways in which measure development can be a collaborative process, which draws on the combined experience, talents and skills of practitioners and researchers. It is also possible to use qualitative methods in the early phases of measure development to generate themes and items for inclusion in a questionnaire (Geller et al., 2010; Rowan and Wolff, 2007).

Anyone who is contemplating developing a new research instrument will need to undertake considerable preparatory study. The most straightforward starting points for information on measure development are Clark and Watson (1995), Barker, Pistrang and Elliott (2002) and DeVellis (2011). Beyond these introductory texts, further technical information can be found in Cronbach (1997), Nunnally and Bernstein (1993) and Rust and Golombok (2008). It is also helpful to look at the procedures followed in recent measure development articles. There are several new therapy measures published each year, and recent studies of this kind serve as a source of ideas about emerging ideas about good practice in this area.

Other sources of information

There are many other types of information that may be included in a systematic case study. In some cases, there may be 'objective' indicators of change that are highly relevant to the progress of therapy, such as exam results, school attendance, sickness absence from work, hospital visits, frequency of alcohol or drug use, binge eating episodes, and so on. Clients can be asked to keep track of this kind of information in a diary, or it may be possible for the researcher to gain access to official records. In some therapies, there may be artefacts that are created, such as drawings, photographs, sculptures or poems, that can become part of the case record. There may also be referral letters or other forms of communication from outside agencies.

Suggestions for further reading

The most comprehensive overview of the issues involved in using tests and questionnaires in counselling and psychotherapy research is to be found in Maruish, M.E. (2004) *The Use of Psychological Testing for Treatment Planning and Outcomes Assessment: Volume 1: General Considerations* (3rd edn). New York: Routledge. Other volumes by the same author examine the use of measures in relation to specific populations, such as children.

The most authoritative source on questionnaire and coding systems for measuring therapy process variables remains Greenberg, L.S. and Pinsof, W.M. (eds) (1986) *The Psychotherapeutic Process: A Research Handbook*. New York: Guilford Press. It should be noted, however, that a number of important process measures have emerged since the publication of their book.

The instruments discussed in the present chapter represent only the tip of a vast iceberg, in respect of techniques for assessing aspects of health and wellbeing. Information about other tools that may be of interest, can be found in:

Bowling, A. (2001) *Measuring Disease: A Review of Disease-specific Quality of Life Measurement Scales* (2nd edn). Maidenhead: Open University Press.
Bowling, A. (2004) *Measuring Health: A Review of Quality of Life Measurement Scales* (3rd edn). Maidenhead: Open University Press.

Companion website material

Many of the instruments outlined in this chapter are supported by websites that include information on the most recent versions of scales, and their application in different contexts. The relevant section of the companion website for this book provides links to several of these sites (https://study.sagepub.com/mcleod).

10

Carrying out a Publishable Literature Review

Introduction

Reviews are the glue that holds the research literature together, and give it some kind of coherence. Every year, several hundred counselling and psychotherapy research studies are published. In the end, the credibility and influence of any single one of these studies will be extremely limited. It is only when knowledge is accumulated across studies conducted by different groups of researchers, across different samples of participants, that it can provide a reliable guide to policy and practice. Literature reviews therefore enjoy a high level of strategic significance in the world of research. The aim of this chapter is to explain how to conduct a literature review project in a manner that will have the possibility of making a genuine contribution to advancing our understanding of some aspect of the process or outcome of therapy. This chapter concentrates on what is required to construct a stand-alone literature review that can be published as a paper, report, book chapter or book. Clearly, smaller-scale literature reviews are carried out by researchers in the context of dissertation chapters, research proposals, and the introductory sections of research papers. The general principles of the review-writing process, outlined below, are also relevant for these other purposes.

What is a literature review?

A literature review is a systematic attempt to analyse a set of studies on a topic, in order to generate reliable conclusions that can inform practice, and can serve as a platform on which further research can be carried out. There are several different types of literature review that can be carried out, depending on the aims of the review and the kind of research that is available for scrutiny. In relation to the type of literature review that might be undertaken for a relatively inexperienced researcher or research team, the most appropriate candidates are:

> *narrative or historical review*: tells the story of the progress of knowledge in a particular area;
>
> *thematic review*: analyses research in a specific topic area in terms of what has been found in respect of discrete themes or areas of focus;
>
> *scoping review*: a map or overview of the literature in a particular area, indicating topics that have been studied in depth, and highlighting areas where less is known;
>
> *practice-friendly review*: analysis of a body of research for the purpose of identifying implications for practice;
>
> *qualitative meta-synthesis*: systematic appraisal of the findings of a set of qualitative research studies;
>
> *meta-analysis*: systematic appraisal of the findings of a set of quantitative studies.

Beyond these forms of literature review, there are two further types of review that are technically more demanding and resource-intensive:

> *Evidence-based practice guideline*: a review carried out by a group of acknowledged experts in the field, based on evaluation of the findings of multiple existing meta-analytic reviews, and other evidence, for the purpose of informing government policy.

> *Meta-narrative review*: a review carried out by expert researchers from different disciplines, into complex evidence derived from different methodological traditions (Greenhalgh et al., 2005).

As with any area of research, it is possible to find genre-blurring review projects that combine or integrate elements of each of these review formats. However, the majority of published reviews can be categorised under one or another of the headings listed above.

Why would I want to do this kind of research?

There are many reasons for devoting time and effort to completing a good-quality literature view. These include:

- *curiosity*: it is possible to use a literature review to channel a passionate interest and 'need to know' in relation to a specific topic or concept;
- *relevance for practice*: individual practitioners, and therapy organisations, often struggle to know how best to proceed in relation to issues around practice;
- *justifying a particular approach*: many reviews are conducted by academics or practitioners who wish to demonstrate that their way of doing therapy is just as good as, or better than, competing approaches;
- *as a political act*: some reviews are carried out in order to document the fact that a specific topic or client group has been neglected in the existing research literature – this type of review has played a vital role in promoting research in such areas as multicultural practice, and therapy for gay and lesbian clients;
- *as a by-product of an empirical study*: a researcher who carries out a study of a particular issue, based on primary data that they collect, may find that in the process of planning their study they have managed to assemble a collection of all of the previously published studies of that topic;
- *as a means of avoiding the necessity to seek ethical approval or collect primary data*: in some circumstances it may be very hard, or even impossible, for a researcher to collect his or her own data.

In addition to these reasons for doing a literature review project, it may be that a literature review represents a stage within a long-term research programme. For example, a research team may carry out a review in order to create a justification for funding to do research in their area of interest. Also, some people are review specialists, who just enjoy the process of doing this sort of work.

What kind of skills and support would I need?

Having access to a good library is a prime necessity in relation to carrying out a literature review. It is not realistic to expect to complete a convincing and comprehensive review by general internet searching. It is essential to be able to view and download full text copies of papers. Training, guidance or mentoring from a specialist subject librarian (i.e., someone who knows about databases in disciplines such as psychology, psychiatry and social work) will be extremely helpful. In terms of personal qualities, individuals who do well in the field of literature reviewing tend to possess a 'detective' mind-set, relishing the challenge of collating information from various sources and finding meaningful patterns. Reviewers also need to be well-organised, in terms of recording and filing information, and willing to spend a lot of time reading stuff that may turn out not to be relevant or useable. The review process also requires a somewhat skeptical attitude to the knowledge claims made by the authors of published studies. Conducting a literature review therefore calls for a considerable degree of interest and awareness around research methodology, in order to arrive at a balanced evaluation of the validity of studies that are being considered for inclusion in a review. Particular types of review demand specific methodological expertise. For example, meta-analysis requires statistical competence, whereas qualitative meta-synthesis depends on an awareness of qualitative methodology. The final requirement in relation to doing a review is to have access to co-researchers. A single-handed review is less convincing than a review in which the value of each study has been independently weighed up by a team of readers. Consumers of reviews are typically on their guard against any hint that the author of a review has an axe to grind, or is consciously or unconsciously biased in some way. The involvement of other co-reviewers goes a long way to allaying these fears. This does not necessarily mean that anyone seeking to undertake a review needs to find one or more colleagues who are willing to commit themselves to an equivalent effort. It is quite feasible to parcel out the work so that colleagues evaluate a subset of the papers being considered, or a research supervisor conducts an independent audit of the overall review process.

Exercise 10.1   Evaluating the usefulness of reviews you have read

Identify some review papers or chapters you have come across that have informed and influenced your practice. If you cannot think of any reviews that you have read, then carry out a search for relevant review papers in your areas of therapy that are of interest to you. What has 'worked' for you, in terms of the ways in which these reviews have been structured and written? What has not worked? What are the implications of these reflections, in relation to how you would approach carrying out a review project of your own?

A step-by-step guide to producing a publishable literature review

Reviewing the literature can be seen as similar to detective work. Even though we live in a world dominated by information technology, it is not possible to enter a key word into an on-line database and come up with all the relevant articles on a topic that is being reviewed. Authors may use different terms to describe the same phenomenon, and all items of interest are never found in a single database. It is therefore essential, when carrying out a review, to allow enough time to follow up leads.

Defining the aims and scope of the review

Just as in any research project, a review needs to focus on a set of specific aims and questions. Some of the aims that can be pursued through literature review investigations include:

- What is the nature and scope of research knowledge on a particular topic? What kind of research has been carried out? Where are the gaps in the existing research literature? (Example: 'What is the evidence base for counselling in schools?')
- How effective is a particular type of intervention in relation to a specific problem? (Example: 'How effective is CBT for depression?')
- What is the relative effectiveness of different types of intervention in relation to a specific problem? (Example: 'How effective are different models of therapy for depression?')
- How effective is a specific intervention (or different interventions) for a specific problem in a specific setting? (Example: 'How effective are psychotherapeutic interventions for depression in primary healthcare settings?')
- How effective is a specific intervention (or different interventions) for a specific problem in a specific client group? (Example: 'How effective are psychotherapeutic interventions for depression in patients with Multiple Sclerosis?')
- What is the role of a particular factor in relation to the causes or treatment of a problem? (Example: 'What is the role of client treatment preference in determining therapy outcome?')
- What do clients experience as helpful? (Example: 'What do people with eating disorders experience as helpful and hindering in the therapy they have received?')
- How valid or practically useful is the knowledge produced by different techniques or methodologies? (Example: 'How sensitive to change are different brief outcome measures?')

When reading through this list of types of literature review aims and questions, it should become apparent that it is possible to continue to narrow the focus. (For example: 'How sensitive to change are brief depression measures used in studies of adolescents with eating disorders?') The narrower the focus, the more likely it is that the reviewer will be able to locate and thoroughly analyse all relevant studies. The wider the focus, the more there is a risk that the reviewer may become overwhelmed with information. A review by Innerhofer (2013) was carried out by a reviewer who had a strong interest in attachment theory. A broad review of the role of attachment in therapy would have produced an extremely long list of papers. In narrowing the review to an analysis of the impact of attachment style on therapy outcome in children, Innerhofer (2013) was able to focus on a more manageable set of 12 articles.

When thinking about the aims of a review, it is also important to consider whether the topic, or one's personal interest, leads in the direction of a more objective type of analysis, or whether it might be more appropriate to frame the review in more exploratory terms. For example, at one extreme are review papers that try to eliminate any possibility of interpretive judgement on the part of the reviewer. A review that counted up the proportion of therapy clients who commit suicide would fall into this category. At the other extreme are reviews where the author is seeking to provide a balanced appraisal of the implications for practice of research in a particular area.

It is sensible to carry out some preliminary searches before deciding on the final version of the aims and questions. A preliminary search can be used to give some idea of the number of papers that have been published, and whether any reviews of the topic have been recently completed. Discovering that a good quality review was published about five years ago is a gift, because it offers something to build on and extend. On the other hand, discovering that a comprehensive review of a topic has been published within the last 12 months may suggest that further work on that topic is not timely, unless some angle can be identified that was not fully pursued in the recently-published report.

Deciding on the style of review

At some point in the process of constructing a review paper, it will be essential to decide on the type or style of review that is being undertaken. For anyone writing a review paper for the first time, it is advisable to stick to either a 'practice-friendly' review or a systematic review. More complex types of reviews, such as meta-analyses and qualitative meta-synthesis (both discussed later in this chapter), are better attempted once an author has gained confidence and competence from the experience of completing a less demanding type of review project.

The style that is selected for a review will depend on the interests and goals of the author, and the intended audience. It is helpful to adhere to one particular review style as mixing styles can be confusing for readers.

The idea of the *practice-friendly review* has been pioneered by the *Journal of Clinical Psychology*, which has published a number of well-received review articles of this type (Comtois and Linehan, 2006; Greenberg and Pascual-Leone, 2006; Knox and Hill, 2003; Logan and Marlatt, 2010; Lundahl and Burke, 2009; Mains and Scogin, 2003; Post and Wade, 2009; Sin and Lyubomirsky, 2009; Solomon and Johnson, 2002). This genre of review can also be found in 'practice-oriented' reviews in the *Journal of Psychotherapy Integration* (Andersen and Przbylinski, 2014; Sullivan and Davila, 2014). Similar types of review, but not explicitly labelled as 'practice-friendly' or 'practice-oriented', have also been published in other journals. The aim of this type of review is not to arrive at an ultimate 'objective truth' in respect of the area being discussed, but instead to consider the potential practical implications of research that has been published on that topic.

The concept of a *systematic review* refers to a review project that is based on a clearly-defined method that specifies how articles have been identified, evaluated and selected for inclusion, and how information from these articles has been integrated into a set of conclusions. Examples of brief systematic review papers produced by novice researchers (and their supervisors) can be found in a special issue of *Counselling Psychology Review*: Antoniou and Cooper (2013); Innerhofer (2013); Michael and Cooper (2013); Oluyori (2013). The British Association for Counselling and Psychotherapy has commissioned a set of longer review publications. These are useful resources for anyone undertaking a systematic review for the first time, because their greater length allows authors the space to explain in more detail how they approached their task. Topics included in more recent reviews in this series include student counselling (Connell et al., 2009), counselling for young people (McLaughlin et al., 2013), psychological interventions for carers of people with dementia (Elvish et al., 2012), the process and outcome of therapy for lesbian, gay and transgender people (King et al., 2007), the effectiveness of workplace counselling (McLeod, 2010b), qualitative studies of helpful and unhelpful aspects of therapy for eating disorders (Timulak et al., 2013), and the role of therapy in suicide prevention (Winter et al., 2009). Some of these reviews are available to download for free from the BACP website.

Accounts of the experience of carrying out a systematic review can be found in Armstrong et al. (2011) and Rojon et al. (2011).

Finding articles

In any type of review project, it will be necessary to locate relevant articles that report on studies. This requires careful detective work using on-line databases, handsearching books, chapters and articles, and possibly even writing to experts in the field. Information about how the research literature is structured can be found in Chapter 2 of this volume, and Chapter 4 of McLeod (2013b). The reason that this part of the reviewing process is best described as detective work is that a lot of the material may be hidden from sight. For example, authors may use different terms or labels to describe the same phenomenon, and articles may be published in unexpected places. For example, there are many counselling and psychotherapy studies published in journals of social work, medicine and education.

Deciding on the criteria for inclusion of papers

The first trawl for articles always brings up a wide variety of items, including general discussion papers and professional update articles. It will be necessary to sift through these, to find the actual research articles that will eventually be included in the review. It is important to keep a record of how many unique items have been identified at each stage of the search process, and the reasons why some have been rejected and others have been allowed to proceed to a more intensive level of scrutiny. Any kind of systematic review needs to include some kind of display or flow-diagram of how a large number of initial 'hits' have been whittled down to a much smaller number of key articles. This information reassures readers of the reliability and validity of the review process by (in principle) allowing for replication to take place. In some situations it can also be of historical interest to know about how many articles were retrieved in a review carried out in 2004 (say) as opposed to 2014.

Some of the criteria that can be used to exclude papers are:

- whether a paper consists of a report of an original research study;
- date of publication (e.g., a review may focus on studies published between 2000 and 2012, on grounds of current relevance, or because an authoritative review already exists of papers published up to 2000);
- the language in which the paper was written (often non-English language papers are not included);
- whether a full-text version of the paper is available on-line;
- whether a paper was published in a peer-review journal (this will exclude student theses and dissertations, and also books and book chapters, none of which will have been through a peer review process);
- the methodological quality of the study (strategies for evaluating the validity of studies are discussed in Chapter 6).

It is generally considered good practice for these decisions to be specified and defined in advance, in the form of a checklist that is then applied by two or three members of the research team, with borderline cases being subjected to more detailed discussion.

Displaying information about the main review articles

Many review articles will include a table that summarises key information about the main research studies that have been selected for review: the author, date, sample, method, main findings. Displaying this information in one place is remarkably useful for readers. Some may regard this table as the single most valuable accomplishment of a review project, because it allows them to look up and read the particular articles that are most relevant to their own research or practice.

Extracting relevant material from studies included in the review

A typical research article is about 7,000 words in length, and includes a great deal of information. In addition, the author(s) of the article will have already decided which parts of the information that they have collected are more or less important, and will have then selectively presented their interpretation of the data as a set of conclusions. A reviewer, faced with such a piece of highly technical writing, needs to be able to do two things. First, the reviewer needs to be able to sum up the 'take-home' message intended by the original author. This is usually included in the summary table described in the previous section. Second, the reviewer needs to be able to go beyond the take-home message of the original author(s) and arrive at his or her own interpretation of a study. This process can be facilitated if the reviewer draws up a list of information that he or she wishes to extract from each paper that is being reviewed. Such a list is helpful in allowing the researcher to detect areas of information that have not been reported, as well as reducing the article to a set of key data points that can be compared against corresponding data points in the other studies being analysed. Examples of areas that might be included in a list are: sample characteristics; proportion of clients who dropped out of the study; Effect Size of change that was measured; length of time of interviews; anomalous findings (results that were not anticipated), etc. At the end of the day, most or all of these areas will become subsections in a review. It is useful to scrutinise published review reports with the aim of identifying the areas that were included in the reviewer's list.

Most reviewers find it helpful to work from single-sided paper copies of the key articles included in the review, rather than pdf files. This allows notes to be written on articles, and for rapid cross-checking of information.

The point here is that in a review it is never possible to take account of, summarise, or discuss, all the information included in source articles. It is therefore essential to develop a strategy for extracting and analysing the information that is most relevant to the purposes of the review.

What can go wrong?

There is a lot that can go wrong. Carrying out a publishable research review is an endeavour that is best learned in apprenticeship mode, under the close supervision of someone who has done this type of thing before. Some of the main weaknesses in review articles include:

- *bias*: the reader cannot escape from a sense that the author is placing some kind of 'spin' on the material being reviewed, in order to support a particular position. An example of this is when the discussion loses contact with the findings, and offers speculative reflection around topics on which little or no evidence was obtained in the review;

- *incompleteness*: the reader knows about studies that have not been included, and cannot understand (on the basis of the criteria that have been applied) why this has happened; the reader may not personally be aware of missing studies, but is not convinced about the comprehensiveness of the search strategy;
- *boring*: it is apparent that the review has plausibly identified a set of relevant studies. However, the findings of these studies are analysed in a superficial or entirely concrete manner – there is no sense of curiosity or discovery, or attempt to develop a conceptual understanding of patterns within findings. Alternatively, the author may stick to merely describing what was found, using long quotes or paraphrasing the abstract of articles that were included in the review.

These weaknesses probably stem from three main root causes. First, it is not uncommon for reviewers to formulate review aims and questions that are too broad. As a result, they become swamped with complex information which is impossible to organise. In such situations, it may be advisable to cut one's losses and focus only on a section or sub-question from within the original project. Second, sometimes reviewers do not adopt a sufficiently structured approach to analysing articles. This is understandable, because in the end all the information in an article is connected in some way to all other information, and imposing a structure runs the risk of destroying the rich network of understanding that is conveyed in a paper. However, it is also a recipe for madness and confusion – at some point it will become necessary to decide which bits of information are the most important. The third source of difficulty in review articles is that the authors have not talked sufficiently to other people about what they are doing. It is through conversations with interested others that reviewers become able to construct and refine the story they wish to tell.

A useful piece of further reading, for review authors, is a short paper by Watts (2011) on the craft of writing a conceptual article. As Watts (2011) points out, most conceptual articles begin by offering some kind of brief review of the appropriate literature, then shift into a more analytic mode that involves building a new way of understanding a topic or phenomenon. In a sense, a review article can be viewed as similar, except that most of the space is devoted to the review and only a little space at the end is devoted to the development of conceptualisation of the material in the review. However, it is often this bit at the end that brings a review to life, and offers the reader something to take forward.

More complex review projects

There are two further types of review project that are highly significant within the literature, but beyond the scope of novice researchers: *meta-analysis* and *qualitative meta-synthesis*. A meta-analytic review consists of the use of Effect Size (ES) calculations to compare the outcomes of interventions for a specific problem or client group. Because meta-analyses are used by governments and healthcare providers as the basis for policy and decision making, they are built around very demanding criteria of statistical rigour, which require considerable sophistication in the use of quantitative methods. A brief, user-friendly introduction to meta-analysis in therapy research can be found in Erford et al. (2010). More comprehensive coverage of this approach is available in Borenstein et al. (2009) and Ellis (2010).

Qualitative meta-synthesis (sometimes also described as qualitative meta-analysis or qualitative meta-ethnography) is a form of systematic review that deals with findings from qualitative studies. In a qualitative meta-synthesis, a systematic comparison is carried out of themes or categories across several studies that have looked at the same topic. The aim here is to differentiate between themes and categories that are consistently associated with the topic, in contrast to those that are less frequently experienced or reported. Within the field of counselling and psychotherapy, qualitative meta-synthesis has been used to explore the structure of helpful events in therapy (Timulak, 2007, 2009), insight events Timulak and McElvaney (2013), and the outcomes of experiential therapy (Timulak and Creaner, 2010). An appreciation of what is involved in carrying out this kind of investigation can be found in Atkins et al. (2008), Britten et al. (2002), Hill et al. (2012), Paterson et al. (2009) and Timulak and Creaner (2013).

It can, of course, be a useful learning experience for a novice researcher to be a member of a team of researchers carrying out a meta-analysis or meta-synthesis project. This kind of experience is highly recommended for anyone thinking about leading such a project at a later date.

A further variant on a straightforward review project is to build and maintain a database of articles on a specific topic, that are then available for other researchers seeking to undertake systematic reviews of aspects of that topic. There are many such databases in the academic community. A recent example can be found in the work of Christensen et al. (2014), who have assembled a database of all research studies on suicide.

How to get published

There are basically three alternative formats that are used in constructing literature review articles:

1. *Thematic.* Material is organised around key themes, issues or questions.
2. *Historical.* Material is organised around a historical narrative of the development of knowledge in an area of inquiry.
3. *Systematic/technical* report. The article is structured along the lines of a research paper, with detailed information provided concerning the methods for data collection and analysis that were utilised.

There are no specific guidelines available for the construction of narrative or thematic reviews. This leaves the author with a lot of freedom, but at the same time means that it is hard to know whether the approach being taken is satisfactory – this can be a difficult situation for novice researchers. By contrast, there is a broad level of agreement around what a good-quality systematic review should look like (Hanley and Cutts, 2013). A typical systematic literature review paper is structured in accordance with the following subheadings and sections:

- *Introduction*: (i) explaining why the topic is important; (ii) overview of the aims of and scope of the review.
- *Method*: how the review was carried out – search procedures; inclusion and exclusion criteria; quality criteria and quality assessment procedures; how data were analysed and synthesised.
- *Results/findings*: summary of included studies; key findings.
- *Discussion*: identify and discuss critical issues emerging from the review, for instance – conflicting findings or theoretical interpretations; pros and cons of methodologies that have been used to study the topic; areas for further research – what should we do next?; implications for policy, training and practice; implications for theory.
- *References*: typically, articles included for review are identified with an asterisk.

Although there do not exist agreed guidelines for writing thematic reviews, anyone considering such a project could do worse than scrutinise the approach taken by authors of 'practice-friendly' reviews in the *Journal of Clinical Psychology*.

The style, length and format of the literature review should be consistent with the journal to which it is being submitted. The majority of counselling and psychotherapy journals are willing to publish review papers.

In some situations it can be appropriate to publish monograph-length reviews of around 30,000 words. Greater word length gives scope for readers to have access to more detailed information, and gain a better sense of the studies that are being summarised. Good examples of longer reviews can be found in a series of systematic review publications produced by the British Association for Counselling and Psychotherapy (BACP) and available through the BACP website (see the list above). In principle, it is possible for any organisation to commission a review and publish it as a paper document and/or through their website. It is perhaps worth noting here that the BACP reviews were all subjected to rigorous quality control procedures in the form of independent peer review. Briefer versions of most of the BACP review reports have also been disseminated as journal articles in *Counselling and Psychotherapy Research*.

Suggestions for further reading

To produce a good literature review paper, it is important to become a connoisseur of reviews, by taking time to read review articles and reflect on how these are structured and written. This chapter has included references to many interesting and informative review papers.

Further guidance on skills and strategies that can be used to facilitate the review process can be found in a wide range of excellent sources, including:

Gough, D., Oliver, S. and Thomas, J. (eds) (2012) *An Introduction to Systematic Reviews*. London: Sage.
Jesson, J., Matheson, L. and Lacey, F.M. (2011) *Doing Your Literature Review: Traditional and Systematic Techniques*. London: Sage.

Companion website material

The website for this book (https://study.sagepub.com/mcleod) includes papers on a variety of aspects of the process of undertaking a review project:

Atkins, S., Lewin, S., Smith, H. et al. (2008) Conducting a meta-ethnography of qualitative literature: Lessons learnt. *BMC Medical Research Methodology*, 8: 21.
Christensen, H., Calear, A., Van Spijker, B. et al. (2014) Psychosocial interventions for suicidal ideation, plans, and attempts: a database of randomised controlled trials. *BMC Psychiatry*, doi:10.1186/1471-244X-14-86
King, M., Semylen, J., Killaspy, H. et al. (2007) *A Systematic Review of Research on Counselling and Psychotherapy for Lesbian, Gay, Bisexual and Transgender People*. Lutterworth: British Association for Counselling and Psychotherapy.
Paterson, B.L., Dubouloz, C., Chevrier, J. et al. (2009) Insights from a metasynthesis project. *International Journal of Qualitative Methods*, 8: 22–33.

11

Using Qualitative Interviews to Explore the Experience of Therapy

Introduction

The most straightforward way to find out about therapy is to ask people. There exists a massive and fascinating literature consisting of research studies based on interviews with clients, therapists, or others with a stake in therapy, such as family members or service managers. This research approach has made a major contribution to the knowledge base for counselling and psychotherapy practice. The present chapter provides a step-by-step guide on how to conduct this form of research, and explores the key methodological choices that arise at each stage of the research process.

What is qualitative research into the experience of therapy?

Qualitative research is an approach to inquiry that collects data in the form of personal accounts, stories and descriptions of experience, and seeks to identify themes or patterns within the information that has been collected. Usually, this type of research makes use of one-to-one interviews as the primary means of data collection. Qualitative accounts can also be obtained through the use of diaries, group interviews, visual data (e.g., photographs or drawings) and collecting samples of naturally-occurring conversation (e.g., dialogue on internet chatrooms, participant observation). The pros and cons of these alternative forms of qualitative data collection are discussed towards the end of the chapter.

There are three key tasks in a qualitative interview study: deciding on which questions to ask and how to ask them; conducting interviews in a way that allows the person to tell their story; and analysing the meaning of the material that has been collected. In addition to these tasks, there is usually a substantial amount of work involved in setting up interviews and transcribing interview recordings.

Qualitative interview-based research in counselling and psychotherapy comprises part of a broader and highly influential tradition of qualitative research in health and social care. Researchers within these fields have used qualitative methods to provide service users with a 'voice', in order to enable their experiences to have an impact on professional training and practice and public policy. This kind of evidence has been valuable as a means of making health and social care more user-focused.

Why would I want to do this kind of research?

There are several reasons why counsellors and psychotherapists find it meaningful and satisfying to be involved in this type of research. At a basic level, research interviews can be regarded as an extension of therapy interviews, and analysing research interviews is similar to arriving at a case formulation. Qualitative research therefore builds on the skills, knowledge and experience that therapists already possess – it is an obvious next step. It is also a next step that provides substantial opportunities for personal learning, and becoming a more effective therapist. There are important practical and ethical differences between research interviews and therapy interviews, and as a result, doing this kind of research can generate valuable reflection around the question of what is 'therapeutic' about a therapy conversation. For example, many research participants report that taking part in a research interview had been 'therapeutic', despite the fact that the interviewer had made no attempt to use any therapy interventions. Another major source of personal learning is associated with the process of transcribing and analysing interviews in which people have been invited to talk about their experience of therapy. What becomes clear, most of the time, is that what people experience, and the way they understand that experience, will not map on to theories of therapy in any straightforward manner. Doing this kind of research has the effect of inviting therapist-researchers to examine their basic assumptions about therapy, and arrive at a deeper understanding.

Research that makes use of qualitative interviews also provides an ideal entry into the field of therapy research as a whole. The experience of undertaking this kind of research project forces a novice researcher to think seriously about a whole range of basic methodological issues, from ethical concerns around confidentiality and avoidance of harm, through to questions of reliability (would that person have told a different story to a different interviewer?) and validity (how can I know whether the themes I have identified in the data are a true reflection of participants' experiences?). Analysing qualitative interviews makes it possible to see why quantification of experience makes sense – yes, every research participant has a unique story to tell, but at the same time there are common themes that can be identified and added up. It also makes it possible to appreciate the limitations of self-report, in terms of the ways in which any source of information about therapy is shaped by the context within which it is collected. Finally, for most people, analysing qualitative interviews leads to a realisation that there exists a level of meaning beyond the overt content of what is said, and that there are significant research possibilities in analysing the structure of a conversation, or the intricate ways that a person uses language.

There are also important reasons for *not* doing qualitative interview research. This is a type of research that can be highly time-consuming. For example, each hour of recorded interview may require up to eight hours to transcribe. It is also a type of research that tends to be a bit messy. Sometimes, what a person says in an interview can be interpreted in several different ways, or may not make sense at all. Also, it is never possible to be absolutely confident that a set of categories or themes comprises a wholly adequate means of representing the data. Embarking on this kind of research therefore requires a sufficient level of tolerance for uncertainty, ambiguity and anxiety.

What kind of skills and support do I need?

The most important source of support, in relation to undertaking a qualitative interview study of the experience of therapy, is a supervisor, mentor or colleague who knows what to do, and is willing to pass on practical knowledge. It is helpful to envisage this as an expert-apprentice relationship. In other words, the supervisor or mentor is not just someone who tells the novice researcher what to do. Instead, they work together on specific tasks (such as designing an interview schedule, listening to a pilot interview, or analysing a transcript). The apprentice then goes off and does the next bit on his or her own, and brings it back to show what they have done.

There are two other crucial sources of support. It is very useful to be able to refer to some kind of external, independent source of consultative knowledge. In a university or college setting, this would normally take the form of a research ethics committee or Institutional Review Board (IRB), and a tutor or committee that would assess a research proposal. If the research is to be conducted outside of a university setting, it may be possible to find experienced researchers who will agree to act as consultants to a project. These external sources provide a 'reality check' on what is being proposed – it is easy for a researcher to be so caught up in his or her own ideas that they lose sight of how their questions might be received by a person being interviewed, or professional gatekeepers such as service managers. It is also very useful to assemble a group of colleagues or friends who would be willing to provide support over the course of a study, as sounding boards for ideas, acting as role-play subjects for pilot interviews, offering their interpretation of segments of interviews, and reading draft reports. Sometimes, students undertaking research studies at the same time will organise themselves into informal peer support and consultation groups. In some academic programmes, research groups are formally organised by academic staff. Such groups may also form part of practitioner research networks.

The process of carrying out qualitative, interview-based research consists of a mix of intense personal immersion in the data, accompanied by dialogue and contact with others. Both of these forms of activity are necessary.

The personal skills and knowledge that are required in this type of research are similar to the competencies associated with being a therapist: the ability to form an empathic and accepting relationship, a capacity to listen, an appreciation of ethical boundaries, and the skill to make sense of the meaning of what the person is saying. Although it is important, as mentioned earlier, to reflect on the differences between therapy interviews and research interviews, qualitative research skills are familiar territory for therapists, and, with practice, most are able to collect good quality interview data.

The academic knowledge required consists of a general understanding of research principles, along with specific knowledge of the specific qualitative research methodology that is being used. For anyone undertaking a qualitative interview study for the first time, it is sensible to stick to a well-defined methodological approach such as thematic analysis, grounded theory, Interpretative Phenomenological Analysis (IPA), or Consensual Qualitative Research (CQR). Within each of these research traditions, it is possible to find guidelines on how to use the approach, how to write up a study, and examples of published studies. Although there are many excellent qualitative studies that have adopted a 'bricolage' approach, in combining elements from these (and other) research methodologies, it is better to begin by following a well-trodden and well-understood path. There is enough to think about, when doing research for the first time, without an added pressure of needing to invent and justify a new or innovative methodological approach.

Suggestions for preliminary reading

There are many excellent articles and books on the topic of how to conduct and analyse research interviews. It is important for each researcher to find a text and author that speak to their own personal imagination. For many qualitative researchers in the field of counselling and psychotherapy, the work of Steiner Kvale has proved invaluable as a source of insight and wisdom in relation to the use of the interview method. His ideas can be found in two books:

Kvale, S. (2007) *Doing Interviews*. Thousand Oaks, CA: Sage.
Kvale, S. and Brinkmann, S. (2009) *InterViews: Learning the Craft of Qualitative Research Interviewing*. Thousand Oaks, CA: Sage.

Both texts cover similar ground, however the later book provides a more comprehensive account of the broader context of interviewing within the field of qualitative research as a whole.

Another author who writes about research interviewing from a psychotherapeutic and humanistic perspective is Ruthellen Josselson:

Josselson, R. (2013) *Interviewing for Qualitative Inquiry: A Relational Approach.* New York: Guilford.

A useful if brief overview of the issues involved in research interviewing is available in:
Knox, S. and Burkard, A.W. (2009) Qualitative research interviews, *Psychotherapy Research*, 19: 566–75.

Exercise 11.1   The interview style that is right for you

In order to use the interview to best effect, it is necessary to ensure that the interviewee is relaxed and comfortable. One of the factors that has a major influence on this process is the capacity of the interviewer to be 'centred' and to come across as genuine rather than playing a role. It can be useful to reflect on your style of being with clients, in your role as a counsellor or psychotherapist, and consider how this way of relating could form the basis for your style as an interviewer. It is also helpful to take part in interviews with colleagues, from both sides of the fence, to develop a first-hand sense of what works for you.

A step-by-step guide to doing a qualitative interview study

At the beginning of any research study, it is necessary to develop an understanding of the nature and development of research in counselling and psychotherapy, in order to be able to understand where and how one's specific project fits into the field as a whole. It is also important to assemble appropriate research support, and identify the aims and research questions that are being pursued (see Chapter 3 for further information on formulating a research question). In relation to undertaking a qualitative interview study, it is also wise to decide early on which method will be adopted (thematic analysis, grounded theory, IPA or CQR). The choice of method will have to be determined partly by the aim of the study, and partly by the research support and expertise that are available. Once these elements are in place, it is possible to construct a research proposal (see Chapter 4), and receive approval to collect data. The research proposal or plan needs to take account of validity criteria for qualitative research (see Chapter 8). In the process of designing a study, it can also be worthwhile to identify one or more published studies that can serve as 'templates' for the proposed research.

Keeping a research journal

Alongside the general research tasks mentioned already, it is also advisable to begin to keep a research diary or journal. A research journal is particularly necessary in qualitative interview research because it serves two vital functions: deepening researcher reflexivity, and building an analytic framework. Researcher reflexivity (see Chapter 8) is a central aspect of qualitative research, because it acknowledges the personal involvement of the researcher in the research process, and seeks to use this involvement to sensitise that researcher to aspects of the phenomenon being studied. By contrast, a lack of attention in researcher reflexivity can lead to research that is perceived by readers as biased. Qualitative research requires summarising or condensing a lot of verbal material, such as interview transcripts, into a succinct statement that will highlight key themes or categories. In order to do this, it is necessary to conceptualise the material in some way. It is a mistake to think that these concepts will only emerge after all the data have been collected, and the researcher is sitting in his or her study reading through the transcripts line by line. Useful concepts can come to mind during or after an interview, while transcribing, in conversation with a colleague, in a dream – that is to say, anywhere. Keeping a journal allows these ideas to be harvested and then fed into the final data analysis stage.

Deciding on the method

There is a large body of research that use open-ended or semi-structured interviews with individuals, followed by analysis of interview transcripts in terms of themes or categories. However, there are different ways in which this general research task can be approached, and these approaches have tended to have been described in terms of specific 'brand names', such as empirical phenomenology or grounded theory. This section offers a brief review of the key features of each of these approaches. They are treated here as 'methods' – sets of procedures that are used to organise a study and are reported in the 'method' section of a journal article. It is important to keep in mind that these approaches can also be considered 'methodologies' because each of them is broader than just a set of procedures, and in fact draws on a somewhat different set of underlying philosophical assumptions. For the purpose of *doing* this kind of research, as a novice or apprentice researcher, what is essential is to be able to understand and follow the relevant procedures. The model of research training/learning that informs this book is that making things (research products) comes first, and it is only when a researcher has had some first-hand experience of the lived reality of doing a particular type of research that the underlying methodological and philosophical principles can begin to make any sense. A clear and helpful guide to the philosophical underpinning of most of the methods outlined below can be found in Ponterotto (2005).

Phenomenology

One of the longest established approaches to qualitative research is *phenomenological analysis*. To distinguish it from phenomenology as a school of philosophy, some qualitative researchers will describe what they do as *empirical phenomenology* (Finlay, 2011). Although all forms of qualitative analysis are informed by phenomenological principles, a study that adopts a specific phenomenological stance is distinctive in aiming to develop a *description* of the 'essence' or essential features of an experience. Compared to other qualitative methods outlined in this section, phenomenology is probably somewhat more challenging, and harder to do well, because it requires at least some degree of engagement with philosophical ideas, and is associated with quite demanding requirements around the depth of analysis that is carried out. Conducting a pure phenomenological study is therefore not necessarily a sensible choice for a novice researcher. However, the writings of leading phenomenological researchers, such as Finlay (2011) and Fischer (2009), have been highly influential within the field of qualitative research as a whole. A further disadvantage of using a phenomenological method is that the aim of producing a description of a phenomenon does not leave much scope or space for the consideration of theory.

Grounded theory

Another long-established qualitative method is *grounded theory*. Initially developed by Glaser and Strauss (1968), the grounded theory approach is probably the most widely-used method in the field of qualitative research. Because it has been applied by so many researchers and research groups, what has happened is that slightly different versions of grounded theory have emerged (see McLeod, 2011, for further discussion). Nevertheless, all grounded theory research follows the same set of basic procedures. The researcher is advised against reading or reviewing the literature ahead of collecting the data, in order to remain as open as possible to subtle meanings conveyed by interview participants. The method is open to any type of qualitative data that might be available, including interviews, observation and documents. Ideally, each interview is analysed before the next one is carried out, so that the interviewer is sensitised to emerging themes that can be explored further in later interviews. As a result, this method uses a flexible, adaptable interview schedule rather than a fixed set of questions. Transcripts are subjected first of all to open coding, in which potential meaning(s) conveyed by 'meaning units' (e.g., phrases, sentences, longer passages) are noted. These codes undergo a process of constant comparison to identify similarities and clarify differences. Through this activity a set of categories will emerge, which are then clustered into a smaller set of perhaps four or five main organising categories. Finally, a 'core category', which captures the meaning of the phenomenon being studied as a whole, is formulated. Grounded theory adopts a distinctive approach to sampling. Rather than deciding the sample size (number of participants) in advance, the aim is to continue collecting data until 'theoretical saturation' has been achieved – in other words, no new codes or categories are being discovered. In the later stages of data collection, 'theoretically interesting' participants are sought out in order to test the robustness of the emerging category structure. The end-point of a grounded theory analysis is a theoretical framework (set of concepts) that is grounded in the everyday experience of participants. In many studies this framework or theory will be expressed in the form of a diagram. The grounded theory method is flexible, well-understood, and supported by a range of textbooks and websites, as well as a critical methodological literature. It has also been used in many influential studies of counselling and psychotherapy (see, for example, Rennie, 2000). The downside of grounded theory is that it calls for certain procedures that can be difficult to follow in practice (for example, continuing with theoretical sampling long enough to achieve saturation, finding a plausible core category). Not reviewing the literature in advance can create difficulties in academic settings where students will need to submit a review before commencing data collection. A further limitation of grounded theory, for some researchers, is that like phenomenology it has an arms-length relationship with theory. Allowing pre-existing theoretical concepts to influence data analysis is not permissible in grounded theory. It is only when an entire grounded theory has been constructed that the links with pre-existing theory are supposed to take place. An additional issue is that grounded theory does not pay much attention to the way in which the participants' experience is constructed through language (for example, if a person described themself as 'bi-polar', that individual can be seen as positioning/constructing themself in relation to psychiatric discourse). Instead, language (i.e., the words spoken during interviews) is regarded as reflecting the inner experience of the informant. In practice, grounded theory is a highly pragmatic means of arriving at practical knowledge, which functions well enough in the absence of giving detailed attention to the ins and outs of language use. But for researchers who *are* interested in language and discourse, it is not a good choice.

Interpretative Phenomenological Analysis (IPA)

Interpretative Phenomenological Analysis (IPA) is an approach that was developed by Jonathan Smith and his colleagues (Smith, Flowers and Larkin, 2009) in the 1990s. In many ways, the IPA method is similar to grounded theory. However, having had an opportunity to watch and learn about grounded theory, the founders of IPA were in a position to create a method that retained the basic virtues of grounded theory (constructing a set of themes or categories that are grounded in lived experience) while avoiding some of the tricky bits, and adding in some valuable new ideas. Unlike grounded theory, IPA does not require researchers to keep going until they have reached a set of categories, and main categories, that will account for all of the data. On the contrary, IPA encourages the use of small samples (often around six participants) and analysis on a case-by-case basis, leading to a discussion of differences across cases as well as common themes. IPA has also developed ways of making use of concepts from pre-existing theory within the analytic process, as well as analysis of language use (e.g., metaphors). The IPA tradition has evolved a style of reporting results of studies in terms of themes that flows well and in many respects is more direct than the category structure used in grounded theory. IPA is also supported by a textbook that elegantly and accessibly explains the philosophical rationale for the approach (Smith et al., 2009), and by useful on-line learning materials. At the present time, these features make IPA a particularly attractive choice for novice researchers.

Thematic analysis

Thematic analysis can be regarded as a minimalist or stripped-down version of grounded theory and IPA. The idea of thematic analysis has been around for a long time, as a general approach to qualitative analysis, but gained prominence following the publication of a paper by Braun and Clarke (2006) which described a set of procedures which could be followed. Their version of thematic analysis allows the researcher a great deal of freedom to analyse qualitative data in a form that is appropriate to their own purposes. What this means is that a researcher who uses thematic analysis needs to explain, in the method section of their study, the analytic procedures they followed. By contrast, a researcher who uses IPA or grounded theory merely needs to claim that they followed the guidelines in Smith et al. (2009) or Charmaz (2013). Thematic analysis is a good choice for researchers who feel confident that they know what they are trying to achieve. For researchers who are less confident, grounded theory or IPA provides more guidance.

Consensual Qualitative Research (CQR)

Consensual Qualitative Research (CQR) is an approach to qualitative analysis that is similar to phenomenology, grounded theory, IPA and thematic analysis, but which includes two additional elements. Unlike other qualitative approaches, which assume that the researcher is working alone, CQR explicitly consists of a team approach. Data are parcelled up to be analysed by members of a small team made up of perhaps three or four people. In addition, the results of these analyses are audited by an expert researcher from outside the team. The intention is that the contributions of all members of the research team combine to yield a consensus analysis which is richer and more plausible than an analysis carried out by an individual working on their own. The other distinctive element of CQR is that theory informs analysis from the start, rather than being considered only at the end. The research team takes existing theory into account when deciding on the 'domains' that will be used to organise the process of data analysis. Interview transcripts are first chunked in terms of domains. Following this, blocks of text within each domain are subjected to open coding and the identification of themes and categories, along the lines of grounded theory. This strategy makes it much easier to make links between the aims and findings of a study, and previously-existing theory and research findings. On the other hand, it can have the effect of restricting the potential creativity of the research process. CQR has been immensely productive, with many counselling and psychotherapy studies completed in recent years using this approach (see Hill, 2012). It fits very well into situations in which there exists a potential pool of researchers, such as a therapy training course or doctoral programme. The role of auditor is also consistent with an apprenticeship-oriented model of research training. Alongside its use with groups of student researchers, CQR is a method that meets many of the needs of experienced practitioners seeking to carry out research-based continuing professional development within a peer group. The CQR research community has generated very clear guidelines about how the method can be applied to different types of research question (Hill, 2012).

Other methods of qualitative analysis

There are many other approaches to the analysis of qualitative interview data. For example, the method of systematic text condensation (Binder et al., 2009; Malterud, 2011) is a phenomenological-interpretive form of analysis that has been widely used in Nordic countries. It is also possible to adopt a 'bricolage' perspective, which brings together analytic ideas and techniques from a range of methods (McLeod, 2011).

The choice of method will depend on a number of factors. Some research questions will be better suited to some methods. For example, questions that involved describing or uncovering the meaning of a specific type of experience, such as 'anger', 'understanding' or 'forgiveness', lend themselves to phenomenological inquiry. Questions that explore action sequences or processes, such as 'living with depression' or 'using metaphor in therapy', are a good fit for grounded theory, IPA and CQR. However, each method can be applied to a range of research topics and questions, so it is important to take time to search in the literature for examples of how different methods have been used in relation to one's own research question, or similar types of question.

Another factor to take into consideration when selecting a method is the nature of support that is available. Probably the single most significant aspect here is the experience and interests of possible research supervisors or mentors. Another aspect is concerned with the coherence and extent of published teaching and training materials. For example, thematic analysis is a flexible and attractive option for many researchers, but at the present time is supported by only one source (Braun and Clarke, 2006). IPA and CQR are relatively easy to learn because they are in effect 'owned' by their founders (Jonathan Smith and Clara Hill) who have maintained a high degree of quality control and consistency around the use of their method. By contrast, as mentioned earlier, grounded theory has fragmented into a number of versions of the method. Anyone seeking to learn about grounded theory is well advised to concentrate on the work of Kathy Charmaz, in the form of her textbook of grounded theory (Charmaz, 2006) and papers published in the *Qualitative Health Research* journal under her editorship.

Having decided on a method, it is necessary to allow sufficient time to learn the method, by reading textbooks and chapters, talking to supervisors, mentors and research colleagues, attending training workshops (if available), and reading and reflecting on articles that have employed that approach.

Deciding on an interview strategy and schedule

The most frequently adopted interview strategy is to use a semi-structured interview schedule, in the context of a one-to-one interview that lasts for about an hour. Ethically, participants need to have received information about the study in advance (see Chapter 5). Usually, however, it will be necessary to devote some time at the start of an interview to checking out that the person has understood what is involved, and is still willing to proceed. This can take a few minutes. Also, some participants may have a lot to say, take time to warm up, or talk slowly. For these reasons, even if the aim is to conduct a 50–60 minute interview, it will be sensible to contract with participants to allow for a longer period of time. There are then some choices that need to be made about how to organise the interview:

- Will the participants receive the questions in advance?
- Should the interview begin with neutral/factual questions, such as age, occupation and so on, or will it be more effective to go straight into the topic, and leave the factual questions until the end?
- How many questions can be asked? Is it helpful to organise these in themes, or as a narrative time-line?
- Is it better to follow a script, in the form of a fixed set of questions, or would it be more effective to begin with a general or 'grand rounds' question and then only use other questions as prompts if the participant misses something that is important to the study?
- How interactive, or personally involved, should the researcher be?
- What does the researcher do if the participant (or the researcher) gets upset, or the participant discloses information about unethical or illegal conduct?
- How does the interview end? Is it useful to know about how the participant experienced the interview? Is it helpful to leave open the possibility of further contact (e.g., if the interviewee has any further thoughts, or the interviewer wants to check on any details)?
- Is there a record made of the interviewer's experience, for example if he or she got angry or felt confused by what the participant was saying?

There are no right or wrong answers to these questions – each one represents a genuine methodological choice-point. What is important is to take the time to consider these possibilities, and consult with others, during the research planning stage. It is also important to remember that the perfect research study does not exist: research always involves arriving at a compromise between competing possibilities and objectives. In deciding on an interview strategy and schedule, it is wise to be guided by exemplar/template studies on similar topics, and build on what has worked for these predecessor researchers.

Refining the interview strategy: carrying out a pilot interview

It is never possible to know whether an interview strategy and schedule will work in the field, without trying these out in a safe situation. Even highly experienced researchers are capable of designing interview schedules that are too lengthy to cover in the time available, or research questions that are not understood by inform-ants. Pilot studies can be carried out with colleagues who play the role of participant (e.g., most therapists can usually get into the role of being a client for interview purposes), or with potential 'real' participants with whom the researcher has a suf-ficiently robust relationship. It can be illuminating to invite some pilot interviewees to act in a difficult or resistant manner. When asking pilot participants for feedback, it is useful to ask them not only about their response to the interview, but also how they believe that other people might respond. It is easier to say 'someone else might have been irritated by that question' rather than 'I was irritated'. It is useful to record pilot interviews, and review them (or parts of them) with a supervisor or members of a peer support group. It is also useful to reflect on the material gener-ated by the interview in relation to the aims of the researcher. For example, it may be that some questions elicit information that is not required, while other questions need to be deepened in order to gain access to the phenomena that matter most. Another aim of the pilot interview phase is to allow the researcher to become more comfortable, confident and fluent in the interviewer role.

A further possibility, at the stage of developing the interview schedule and strat-egy, is for the researcher to be interviewed by a colleague. It is likely that the researcher will be able to draw on some areas of personal experience that are rele-vant to the topic of the study. Alternatively, the researcher can role-play an imagined informant. This exercise provides a researcher with a valuable alternative perspec-tive on the interview process, as well as contributing to the enhancement of researcher reflexivity.

Doing the interviews

To a large extent, the success of a qualitative interview-based study will depend on the richness and authenticity of the interviews. Even the most expert and careful analysis can only work with what is in the transcript. If informants have not felt safe enough to open up, or have been asked irrelevant questions, the resulting transcripts and analysis will inevitably be somewhat limited.

In principle, counsellors and psychotherapists have the potential to be highly effective research interviewers, because they are good at listening, have a capacity to tune in to non-verbal cues, and are practised in using their own emotional response to the person as a source of information. Some people, confronted by the task of carrying out a semi-structured interview, will resort to a kind of market research strategy of rattling through a fixed set of questions. Therapists doing research interviews are not like this – they are generally able to create space for the person to tell their story. Nevertheless, there are two important areas in which therapist-researchers can find it hard to make the transition from therapy dialogue to research interviewing. Sometimes therapists will allow themselves to be drawn in to responding therapeutically, for example by helping the informant to resolve an issue. Sometimes therapist-researchers can be too non-directive, and come away from an interview having neglected to ask certain key questions. These are areas that can readily be addressed in research supervision.

It is important to recognise that there are many different styles of qualitative interviewing, and that it is necessary for each researcher to find a style with which they are comfortable. For example, some interviewers find that it is helpful for them to take notes, or draw diagrams during an interview (in addition to recording the interview), because doing so helps them to keep track of what is being covered. For other interviewers, taking notes would be an intrusive distraction. Some like to start with a 'grand rounds' general question ('I'd like to know what this episode of therapy meant for you'), and then use further probe questions if there appear to be key areas or issues that the informant may seem to have skipped. Other interviewers are more comfortable adopting a step-by-step approach, working through a set of questions. For some interviewers, it is useful to share some of their own experience of the topic being explored. Some interviewers will make use of 'projective' questions, such as 'If your therapist was an animal, what would they be?' There are many, many ways to personalise the interview process. There is actually substantial room for manoeuvre in qualitative interviews. It is therefore really useful to take some time to study qualitative interview texts and guidelines, and practise with/on colleagues.

A crucial aspect of any qualitative interview is the commitment to take care of the informant, in terms of time boundaries, confidentiality, monitoring level of distress in relation to sensitive topics, and making sure that there is a sufficient degree of closure at the end of the interview. It is always useful to include, at the end of an interview, an invitation to the participant to add anything that has not been covered and which they feel might be relevant to the study, and to ask about what it was like to be interviewed and how the interview approach might be improved for future participants. A useful technique here is to ask not only whether the person found any of the questions confusing or difficult, but also whether they think that another person might find them confusing or difficult; there can be a certain amount of embarrassment about admitting to not personally understanding something. These closing questions can also provide useful information about the authenticity and meaning of the interview for the informant. If an informant states that they found the interview to be an interesting experience, which helped them to look at a topic in a fresh way, then this usually indicates that the information they provided was a genuine reflection of how they feel. If, on the other hand, an informant does not convey a sense of having been involved, during the interview, in a genuine process of inquiry and exploration, then this may indicate that the informant was holding something back, or was ambivalent about some aspect of the topic of the research.

Taking care of the informant may be facilitated by the order in which questions are asked. For example, many interviewers will begin with relatively factual questions, that are easy to answer, before moving into more sensitive areas of questioning. Questions about the interview experience, and then the collection of demographic information, can be used right at the end to close off the interview. Taking care may also be facilitated by using early, pre-interview contact to begin to establish a research relationship or research alliance, for example by personalising communication and being sensitive to participants' needs around the venue and timing. Another element of taking care is to invite a participant to make contact after the interview, if there is anything further they wish to add to what they have said. In some studies, it can also be appropriate to provide details of counselling and support services, helplines, etc., that the person might wish to consult.

In qualitative interview-based research, the researcher is the main research instrument or tool. The previous paragraphs in this section have looked at ways in which the interview schedule and strategy can be designed to be consistent with the style and personal values of the researcher. There is also a more direct way of using the interviewer as an instrument, which is to pay attention to one's own responses to the interviewee, and note these down after the end of the interview. The kind of things that might be useful to note include: feelings, emotions, images and fantasies that came into awareness during the interview; the appearance, voice quality and physical presence of the interviewee; the impression that the interviewee seemed to be trying to convey. This kind of information can be really helpful in enabling a deeper understanding of the material in an interview transcript, by sensitising the researcher to the implicit or hidden dimensions of an informant's account.

A final point about interviews is that not all of these are equally informative. In most studies, there will be some interviewees who talk vividly and honestly about their experience, and contribute a wealth of insights and quotable statements. Other interviewees will offer less, either because they do not feel safe, do not develop rapport with the interviewer, are not ready to talk, or because of innumerable other factors. This is just the way it is. Obviously, it is essential for a researcher to give equal consideration to take the contribution of every informant. Sometimes, there can be massively important ideas buried in throwaway comments by informants who have not said much.

Transcribing

Interviews need to be transcribed. It is possible to take notes while listening to a recording or watching a video of an interview, but it is then awkward to check back to the source, when comparing ideas from different interviews. Also, taking notes when listening to a recording usually involves transcribing passages that are of special interest. So, in the end, most qualitative researchers will convert recordings into transcripts.

Transcripts are also ethically safer, in terms of confidentiality, because names, places and other identifying information can be changed.

If possible, it is a good idea for the researcher to do the transcribing, and to make notes as they go along. The discipline of transcribing forces the researcher to listen closely to what was said, and enables the researcher to become immersed in the data. Sometimes, because of time pressure, typing ability or whatever, transcribing will have to be done by someone else. It is essential that the person doing the transcribing fully appreciates the confidentiality of the material with which they are working. Ethics committees will sometimes want the transcriber to be named, so they can be sure that ethical considerations will be handled properly. For example, sending recordings to be transcribed by a commercial office services company would not be appropriate. It is necessary to decide, at the outset, on the transcribing rules that will be followed. In conversation analysis studies (not the type of study being described in the present chapter), it is essential to use a complex, detailed and time-consuming set of transcribing rules that convey information about voice quality, exact length of pauses, talkover sequences, and much else. This level of detail is required if specific linguistic and conversational processes are being analysed. Usually, qualitative interview-based studies are more concerned with analysing meaning, rather than analysing linguistic features. It is therefore sufficient, when transcribing, to include the words that were said, and to indicate silences and emotions (e.g., if the person seemed angry or was in tears). However, these simple rules need to be defined to ensure consistency across a series of transcripts.

Some researchers will send a copy of the transcript to each interviewee, with a request to make corrections and indicate any passages that they would not want to be quoted in research reports. However, probably the majority of researchers will not follow this procedure. Sending a transcript opens up the possibility of the person being upset when they see what they said in the interview. This occurs in a situation where the researcher is not on hand to offer support. Also, there is a possibility that the transcript may be read by another member of a person's family. It is therefore important to consider these factors, and discuss them with informants, before agreeing to send out transcripts. It may also be the case that some informants strongly wish to receive a transcript, as a form of documentation of a significant experience in their life.

The format and layout of a transcript need to be prepared for analysis. It is useful to insert line numbering, so that the location of interesting quotes, or instances of codes/themes, can be readily identified. If analysis is carried out on paper copies, it may be helpful to display the text double-spaced, or to use wide margins, to allow notes to be written on to the page.

Transcribing takes time. It is important to include a realistic estimate of the time requirement during the planning phase of a study. If time constraints are a significant issue, it may be better to choose a different type of research or method of data collection. Within a qualitative research approach, it is possible to collect data using diaries, open ended-questionnaires, or other forms of written report that do not need to be transcribed.

Analysing

The process of analysing transcripts of qualitative interviews should adhere to the procedures specified within the qualitative method that is being followed (e.g. grounded theory, IPA, CQR). All of the widely-used methods are supported by clear instructions and worked examples around how transcript data should be analysed. These instructions need to be studied carefully, and discussed/practised with a research supervisor or mentor. The comments below are intended as a supplement to the guidelines associated with grounded theory, IPA, CQR or other established qualitative methods, and not as a replacement for them.

The first step in qualitative analysis is to become immersed in the data, to upload these into your imagination and working memory. This happens by doing interviews, transcribing interviews, and reading transcripts. This process can also be aided by constructing a location for the data. Paper-based analysis may involve spreading notes or file cards on the floor, on a table top, attaching them to walls, or clipping them to loops of string stretched across a room. Screen-based analysis may involve creating and organising folders in WORD, or becoming familiar with the operation of a qualitative analysis package such as NVivo.

It is then necessary to make best use of the time available. Arriving at a robust and coherent analysis of qualitative transcript texts takes a lot of time. Typically, students who are under pressure to complete their dissertation or thesis do not have a lot of this, and in some cases may not have enough to get to a point of being fully satisfied with the job they have done. There are two types of analytic time. There is a kind of rhythmic use of time, where the researcher dips in and out of the material for fairly short periods, for example when transcribing, or discussing specific transcripts with their supervisor or peer group. It is important to keep a note of the analytic ideas (codes, themes, connections with theory and previous studies) that arise during or following each of these visits to the data. These notes constitute the elements or building blocks of the ultimate analysis. At the time of making the notes, it may not be clear where they fit into an overall scheme. That does not matter – the overall scheme comes later.

The other type of time is a block of time, of at least several days, towards the end of the project. Some researchers will go away for a few days, or take a holiday from work, to make sure that they have a block of undisturbed time. (This can be unpopular with family members.) By this point, all the interviewing and transcribing will have been done, and a great many notes compiled. The task now is to connect everything together and begin to write it all down. It is probable that most of what is written will need to be edited and polished. The aim is to emerge from this block of time with a version or working draft. In my experience, qualitative researchers who manage to create this kind of block of time report that they are excited and energised by the experience, and feel that they have achieved something worthwhile. Those who proceed on the basis of analysing the data on two evenings each week, or every second Saturday, tend to accumulate high levels of stress and frustration. This is because it is enormously difficult, at a cognitive and emotional level, to re-enter this material at depth over and over again.

In terms of the actual process of analysing transcript data, all of the widely-used methods of qualitative analysis, such as grounded theory or IPA, require researchers to work through the material, on a line-by-line or statement-by-statement basis, and allocate a code or descriptive label (or multiple codes/labels) that convey the possible meaning of that little segment of the data. The idea is that the interview as a whole has given the person an opportunity to express what it means to him or her to be a client, or a therapist, or to sit in silence, or write answers to a feedback questionnaire or whatever the research topic might be. Within that totality, each line of transcript or statement reflects a fragment of the total meaning. This procedure lies at the heart of qualitative analysis. A good way of thinking about what happens next is that each meaning-code is then written on a card. These cards are then compared with one another to allow all the cards with a similar meaning to be together to form categories or themes. In practice, not all researchers use actual cards – an equivalent process can be replicated with computer files, diagrams, and other means of display.

However, qualitative analysis is not merely a matter of accumulating and sorting out codes. These codes come from the mind of the researcher. One of the major lessons of cognitive psychology is that, confronted by a complex array of information, people tend to see patterns and jump to conclusions. In such a context, the discipline of coding line by line is an effective means of subverting and challenging any pre-existing or early assumptions and imagined patterns that the researcher might hold. Micro-coding forces the researcher to pay attention to what is there, or more probably, *what else* might be there. Within the phenomenological tradition, this is the activity known as 'bracketing-off' (Fischer, 2009). It is only very rarely, or perhaps even never at all, that a researcher is able to lay aside all of his or her assumptions, and be fully open to the essential meaning of something said by a research participant. But each moment of willingness to bracket-off gives a researcher the opportunity to make a new discovery, learn something new, extend their interpretive horizon, deepen their understanding.

This activity of micro-coding is cognitive: it involves thinking, reasoning and using concepts and words. It also involves emotional responses to the material and 'felt sense' of the message that the participant was communicating. These are bodily phenomena. It can be valuable for qualitative researchers to make use of their physical, bodily response to what they hear in a recording or read in a transcript. Fergus and Rennie (2006) have written about coding 'from the gut'. What they mean is that, by being immersed in the data, the researcher develops a gut feeling around what the speaker might have meant. The task is then to find the words, phrases or images that best capture this felt sense. This can happen when the researcher is working on their own with the material. Another way of accessing a bodily level of appreciation of the meanings being expressed in an interview is to read the transcript aloud, listen while a colleague reads it back, or listen while different colleagues read the same passage aloud.

It is important to accept that the process of qualitative analysis is not linear. It is not a matter of gradually accumulating more and more codes and meanings, until a structure or overall picture emerges. Unfortunately, it is a process that goes backwards as well as forwards. In any qualitative research, the investigator begins with some kind of pre-existing understanding of the phenomenon being studied. A genuine process of exploration and discovery requires that this prior structure of understanding should be dismantled and rebuilt. This can be scary. Many qualitative researchers report that, during data analysis, they went through a period or periods of what some therapists describe as 'not-knowing' and what ordinary people describe as 'getting really confused'. This is scary because by that point the researcher will have invested many hours on the project, and will be aware that they need to 'come up with something' if they are to get their degree or produce a publishable study. It is crucial in this situation to accept that being confused is actually a good sign, a progress marker. It is also crucial to recognise that the way forward may not necessarily be to facilitate by working harder at the analysis. It may be useful to keep going with the analysis, because there may be a little nugget of a quote in the next transcript that triggers an 'aha' moment. But is also a good idea to pay attention to one's own sources of creativity, whatever these might be – art, music, dreams, nature, reading, meditation. Another way of looking at it, is that arriving at a coherent and satisfying analysis of interview data calls on a belief in, and acceptance of, one's own capacity to understand.

The level of understanding of qualitative data that is possible now may be different from the understanding that is possible in two years time or indeed ten years time. This is something that is very apparent to many students who are under a deadline pressure to complete their dissertation or thesis. They know that they have made a good effort to analyse their data, but they also know that there is 'more to it' that is just outside their grasp. My own advice is to go with what you have, and be willing to come back to it later. One practical strategy here is to publish (or submit) an analysis that consists of a largely descriptive account of all of the themes or categories that emerged in analysis. Because space in journal articles is tight, a researcher only needs to provide a brief description of each theme or category, backed up by one or two well-chosen examples. There is not space to unpick complex aspects of the data that, at this point, the researcher may not fully understand. At a later date, when some of these complexities become clearer, it may be possible to write about these aspects of the analysis in more depth, referring back to the original paper as a source of information about the overall analysis as a whole. A classic example of this strategy can be found in the research carried out by David Rennie into the client's experience of therapy. The earliest publications to emerge from this project were based on providing an overview of the grounded theory category structure as a whole (Rennie, 1990, 1992). Later publications then presented more detailed analyses of specific categories, such as client deference (Rennie, 1994a), storytelling (Rennie, 1994b) and resistance (Rennie, 1994c).

An alternative strategy, when faced with complex results, is to wait until it all becomes clear. My advice is not to do this, because it can take a long time – years – for this to occur. Also, it may never happen.

A final practical tip in relation to data analysis, which in my opinion is not given sufficient emphasis in many qualitative research textbooks, is to make use of other people. In our society, anything that is connected to psychology is likely to get sucked into a vortex of individualism. In respect of qualitative analysis, this leads to a reliance on the implementation of an analysis protocol by an individual researcher. Important exceptions to this rule can be found in CQR (Hill, 2012) and dialogal research (Halling et al., 2006). However, I would suggest that it is valuable for any qualitative researcher, no matter which method they are using, to involve other people. An activity that can be extremely useful, following a period of immersion in the data and coding, is to meet with others and just talk about what has been found, with no requirement to label any of this as categories or different levels of category. It can also be helpful if a member of the group writes down what the researcher says, and how he or she responds to questions. The act of just freely talking about what has been found, calls for the researcher to articulate ideas that up to that point were implicit. Talking in a non-judgemental environment means that self-censorship is minimised, and self-contradiction is permissible. After such a conversation the researcher will need to sift through what has emerged, including systematically checking on whether what they were able to say represented all of the data, and whether there might be counter-instances in the data that did not fit into the implicit themes that were articulated.

There are many other ways that other people can play a part in data analysis. It is instructive for a small group to spend at least 90 minutes sharing their interpretations of a portion of a transcript. It is certain that an enormous amount of ideas will be generated, and that some of these ideas will be completely new to the researcher, no matter how much time he or she has already spent on that material. It is then up to the primary researcher to determine whether these ideas are relevant to the dataset as a whole. The members of a discussion group need not all be other researchers, or from the same discipline. Academic researchers, particularly within a single discipline, tend to make reference to the same set of ideas – lay people, inexperienced students, or people from other areas of the university, are likely to offer interpretations that are more creative and diverse. A further way in which other people can be involved is by acting as auditors. At the point where a reasonably complete draft of an analysis has been assembled, it will be helpful for a 'critical friend' to go through this to check whether the quotes/examples are convincing as illustrations of themes/categories, and whether the themes/categories that have been clustered together into main/superordinate groupings seem to be plausibly connected to each other. This task needs to be carried out by someone who is an experienced researcher, but is not necessarily all that time-consuming. For example, if a quote that is used as evidence to back up a category can readily be interpreted as carrying a meaning that has not been picked up by the researcher, then something is badly wrong. Other forms of auditing may involve the auditor analysing one or more transcripts, and then comparing their themes/categories with those of the primary researcher.

The involvement of other people in the process of qualitative analysis represents a manifestation of the *ethic of care* that was discussed in Chapter 1. These other people, whether an individual supervisor or a peer support group, need to care in the sense of being genuinely interested in, and respectful of, the researcher and what he or she is trying to achieve. They also need to care enough to challenge the researcher, even if this involves being critical or saying things that may come over as somewhat harsh.

Writing

Writing a qualitative paper or dissertation/thesis comprises an extension of the process of data analysis. The stage of writing up a study functions as a test of the coherence of the analysis that has been carried out. A structure of themes or categories that make sense on the whiteboard or during conversations within a research team can fall apart when it begins to be articulated on paper. A written report requires a logical sequence or narrative flow from one idea to another. Sometimes it can be hard to arrive at a satisfactory way of structuring the material to achieve an acceptable degree of linearity. This is a fundamental issue in all qualitative research, rather than being a sign of the inadequacy of any particular researcher. Qualitative interview-based research asks participants to share their experience of some specific part of their life. The themes that are then generated can be viewed as different aspects of that experience, which do not necessarily have a causal or linear relationship with each other. However, a results/finding section in a paper, that jumps abruptly from one theme or category to the next, will prove hard to read.

The most effective strategy for writing a results/finding section is to begin by offering the reader a brief summary of what was found, as a means of orienting and preparing them for what is to follow. Sometimes this summary will take the form of a table made up of themes/categories, or a diagram showing how the themes/categories are connected with each other. Sometimes the summary will just consist of a brief paragraph. The actual presentation of findings, which comes next, is then structured in terms of the story that the researcher has decided to tell. This story might start by explaining the key 'headline' finding of the study in some detail, before moving on to describe less important themes/categories in less detail. An alternative story structure is to organise the material around stages or phases in an unfolding experience. Results/findings sections in which the researcher does not tell a story, but instead offers a list of themes/categories in no particular order, or (worse) zig-zags back and forward between themes, or (even worse) relies on long quotes with little or no commentary, will have the effect of leaving the reader with a sense that the researcher has only collated the material and then left it up to the reader to analyse this.

In a qualitative article there are two stories that are being told. The first story is an account of what participants had to say on the topic under investigation. The second story consists of a narrative of how these findings fit into, confirm or contradict previous knowledge of the topic. In well-written qualitative articles, these different levels of narrative will dovetail together in a seamless fashion. In poorly-written papers, these narratives will either be bolted together or one of them will be subjugated to the other. When writing a qualitative paper, it is therefore particularly important to pay careful attention to the points of connection between the 'literature story' and the 'participant story' – the bridge passage between the introductory literature review and the method section, and the part of the discussion section where the findings of the study are looked at in relation to previous research. These transitions are handled very well, in my view, in most articles published in *Qualitative*

Health Research, and in many IPA articles. By contrast, these transitions are deeply problematic for many authors publishing in therapy journals, because it is almost certain that the background/introductory literature will consist of quantitative studies. In such a situation, it is possible to deal with the first transition by arguing that qualitative research has the potential to open up new ways of understanding a topic that has hitherto been studied using quantitative methods. But it is much harder, towards the end of a paper, to do the comparing task. It is like comparing apples and oranges, but without the space to clarify or explain the concept of an apple or the concept of an orange. As always, it is vital for novice researchers to look at how these technical writing tasks are handled by more experienced authors. These are not always done well.

There is, of course, a third story that can be told in a qualitative study – the researcher's story. The issues outlined in the previous paragraph should help to make it clear why it is so hard to integrate researcher reflexivity (the researcher's story) into a conventional research paper. This third narrative thread introduces a degree of complexity that is hard for most writers to handle. As a result, most journals have over the years arrived at their own specific 'house style' in respect of reflexive writing. This can be frustrating for qualitative therapy researchers who accept the role of reflexivity but are aiming to publish in therapy journals that have opted for minimal researcher self-reference in the form of a brief section in the method part of an article. It can be easier to include reflexive writing in a dissertation or thesis, because there is enough space to include different forms of writing, and also enough space to explain the rationale for these rhetorical choices.

It is worthwhile paying attention to the challenges of qualitative writing from the outset of a project. There are three activities here that can be particularly helpful. When reading the literature and compiling a literature review, it is useful to reflect on the effectiveness with which different articles are written, and build up a catalogue of 'good ideas for writing'. It is also valuable to write as you go along. It is easier, at the end, to be in a position of editing text that already exists, rather than staring at a blank laptop screen. Finally, when transcribing interviews, be on the lookout for quotes that are luminous, evocative, memorable, etc. These 'nuggets' or 'gems' (Smith, 2011) are useful in two ways. First, they have the potential, judiciously placed, to light up a manuscript or article. Second, they invite reflection on the part of the researcher: 'Why am I drawn to that statement?', 'What is it that makes it so memorable?'

In the findings/results section of a paper, a powerful and persuasive way of communicating qualitative insights is to look for ways of combining 'telling' (information about themes/categories) and 'showing' (brief stories that capture and exemplify that theme). This distinction has deep roots in the psychology of knowing, in the form of the contrast made by Jerome Bruner between 'paradigmatic' and 'narrative' forms of knowing. Research papers, on the client's experience of therapy, that were produced by David Rennie contain many beautifully crafted examples of how narrative and paradigmatic knowing can be woven together when presenting findings from qualitative research. The creative tension between these ways of knowing is further explored in a book by Toukmanian and Rennie (1992). It is important to emphasise here that effective narrative knowing or 'showing' demands more than just a brief informant quote such as 'I trusted my therapist at a deep level'. True narrative knowing, around this theme, would consist of a story told by the client that exemplified a concrete incident or episode that conveyed the depth of his trust. Having access to this kind of material has implications for the ways in which interviews are structured and conducted. In general, informants will want to tell stories. By contrast, researchers may become frustrated when an informant embarks on a bout of storytelling ('When will he get to the point and answer the question?') and will often cut the story off before it reaches its climax or conclusion. The importance, in qualitative interviews, of adopting a narrative-friendly approach, is discussed by Mishler (1986), Riessman (2008), and many other sources.

At the point of actually writing a qualitative paper, it is important to be mindful of the aims of qualitative inquiry and the type of knowledge that is generated. The quantitative, 'positivist' tradition is based on an underlying model of the world as consisting of causal 'factors'. The counselling and psychotherapy research literature is largely organised around this way of thinking. Examples would be, research into the *effect of* interventions on outcome, or the *impact of* working alliance on dropout. Qualitative research, by contrast, is based on a rather different set of underlying assumptions, which posit the world (or at least, the social world) as organised around purposeful collaborative action carried out by self-aware agents. The report of a qualitative study needs to be written in a way that reflects this philosophical stance. Careful reading of well-written qualitative articles will reveal the many ways in which this has been accomplished. Themes and categories are best formulated as action statements or 'doing' words. For example 'searching for a therapist voice' works better than 'counsellor identity' as a label for a theme. Although both labels are accurate, and convey meaning, the former implies a self-initiated process, while the latter is a 'thing' or static concept. A short paper by Sandelowski and Leeman (2012) provides an invaluable account of the subtle implications of different ways of labelling themes and categories. An example of a qualitative therapy research study that has explicitly adopted an 'action language' approach to theme-labels can be found in Levitt et al. (2006). Another form of writing that conveys lived experience involves the judicious use of statements from informants, not only to illustrate themes and categories, but also as the titles of themes and categories and possibly also within the title of an article. Images or phrases from informants can be highly evocative. They also function to remind the reader that the research is based on the experiences of specific people rather than a 'sample'. The use of diagrams that model the inter-relationships between categories is another way in which authors need to be careful. A diagram can all too easily be interpreted as a way of displaying the 'factor structure' of the findings of a study. Diagrams can be useful in qualitative research writing, but only if they convey action-sequences.

Further consideration of the issue of writing qualitative research can be found in a later section of this chapter, in the context of what is involved in writing for publication.

What can go wrong?

There are many practical things that can go wrong in interview-based qualitative studies: participants do not turn up for interviews, recording devices break down, transcribing takes much longer than anticipated, and so on. Other things that can go awry can be understood as part and parcel of the challenge of any research, rather than intrinsic to this particular type of study, such as not reviewing the literature carefully enough, or lack of clarity in writing. It is possible to identify two main pitfalls that are specific to interview-based qualitative research studies: a lack of analysis and a lack of focus.

Usually, the researcher in this type of research begins by generating a series of questions that they want to explore in interviews with informants. Even if the researcher adopts a largely unstructured, exploratory style, there is typically an interview schedule somewhere in the background. During the analysis phase, there is a tendency for novice qualitative researchers, who lack confidence, to make lists of the answers to each question. The results section is then organised around the subheadings for each question, followed by an itemisation of how many people answered in one way, and how many in a different way. Sometimes the researcher just presents a series of quotes from each participant. A further form of lack of analysis occurs when qualitative researchers code their interview material in terms of content categories (i.e., the topic that was being referred to). In practice, this ends up being rather similar to an analysis that is organised around interview questions, because topics or content areas largely correspond to interview questions. In a study of therapist experiences of training, for example, it is fairly straightforward to go through a transcript and highlight the topics that are being discussed: personal therapy, placement, time demands, reading, writing assignments, and so on.

These ways of doing qualitative analysis do not work. When responses are collated in relation to questions, the analysis (a) misses the chance to identify underlying themes and meanings that weave through answers to several questions, and (b) gives the impression that the researcher has not really discovered anything, but remains rooted in the understanding of the phenomenon that they had at the start of the inquiry process. Analysis in terms of content categories does not offer an understanding of the *meaning* of these topics for informants. For example, in a study of therapist experience of training, probably all informants will have something to say about personal therapy. This is not telling us much. What the reader wants to know is what the personal therapy meant to those informants, how they felt about it, the strategies they employed to cope with this demand on their time, and so on.

It is important to emphasise that collating answers to questions, and identifying content categories, are valid research procedures. Collating answers is central to survey research. Content categories are central to media analysis (e.g., the number of minutes of TV news coverage that were devoted to different topics). However, qualitative research always involves some form of conceptualising the data, because the purpose is to understand how meaning is constructed. Collating and content counting may represent an early step in sifting through complex qualitative data, but a convincing qualitative analysis always involves going further than this.

Another way that qualitative interview-based research can go wrong is through a lack of focus. A lot of qualitative research is motivated by a wish to explore the 'experience of' some aspect of therapy. Informants are recruited to provide accounts of their experience. But 'experience' is a somewhat all-encompassing concept. If I start talking about my experience of something, where do I stop? This is one of the reasons why it is useful for researchers to get a sense of what it is like to be an interviewee. For example, if I am asked about my experience of receiving person-centred therapy following a bereavement, I know that the meaning of that therapy was shaped by the nature of the loss, my earlier experiences of loss, the way that death and loss are handled in my family and culture, and so on and so on. This is even before talking about how I felt about choosing a therapist, meeting her for the first time, being in the therapy room, and on and on through several weeks of therapy sessions. Most people who agree to be interviewed want to be helpful, and are willing to open up many layers of the meaning of the topic that is being investigated. The result of this is that the researcher can end up with a large number of emergent themes. It can then be very hard to do justice to the richness of the material in an article-length report or even in a longer dissertation or thesis. It can also be hard to pinpoint how important themes might be if they are only mentioned by some informants. For instance, one participant might talk at length about the layout and décor of the therapy room, while other informants might say nothing about this aspect of their experience of therapy.

A recurring piece of advice in this book has been to read research articles. In relation to the notion that many qualitative studies lack focus, it is instructive to take some time to read a sample of published qualitative interview-based studies. How many studies describe a large number of different themes, and end up not being able to explore any of them in sufficient depth? Are there studies in which the complexity of what was found ends up confusing the reader?

The following section highlights some qualitative studies of the experience of therapy that I believe have represented particularly successful and effective examples of this genre of research. In some of these studies the researcher has decided on a specific focus from the start, or has chosen, within a particular paper, to focus on a specific aspect of their findings. In other studies the researcher has found effective ways to manage complex findings.

Exemplar studies

The exemplar studies that are briefly discussed in this section are not intended to be representative of the entire body of literature on qualitative interview-based research into the experience of counselling and psychotherapy. Instead, the aim is to provide some examples of what can be achieved with this methodology.

The experience of disadvantaged or marginalised clients. The therapy research literature as a whole largely consists of studies of white, middle-class, able-bodied clients. Qualitative interview-based research has made a major contribution to the field, by giving a voice to clients who do not fit into these mainstream categories. For example, there have been many powerful studies on the experiences of black and ethnic minority clients. Notable within this literature are studies by Chang and Berk (2009), Chang and Yoon (2011), Thompson, Bazile and Akbar (2004) and Ward (2005).

The ideas of clients around what makes therapy helpful. An important and influential subset of qualitative interview-based studies consists of investigating the views of clients around what has been helpful or unhelpful to them in their therapy (see Binder et al., 2009; Binder et al., 2011; Clarke et al., 2004; Gostas et al., 2013; Levitt et al., 2006) and the related topic of clients' theories of change (Lilliengren and Werbart, 2005; Philips et al., 2007).

The client's view of specific therapy approaches. Several qualitative studies have used interviews to explore what it was like for clients to receive particular types of therapy from the client perspective. These investigations have looked at a wide range of therapy models: CBT for fear of flying (Borrill and Foreman, 1996); CBT for depression (Glasman et al., 2004); psychodynamic therapy for eating disorders (Poulsen et al., 2010; Proulx, 2008; Toto-Moriarty, 2013); 'minimal' therapy based on a self-help manual (Macdonald et al., 2007); psychotherapy for chronic pain (Osborn and Smith, 2008); psychotherapeutic support in cancer care (MacCormack et al., 2001). Perhaps because mindfulness training is a therapeutic method that has emerged in recent years, at a time when qualitative research was becoming more widely accepted, probably the largest single area of qualitative research into the experience of a specific therapy has occurred in respect of mindfulness interventions (Allen et al., 2009; Chadwick et al., 2011; Fitzpatrick et al., 2010; Mason and Hargreaves, 2001; Morone et al., 2008).

The experience of being a therapist. Researchers have used qualitative interviews to document therapist experience around such topics as the characteristics of 'master therapists' (Jennings and Skovholt, 1999), learning from clients (Nielsen, 2008), assessing change in clients (Daniel and McLeod, 2006), integrating new techniques into their therapy approach (DiGiorgio et al., 2004), working with suicidal clients (Rossouw et al., 2011), using psychotherapeutic skills in medical consultations (Davidsen, 2009), negotiating informed consent (Goddard et al., 2008), working with bi-lingual clients (Santiago-Rivera et al., 2009) and dealing with sexual attraction in the client-therapist relationship (Martin et al., 2011; Rodgers, 2011). Other therapist-focused research has looked at ways in which therapists deal with the pressures of their work, for instance by using yoga (Valente and Marotta, 2005) or mindfulness meditation (Christopher et al., 2011). There also exists a large body of qualitative research into therapist experiences of personal therapy (see Geller et al., 2005).

Specific aspects of the structure of therapy. Qualitative research has explored the client's experience of particular activities and moments within therapy, such as receiving a letter from their therapist (Hamill et al., 2008), missed appointments

(Snape et al., 2003), moments of therapist self-disclosure (Hanson, 2005; Knox et al., 1997), giving the therapist a gift (Knox et al., 2009), the impact of the therapy room (Fenner, 2011), filling in feedback questionnaires (Unsworth et al., 2012), and the ending of therapy (Knox et al., 2011).

How clients define and evaluate the outcomes of therapy. An area of qualitative research that has significant implications for policy and the provision of services, consists of interview-based studies of the ways in which clients assess the outcomes of the therapy they have received. Exemplar studies within this area include work by Binder, Holgersen and Nielsen (2010), Knox et al. (1999), Kuhnlein (1999), Nilsson et al. (2007), Perren et al. (2009) and Valkonen et al. (2011). The findings from these studies have made it possible to see that it is not adequate to define outcome purely in terms of a change in scores on quantitative symptom measures (McLeod, 2011).

These are just some of the qualitative-interview based studies that have been published in the field of counselling and psychotherapy. There are many other excellent studies that might have been included. Bibliographies are available of grounded theory therapy studies (Rennie, 2000) and CQR studies (Chui et al., 2012). There are also similar studies, on therapy-relevant topics, that can be found within the health psychology and psychiatric survivor literatures. In addition to interviewing clients and therapists, it is also possible to carry out interview-based research with 'significant others' (Roberts, 1996) or members of the public (Weatherhead and Daiches, 2010).

The exemplar studies highlighted in this section offer a wide range of examples of how well-established qualitative methods, such as grounded theory, empirical phenomenology, IPA and CQR, can be used to generate articles that are readable, interesting and credible, and which make a meaningful contribution to the evidence base for counselling and psychotherapy. Conducting such a study is within the scope and resources of most practitioners and students.

One of the key features of the studies that have been listed is that all of them focus on a specific and concrete aspect of the lived experience and practice of therapy. While it is possible to use qualitative reviews to explore the meaning for clients and therapists of theoretically-defined phenomena such as 'empathy' or 'transference', it is typically quite difficult for people to talk about such entities because they lack a concrete experiential anchor from which to speak. There is a risk, as a result, that therapists being interviewed about 'conceptual' phenomena will draw on their theoretical understanding, rather than their lived experience, and clients being interviewed about such phenomena will try to figure out what it is that the interviewer wants to hear. Examples of studies that have overcome these issues include Cooper (2005), Knox (2008), and Schnellbacher and Leijssen (2009). On the whole, qualitative interview-based research into the experience of clients and therapists is a methodology that is best suited to investigating concrete moments in therapy or broader themes that can be described in ordinary language (e.g., 'What was helpful?'). Within such an approach, the role of therapy theory and concepts is to provide a basis for the interpretation of findings, within the discussion section of a paper or dissertation.

Variants on interview-based qualitative research into the experience of therapy

The step-by-step guidelines, and exemplar studies, that have been suggested in this chapter, have centred on the use of individual, face-to-face interviews in which the participant, drawn from some kind of representative group, responds to a set of questions. Within this broad approach, there are several important additional strategies that can be adopted.

Adding visual techniques. It can be valuable, in enabling informants to generate richly-described accounts of their experience, to make use of visual imagery and methods. Many interviewers include, in their list of questions, invitations to 'imagine' – for instance, if your therapist was an animal, what kind of creature would they be, and what would they look like? McKenna and Todd (1997) used a visual time-line to help clients map out the sequence of multiple therapy experiences over their lifetime. Rodgers (2006) invited clients to depict their 'life-space' in the form of a map or drawing, and then talk about the image they had created. These applications of visual methodologies reflect a wider movement within the field of qualitative research as a whole.

Using stimulated recall. Several studies have made use of a technique known as *Interpersonal Process Recall* (IPR) to make it possible for informants to talk in detail about specific moments or episodes in therapy. IPR involves making a recoding (usually audio) of a session, and then asking the client or therapist to listen to it, with a request that they pause the recording whenever they recall what they were thinking or feeling at the time. If carried out soon after a session, the assumption is that this kind of 'stimulated recall' technique will make it possible for the person to re-enter their original experience and describe it in detail. Guidelines for using IPR can be found in Elliott (1984) and Larsen et al. (2008). Therapy research studies that have used this technique include investigations of the client's experience of therapy (Rennie, 1990, 1992, 1994a,b,c), collaborative use of metaphor (Angus and Rennie, 1988, 1989; Rasmussen and Angus, 1996), and change processes (in counselling for alcohol problems: see Moerman and McLeod, 2006). IPR is a powerful method, which functions as a kind of experiential microscope. However, it can be hard to set up an IPR study, which requires a high degree of time investment from participants. There are also ethical sensitivities arising from the risk of intruding on the therapy process. These issues can be overcome, but mean that IPR has been used in relatively few studies to date.

Individual face-to-face interviews are not the only way to collect qualitative data. It is possible to collect similar data using telephone interviews, group interviews (focus groups), email, and open-ended questionnaires. The pros and cons of each of these interview strategies can be readily explored within the research methods literature.

In a private one-to-one interview, the informant may be strongly influenced by the presence of an authoritative expert other (the interviewer). The *focus group* technique (Bloor et al., 2000; Greenbaum, 1998; Krueger and Casey, 2008) is a means of conducting systematic small group interviews with sets of around seven to twelve people. In these groups, the interviewer acts as a facilitator to draw out the beliefs and attitudes of group members concerning the topic under examination. The group discussion is tape recorded and represents a rich source of qualitative data. In the focus group setting each member of the group is exposed to an open social situation, one in which the views of the researcher will be less significant as a potential source of influence. The group facilitator or director must, of course, skilfully conduct the session to prevent any members of the group dominating the discussion. A study by Karakurt et al. (2013) provides a typical example of the application of focus group methodology to the investigation of therapist experiences in working with a specific client group.

In some circumstances, the *open-ended questionnaire* can be a valuable research tool. Because questionnaires are easy to distribute, a wider coverage of informants can usually be achieved by using this technique compared to the use of interviews. Short, open-ended questionnaires are normally experienced by research participants as straightforward, unintrusive and unthreatening. From the point of view of the researcher, there is also the major advantage that qualitative questionnaire data do not need to be transcribed. Open-ended questionnaires have been used in several studies of the experience of therapy. Lietaer (1992), for example, asked clients in client-centred therapy to write at the end of each session about what they had found helpful and what they had found hindering to them in that session. Bloch et al. (1979) and Llewelyn et al. (1988) have also used written accounts of 'the most help-ful event' to explore the perceptions of clients in various forms of individual and group therapy. Bachelor (1988) asked both clients and non-clients to write about their experiences of 'being understood', and used this qualitative material to con-struct an analysis of 'received empathy'. Bachelor et al. (2007) invited clients to write about their experiences of working collaboratively with their therapists.

It is possible to include qualitative and quantitative data in the same study. However, mixed-methods studies are not recommended as a first-choice option for novice researchers. It requires a certain amount of methodological sophistication to take account of the different epistemological requirements of quantitative and qualitative sources (e.g., in general, quantitative research works best with large sam-ples, while qualitative research works best with small samples). There are also difficulties associated with writing up a mixed-method study (e.g., more space is needed to describe the method of data collection and analysis).

Finally, it is worth emphasising that the aim of most qualitative interview-based studies is to explore the experience of a single, fairly homogeneous group of informants. Comparative studies are quite rare within the field of qualitative research and are hard to do well. This is because it is difficult to be certain that the meaning of a theme or category within one group of participants is similar to its meaning in a comparison group. Many novice researchers are drawn to the idea of comparing client and therapist experiences of therapy, or of some specific aspect of therapy. This kind of research design tends not to have a happy ending. A classic finding, from such a study, is that clients say that they really appreciated the 'advice' offered by their therapists – but the therapists do not mention 'advice' at all. It is then not at all easily to find a credible way of reconciling these contrasting perspectives while at the same time honouring the standpoint of both parties. The other problem with this type of design is that it can leave the reader frustrated, because they have not been able to get close enough to the experiences of either group of informants. Anyone considering carrying out a comparative qualitative study is recommended to pay close attention to the study by Nilsson et al. (2007) comparing client experiences of the outcomes of either psychodynamic psychotherapy or CBT. This is an important and persuasive study, but only because of the very high level of technical expertise and discipline exerted by the members of an experienced team of researchers.

How to get published

Writing-up a qualitative research study for publication presents a number of challenges:

- Condensing many thousands of words of interview transcript into a results/findings section that is perhaps no more than 1,500 words in length, and at the same time providing enough examples of informant statements to ensure that the conclusions are grounded in data.
- Making sure that the 'voice' and standpoint of participants are honoured.
- Reporting on the reflexivity of the researcher, and how this has influenced various aspects of the research process – first-person ('I') writing is not usually found in scientific articles.
- Reporting on method (how the data were collected and analysed) in sufficient detail, without losing the reader's interest.
- Writing a paper that commences with a review of the literature, following a study that started with an exploratory question and in which it was only possible to identify the relevant literature after the data had been analysed.

As a response to these issues, several articles have been published that offer recommendations and guidance on how to write qualitative articles (Caulley, 2008; Choudhuri et al., 2004; Elliott et al., 1999; Ely et al., 1997; Golden-Biddle and Locke, 2006; Holliday, 2002; Knox et al., 2012; Ponterotto and Grieger, 2007; Sandalowski, 2012). A useful paper by Woo and Heo (2013) reports on an analysis of the characteristics of qualitative research articles published in a subset of counselling journals in recent years. This paper provides a picture of the 'state of the art' in qualitative research in therapy, and makes recommendations regarding the importance of reporting validity procedures and reflexivity.

It can also be helpful to make an effort to look at the writing style adopted by authors who have used the same method, and who have published in potential target journals. There are distinct differences between the reporting style of grounded theory, IPA and CQR studies, and in the way qualitative material is handled in various journals. Some of these differences are very obvious – for example the highly reflexive articles published in *Qualitative Inquiry*, compared to the minimally reflex-ive writing in most counselling and psychotherapy journals. Other differences are more subtle, such as conventions around how to report on the proportion of par-ticipants who contributed to a particular category, the number of participant quotes that are provided, or the use of figures and tables. For a novice researcher, it would be sensible to find a published article that could function as a template, and then use that structure to organise one's own material.

In recent years, the majority of counselling and psychotherapy journals, and journals in cognate disciplines, have published qualitative interview-based research. However, to the best of my knowledge, some influential journals, such as the *Journal of Consulting and Clinical Psychology* and *Psychological Medicine*, have never pub-lished qualitative papers. Several qualitative studies on therapy topics have been published in non-therapy journals such as *Qualitative Health Research*, *Qualitative Social Work*, and *Qualitative Reports*.

An alternative to publishing a qualitative study as a journal article, is to write a longer report, that can be published as a monograph (a short academic book of around 30–50,000 words) or by the sponsoring organisation. Examples of this kind of publication includes books by Etherington (2000) and O'Neill (1998). It is interest-ing to compare the experience of reading these reports with the experience of reading article-length studies. Longer reports do seem to have the potential to convey more of the richness of qualitative research. It is perhaps instructive that the historical origins of qualitative research are in social anthropology, which has always favoured the monograph-length reporting of fieldwork. Examples of organisationally-published qualitative studies include Morris (2005) and Netto et al. (2001). These are highly effective pieces of writing. The Morris (2005) study is also available through the website of the organisation that sponsored the research.

There are however some limitations associated with publishing research in the form of books, monographs and organisational reports. One of the strengths of journal publishing is that manuscripts are subjected to peer review which ensures quality. This is less likely to take place outside of the structure of journal publishing. Although it is always possible to ask experts to review a study, there is obviously a lot more work involved in reviewing a 50,000 monograph compared to a 6,000 word article. Another limitation is that journal articles are more accessible, and also more likely to be listed on on-line databases. These factors increase the likelihood that the work will be found and read by interested others. An emerging form of dis-semination of research studies is through on-line publishing, for example on Kindle.

Suggestions for further reading

This chapter has included many suggestions for exemplar qualitative studies. Anyone who is planning to undertake this type of investigation would be strongly advised to find one or more exemplar studies that are inspiring, and which offer a template for how to proceed.

The chapter has also recommended that the starting point for carrying out a qualitative interview-based study should always be one or another of a small set of tried and trusted approaches, such as grounded theory, IPA and CQR. Making this choice involves reading three key texts:

Charmaz, K. (2013) *Constructing Grounded Theory* (2nd edn). Thousand Oaks, CA: Sage.
Hill, C.E. (ed.) (2012) *Consensual Qualitative Research: A Practical Resource for Investigating Social Science Phenomena*. Washington, DC: American Psychological Association.
Smith, J.A., Flowers, P. and Larkin, M. (2009) *Interpretative Phenomenological Analysis: Theory, Method and Research*. London: Sage.

Companion website material

The companion website for this book (https://study.sagepub.com/mcleod) gives direct access to a range of different types of qualitative interview-based studies:

Christopher, J.C., Chrisman, J.A., Trotter-Mathison, M.J. et al. (2011) Perceptions of the long-term influence of mindfulness training on counselors and psychotherapists: a qualitative inquiry. *Journal of Humanistic Psychology*, 51: 318–49.
Gostas, M.W., Wiberg, B., Neander, K. at al. (2013) 'Hard work' in a new context: Clients' experiences of psychotherapy. *Qualitative Social Work*, 12: 340–57.
Morris, B. (2005) *Discovering bits and pieces of me: research exploring women's experiences of psychoanalytical psychotherapy*. London: Women's Therapy Centre.
Rennie, D.L. (1994) Clients' accounts of resistance in counselling, a qualitative analysis, *Canadian Journal of Counselling*, 28: 43–57.
Schnellbacher, J. and Leijssen, M. (2009) The significance of therapist genuineness from the client's perspective. *Journal of Humanistic Psychology*, 49: 207–28.
Toto-Moriarty, T. (2013) A retrospective view of psychodynamic treatment: Perspectives of recovered bulimia nervosa patients. *Qualitative Social Work*, 12: 833–48.

12

Evaluating Outcome: Practice-based Research

Introduction

The question of the outcome of therapy represents the single most important research topic within the counselling and psychotherapy research literature. Many organisations, institutions and governments have invested substantial resources on research into the effectiveness of therapy. Partly, this investment has been motivated by a desire to ensure that the kinds of therapy that are offered are both helpful and cost-effective. This line of research has also reflected the reality that the field of psychological and mental health care comprises a crowded and contested market-place. There are many competing ideas about why people become depressed or anxious, and how these difficulties can be alleviated. Outcome research can be used to develop an appreciation of which approaches to therapy might be most effective for particular types of problem

Historically, randomised controlled/clinical trials (RCTs) have been regarded as the most reliable source of evidence in respect of therapy outcome. In an RCT clients are randomly assigned to different treatment conditions. The aim is to discover whether clients in one of the intervention conditions demonstrate higher levels of improvement, compared to those who have received other types of therapy (or have been in a waiting list condition). If one of the intervention conditions is associated with significantly higher levels of change, there is a strong logical case to be made for the efficacy of that model of therapy, because the randomisation process has ensured that all other relevant factors have been held constant. While the RCT design remains hugely influential within the field of counselling and psychotherapy research, there is also a growing appreciation of the limitations of this type of study:

- The procedures that are necessary in order to ensure rigorous randomisation can mean that clients in RCTs tend to be rather different from clients seen in routine practice.
- The need to closely define and monitor the type of therapy that is delivered may leave little space for therapist flexibility, responsiveness and use of clinical judgement.
- RCTs are expensive to run, with the consequence that many plausible and probably effective therapy interventions have never been evaluated in this way.

As a result of these factors, a great deal of effort has been devoted to the development of reliable and valid methods that can be used to evaluate the effectiveness of therapy in everyday routine practice, rather than in the artificial conditions of an RCT.

Practice-based or *naturalistic* research into the outcomes of counselling and psychotherapy typically uses brief self-report symptom questionnaires to monitor client outcome over the course of therapy. The strength of such studies is that they provide evidence of the effectiveness of therapy as it is generally practised. The limitation of naturalistic studies is that they lack the level of control that is inherent in an RCT design, with the result that there may be a lack of certainty about how findings should be interpreted. However, in recent years a range of methodological innovations has been introduced to strengthen the methodological robustness of practice-based research.

There are two types of practice-based outcome research that have been developed. The first type makes use of massive databases consisting of data from thousands of clients receiving therapy within large-scale healthcare systems.

Examples of such studies include Kraus et al. (2011) and Stiles et al. (2007, 2008b). The organisational complexity and time-scales associated with this form of 'data-mining' research mean that it is beyond the scope of novice researchers. This chapter focuses instead on a second type of practice-based outcome research which analyses the outcomes of therapy delivered within a specific agency or local/regional network of practitioners. This second type of practice-based outcome research provides many opportunities for novice researchers to make a contribution to the literature on the effectiveness of therapy, while at the same time providing valuable feedback for the therapy clinics or agencies sponsoring the research.

What is a practice-based outcome study?

A practice-based outcome study involves the collection of data on the symptoms, problems, well-being or goals of clients before they commence therapy, at the end of therapy, and perhaps also at follow-up. The primary aim of this sort of research is to provide evidence of the effectiveness of therapy.

Why would I want to do this kind of research?

There are strong organisational reasons for undertaking this type of study. Most counselling and psychotherapy services and agencies need to be able to demonstrate, for example in annual reports, that they are achieving a satisfactory level or results. In some instances, continued funding may be contingent on results. In addition, evaluating the outcomes of routine practice can enable a service to do better work, for example by identifying groups of clients who may need longer therapy or a different approach. Finally, the skills and knowledge that are required to carry out a practice-based outcome study are relevant for therapists in respect of evaluating their own work with clients, and using feedback from clients to guide the therapy process.

What kind of skills and support do I need?

This type of study requires competence in basic statistical techniques, either on the part of the lead researcher or another member of the research team. Collecting data will usually require a high level of collaboration from the counsellor or psycho-therapists who are seeing the clients, and/or administration and reception staff. A sufficient degree of organisational ability is also necessary to design and implement the systems for storing data and checking that forms have been distributed to the relevant people and then completed on time and filed.

Exercise 12.1   Mapping a practice-based study – who wants what?

If you are considering introducing practice-based outcome monitoring into an established counselling or psychotherapy service, it is important you construct a stakeholder map. Take a large piece of paper. Around the outside edge place all of the key stakeholders – the management, the funders, clients, counsellors, etc. Beside each group, make a list of (a) what they want in terms of information and possible eventual improvements to the service, and (b) what they are willing to give in terms of time and resources. Use the centre of the page to identify areas of agreement and areas in which further discussion and negotiations will be required.

A step-by-step guide to doing a practice-based outcome study

It is important to allow time, and consult widely, on the aim and purpose of a practice-based outcome study. Some of the factors that will need to be considered are as follows:

- What research questions are being pursued?
- Which clients are being targeted?
- What kind of consent will clients be asked to provide?
- Which outcomes are being measured?
- Are all possible therapists, and cases, included in the study, or just a sample?
- How will the data be collected and stored?
- How will any missing data be handled?
- What is the time-period for the study?
- How much will it cost?
- How will the data be analysed?

As with any other type of research, it is vital to be guided by examples from studies that have already been completed and published. Rather than attempt to design a practice-based outcome study from the ground up, it is sensible to look at what has worked (or not worked) in previous studies, and assemble a research protocol that is comprised, as far as possible, of proven elements. These issues are explored in more detail below.

Identifying research aims and questions

The main aim of a practice-based outcome study is to evaluate the effectiveness of the therapy that is being offered. In many studies, this aim translates into a research design in which all clients, over a specific period of time, are invited to complete a general symptom measure such as the CORE-OM, ORS or OQ-45 (see Chapter 9 for further information on these and other measurement scales). However, there are many secondary research questions that may also be relevant. For example, it may be of interest to look at the outcomes of trainee counsellors, or counsellors who have received different forms of training. It may also be of interest to focus on outcomes in clients with different types of problem, such as eating disorders or depression, or who vary in problem severity, or who require a greater or lesser number of sessions. There are many theoretically interesting and practically relevant types of question that can be asked with a standard practice-based outcome design. To explore these questions it is necessary to be able to think ahead and anticipate the types of analysis that might be carried out on the data, and then ensure that the relevant information on these factors has been collected. For example, if the aim is to discover whether clients with eating disorders (or whatever) achieve outcomes that are better or worse than those for other clients, it will be necessary to (a) be able to identify which clients have eating disorders; (b) make sure that enough of this type of client are captured in the sample; and (c) use a measure that is credible as a way of assessing change in clients with dysfunctional eating.

Some of the main research questions that have been explored through the use of practice-based outcome studies included the following:

1. *How effective is therapy?* The intention to document the effectiveness of therapy underpins the whole practice-based evidence movement. In many practice-based outcome studies, the aim is merely to evaluate the overall effectiveness of the particular form of therapy being offered by a counselling centre or therapy provider (see for example Archer et al., 2000; Balfour and Lanman, 2012; Gibbard and Hanley, 2008; Lindgren, Werbart and Philips, 2010; McKenzie et al., 2011; Ogrodniczuk et al., 2012; Weersing and Weisz, 2002; Westbrook and Kirk, 2005). In other studies, the aim has been to compare the effectiveness of alternative therapy approaches (e.g., person-centred and CBT) offered within the same service (see for example Marriott and Kellett, 2009; Stiles et al., 2006, 2007; Werbart et al., 2013). A further variant around the question of effectiveness involves focusing on the outcomes associated with a particular group of therapists, such as novice counsellors (Armstrong, 2010), or to compare the relative levels of effectiveness across a set of therapists (Okiishi et al., 2003).

2. *Are there subgroups of clients who are more or less likely to find therapy beneficial?* If a practice-based database includes a sufficient number of cases, it may be possible to identify groups of clients who do better in therapy, or report lower levels of benefit. For instance, in practice-based research, Weersing and Weisz (2002) found that ethnic minority clients recorded lower levels of change than white clients, and studies by McLeod et al. (2000) and Saxon et al. (2008) found lower levels of change in clients who were unemployed. Cairns (2014) used practice-based research to explore the characteristics of clients who found it hard to engage with therapy. In practice-based studies where clients complete measures at each session, it has been possible to identify characteristics of those clients who exhibit sudden gains (Stiles et al., 2003; Stulz et al., 2007).

3. *What proportion of clients drop out of therapy?* Clients who do not attend (DNA) therapy, drop out of therapy, or do not have planned endings, have represented a significant focus for practice-based research. It seems probable that the majority of clients in this category are not being helped by the therapy they have been offered, or do not perceive it as being potentially helpful to them. The occurrence of missed sessions represents a major cost to services, which has the effect of increasing waiting times for those who are seeking therapy. Practice-based studies that made a major contribution in drawing attention to the high DNA levels associated with some services and client groups include Connell et al., 2006; Gilbert et al., 2005; Scheeres et al., 2008; and Schindler et al., 2013.

4. *What are the characteristics of clients who receive therapy?* The planning, co-ordination and funding for therapy services require information about the types of clients who use various services. Practice-based studies have shown that clients who are seen within voluntary sector counselling agencies in the UK are similar in symptom profile and severity to patients within National Health Service (NHS) out-patient services (Caccia and Watson, 1987; Moore, 2006). Werbart and Wang (2012) have used practice-based data to analyse the attributes of clients who are not accepted for therapy within a specific service.

5. *How many sessions do clients need?* Analysis of practice-based data can be used to explore questions around the number of sessions used by clients, and the number of sessions that are necessary in order for meaningful change to occur. All practice-based studies should provide information on the number of sessions used by clients, and several studies have examined the relationship between length of therapy and outcome. This information can be valuable for therapy clinics and agencies looking to make decisions about whether to introduce limits on the number of sessions. One of the interesting discoveries to emerge from this area of research has been evidence that there does not appear to be an 'optimal dose' of therapy that can be predicted in advance, on the basis of problem severity and chronicity. Instead, clients and therapists seem to be responsive to the accomplishment of change, and tend to bring therapy to a close when the client has arrived at a 'good enough' level of functioning (Stiles et al., 2008a).

6. *How can practice-based evidence be used by a therapy agency to inform the design of more effective services for clients?* Ultimately, the aim of practice-based research is to contribute to the development of better services. At a general level, the practice-based literature as a whole can be regarded as informing the design of services. However, it is also possible to apply a practice-based approach to research in ways that have a more direct and tangible impact at a local level. The most widely-studied example of this kind of thing can be found in the use of brief outcome and process measures in client monitoring and tracking. In these initiatives research data are not just collected centrally, but are also immediately fed back to the therapist (and in some instances also the client). There is now a great deal of evidence that this way of using research information helps to keep therapy 'on track' and enhances outcomes (Lambert, 2007, 2010). Another way in which practice-based findings can be used at a local level is to inform the redesign of services. For example, if routine outcome monitoring identifies unemployed clients as a group that does not do particularly well in therapy, it would be possible to offer some kind of augmented model of therapy to this set of clients, such as a support group alongside one-to-one sessions. It would then be possible, in the next time period, to look at whether this initiative had made a difference to the outcomes of therapy for this client group. It is probable that

many therapy clinics and agencies do make use of practice-based findings as a basis for 'action research' along these lines. However, to the best of my knowledge there are relatively few published examples of such studies or projects within the current literature. Examples of the possibilities associated with such an approach can be found in Holmqvist, Philips and Barkham (forthcoming) and in a special issue of the *European Journal of Psychotherapy and Counselling* (volume 8, issue 2, 2006). Further information on the potential value of action research strategies in counselling and psychotherapy research can be found in McLeod (2011).

These questions represent the primary areas in which practice-based methodology has been applied within the field of counselling and psychotherapy research. A valuable example of how these sources of information can inform the development of services can be found in a report, published on-line, from the Royal College of Psychiatrists (2011). Later in the chapter, we also consider some examples of how practice-based outcome research can be augmented through the concurrent use of other research approaches, such as qualitative interviews and case studies.

Choosing outcome measures

Within the wide range of methodologies that are used in counselling and psychotherapy research, the key distinctive feature of practice-based research is that it aims to capture information about what is happening in routine practice. It is therefore essential that the data collection procedure intrudes as little as possible into the naturally-occurring process of therapy. What this means, in practice, is that data are collected through a combination of forms filled in by staff (therapists and administrators) and brief self-report measures completed by clients. One of the goals of this type of research is to allow connections and inferences to be made between a particular set of data and broader trends within the field. As a result, it is best if data are collected in a standardised format that allows comparison with other studies and data-sets. Chapter 9 provides information about brief outcome measures that are suitable for use in practice-based research. In general, it is not sensible to try to design one's own outcome questionnaire, or to modify existing questionnaires – either of these strategies will mean that it is difficult or impossible to compare one's findings with the results of other studies. In addition, developing a new measuring instrument is a highly time-consuming task.

Before embarking on a practice-based outcome study, it is important to look carefully at the intended use of the data. It is also helpful to imagine what a subsequent article or report might look like, and the areas and questions that would be of interest to particular sets of stakeholders, such as clients, funding bodies, managers, therapists, trainers, supervisors, and the wider professional community. If possible, it would be useful to consult these people directly and ask them what they think. It would also be worthwhile to read published practice-based outcome studies from a critical perspective to get ideas about how other groups of researchers have resolved these issues.

Describing the therapy

From the point of view of supporters of RCT methodology, one of the main weaknesses of the practice-based outcome literature is that studies do not provide sufficient information about the therapy that is being delivered (Clark, Fairburn and Wessely, 2008). In RCTs and also in case studies, a lot of attention is devoted to defining the therapy that is offered and the characteristics of therapists (e.g., training and experience). Such information tends to be missing, or thinly reported, in practice-based studies. This is doubly unfortunate, because (a) the distinctive contribution of practice-based research is diminished if the actual practice is not described, and (b) this makes it hard for practitioner-readers to know whether the results of a study apply to their own practice setting.

It is possible to identify two broad categories of practice-based outcome research: the construction and analysis of data-sets based on thousands of cases, and smaller-scale projects that evaluate the work of a specific therapy agency or group of practitioners. This chapter is more concerned with the latter category. In such studies, it is helpful to report as much factual information as possible:

- How clients make contact, how they are assessed, how client preferences are accommodated.
- Location, duration and frequency of therapy; cost of therapy; therapy modality (individual, couple, group).
- Client demographic characteristics, presenting problems/diagnoses, chronicity of problems, client past/current use of therapy and other services.
- Therapist demographic characteristics, training, experience, supervision.
- Type(s) of therapy being delivered.
- Values/principles espoused by the organisation.

It may be useful to refer readers to publications that describe the work of the agency or clinic. In some instances it may be relevant to invite therapists to describe their practice using a brief questionnaire (see for example Hill et al., 2008). The CORE outcome evaluation system includes forms completed by therapists that cover many of these areas. These forms provide a useful starting point, but it may be that in particular circumstances additional information needs to be collected.

An associated issue, which also needs to be considered at the outset, is how the ending of therapy will be defined, and how information on that ending will be collected. Some of the possible approaches to this question are discussed by Connell, Grant and Mullin (2006).

When describing the therapy that is offered, it is valuable to think about the ways in which readers of an article will seek to assimilate the findings of the study into their interests and their existing 'map' of therapy. For example, readers will want to know about aspects such as 'Is this CBT?', 'Are these minority/disadvantaged clients?' or 'Were these people depressed?'

Collecting data/minimising attrition

Clients are entitled to receive an explanation of why they are being asked to complete questionnaires, and what will be done with the information they provide. It should always be made clear that a client has the right not to complete questionnaires, without prejudice to their entitlement to therapy. It is good practice to offer appropriate assistance to people who have difficulty in completing questionnaires, for example because of literacy problems or visual impairment.

In most therapy settings, the collection of routine outcome data is defined as an 'audit' rather than 'research', with the consequence that formal ethical approval is not required. However, it is always important to check this out. Any research, including analysis of an existing data-set, being carried out by a student, will always require ethical approval from the relevant university committee. Research designs that go beyond a routine audit (e.g., interviewing clients, or randomly assigning clients to alternative therapies) would always require formal ethical approval.

No matter whether formal ethical approval is obtained or not, it is always essential to collect and store data in a manner that respects client confidentiality, autonomy, wellbeing and human rights. One specific area that may need attention in this respect is the inclusion in many scales of 'risk' items (e.g., the intention to do harm to the self or others). It is reasonable for clients to expect, no matter what they are told about how questionnaires are processed, that if they indicate an intention to harm on a questionnaire then someone will listen. This issue does not arise often, because relatively few therapy clients are suicidal or otherwise at risk. But it certainly can happen that a client will indicate risk, on a measure, while not disclosing this issue to their therapist.

It is instructive to look closely at the method sections of practice-based outcome studies to learn about how the data were collected. The most common procedure is for questionnaires to be completed just before or at the end of the first meeting with a therapist (which could be an assessment session or a first therapy session), and then at the end of the final therapy session. Often the questionnaire will be collected by a receptionist or administrator. If it is collected by the therapist, the client is usually told that the therapist will not read it, and it is placed by the client in a sealed envelope. A variant on these arrangements can involve the client completing a questionnaire on a PC or laptop, rather than being given this in paper form.

While this kind of procedure is relatively straightforward to administer, it is problematic on research grounds. The main limitation is that many clients (as many as 40%) may have unplanned endings, and as a result will not complete end-of-therapy measures. This means that it becomes difficult to interpret the meaning of any change statistics that are generated by the study. The probability is that the majority of clients with unplanned endings were dissatisfied with therapy. But you never really know. A second limitation is that nothing is known about the lasting effects of therapy. A third limitation is that there is evidence, from many studies, that clients start to improve as soon as they have made an appointment to see a therapist, probably because they feel more hopeful and are proud of themselves for taking action. As a consequence, measuring symptoms at the first session will underestimate the overall effectiveness of therapy – if the data were collected at the first point of contact, a higher degree of benefit would almost certainly be recorded.

In response to these difficulties, it makes sense to consider some strategies for augmenting the standard data collection model:

- Administering a brief telephone measure during the first contact with the agency, or mailing out a questionnaire (and return envelope) with an information pack immediately following first contact.
- Asking clients to complete measures just before the start of every session. If they complete measures at the end of sessions, their answers will likely be coloured by a short-term relief effect and having spent an hour with a nice person; if they take the questionnaires home they will often forget to fill them in. This procedure may also make a positive contribution to outcome – many clients report that filling in a scale just before the start of the session helps them to collect their thoughts, identify priorities and self-monitor change.
- Asking clients at the start of therapy if they would be willing to complete a mailed or on-line follow-up questionnaire at some point following the end of therapy. It is likely than many of them will not complete this measure, but at least some follow-up data are better than none. Also, by that stage, a lot of information is available about clients, so it is possible to make detailed comparisons to determine whether those who did complete follow-up scales were representative of the sample as a whole.

Of these strategies, the single most valuable and important one is weekly completion of scales. If a client drops out of therapy, the last questionnaire they completed can be used as a measure of change.

Attention also needs to be paid to the processing of data. If clients are completing a questionnaire every week, it is costly, time-consuming and unnecessary to enter all of that information onto a database, if in the end all that is being analysed is the difference between start-of-therapy and end-of-therapy scores. It may be sensible to store forms until the end, and just enter the information from the last measure (this issue does not arise if the client is completing scales on a PC, tablet or laptop). However, it would be useful to record each time a measure is completed, as a means of checking on the efficiency with which therapists or administrators are collecting data. Therapists and administrators are busy people with many other tasks to fulfil, and thus may need support and encouragement to persevere with data collection. Connell et al. (2006) found major differences across therapy agencies in relation to the proportion of clients who completed practice-based measures.

A further issue that calls for consideration on the part of novice researchers, or counselling and psychotherapy agencies seeking to evaluate the effectiveness of their practice, is the size of the sample of cases being collected. Many agencies have attempted to collect all the data on all clients. This can be a stretch, and lead to missing and incomplete data, for the reasons outlined above. It may make sense to focus a particular effort on all clients who start therapy during a specific time period, or all clients seen by therapists who are experienced and competent, and explicitly espouse the values and approach of the agency. In some practice-based studies, data are collected on clients seen by placement students or counsellors who will quickly move on to other pastures. The work of these counsellors may not fairly reflect the approach taken by the agency as a whole. In making decisions to reduce the number of cases being analysed, it is unwise to adopt a strategy of only collecting data on every second or third client. Consumers of research may be suspicious that such an approach could subtly or unconsciously produce a situation of cherry-picking the best clients. It may be valuable to continue an on-going collection of baseline data (e.g., pre-therapy and post-therapy measures) at the same time as devoting special attention to a subgroup of clients (e.g., clients seen by more experienced practitioners). In most agencies, it is relatively straightforward to collect intake/pre-therapy data on >95% of clients. Possessing such data makes it possible to demonstrate that the smaller group of intensively-studied clients are representative of the client population as a whole. A focus on a specific group of clients or therapists also makes it easier to collect high-quality information on client and therapist characteristics.

Allied to the choice of sample is the question of the timing of a practice-based study. An effectiveness study on a new therapy service may well produce different results compared to an analysis of that service two or three years later. There is often an initial burst of enthusiasm for a new service that may then diminish over time. Conversely, there may be early teething problems that get ironed out. The effectiveness of a team of therapists may be quite different at a time of funding cuts and management conflict, compared to a period of funding stability and inspiring and supportive leadership. These are all contextual factors that need to be taken into account when designing a study and reporting/interpreting findings.

In deciding on whether, and how, to focus on a restricted sample of cases, it may be worth reflecting on two general research truths. First, while 'big is better' in terms of sample sizes for quantitative research (because of the greater statistical power to detect difference), analysis of debates around the value of practice-based research shows that some leading figures in the therapy worlds have criticised this approach on the grounds that the information that is collected is too broad-brush, for instance in not providing a clear enough picture of the type of therapy that is delivered. The second truth is that therapists and clients in RCT studies are very carefully selected. In practice-based research, by contrast, an inclusive approach has generally been adopted, in which data are collected on all clients seen by all therapists. It would seem sensible to find ways to combine the rigour of RCT methodology with the real-life authenticity of practice-based inquiry.

Analysing data

In any practice-based study, it is important to provide as much factual information as possible on clients, therapists, attendance rates and social/organisational context. This information is invaluable in making it possible for readers to assess the relevance and generalisability of the study to their own practice setting, and to compare the findings of the study with other comparable projects. It is always useful to take some time to think about potentially relevant information that might be available in agency files rather than having been collected specifically for the purposes of a study. For example, Self et al. (2005) used client postcodes to generate estimates of social deprivation in their analysis of rates of unplanned endings in routine therapy in an NHS clinic. It is usually helpful to use tables to present this information in an accessible manner.

It is also valuable to provide readers with information about the number of clients who approached the agency, the number/percentage of those who underwent assessment, the number/percentage who started therapy, through to the number/percentage who completed end-of-therapy measures, and to provide information, if available, on why the numbers reduced at each stage. For example, some people who underwent assessment may have decided not to proceed with therapy, while in other cases the assessor may have deemed them unsuitable for therapy. At key points in this flow-diagram or chart where there is a major drop-off in numbers (for example 100 clients start therapy and complete CORE, while only 40 complete CORE at the end of therapy), it is usual to carry out an analysis of the representativeness of those who were retained, in relation to age, gender, earlier score, etc.

There are two basic strategies that are generally employed in practice-based studies for reporting outcome. The *Effect Size* (ES) statistic is used to provide an estimate of the overall magnitude of change. In addition, percentages of clients who have reported clinical and/or reliable change (or deterioration) are reported. On the whole, it is not particularly informative to look at whether there is a statistically significant difference between pre-therapy and post-therapy scores. If the sample is large enough, it is possible to detect statistically significant change in situations in which relatively little change has occurred. Low-magnitude change can be explained by a wide range of factors, such as differential attrition from the study of less satisfied clients, or the effects of repeated completion of a measure.

It is essential to think about the meaning of the information that is being analysed rather than just regard a stats package as an automatic knowledge-generating machine. For example, high or low effectiveness ES rates may be due to a small number of outlier cases. It can help readers to understand what has been found if the existence of these outliers is explained. In practical terms, a client shift towards the healthy end of a symptom scale may be less important than client attrition rates, or figures on the number of clients who get worse.

Comparisons between subgroups of clients (for example those who saw a CBT therapist versus those who saw a person-centred therapist) can be accomplished by using the appropriate version of analysis of variance. If a sufficiently large data-set has been assembled, more complex forms of statistical analysis, such as linear modelling, will come into play. Further discussion of issues and options around analysing practice-based data can be found in Barkham et al. (2012) and Leach and Lutz (2010). One issue that may need to be considered concerns the format in which data have been entered. Increasingly, the groups and organisations that develop measures, such as CORE, also provide databases that therapy clinics can use to enter and store data. This is convenient, but it may restrict the kind of analysis that can subsequently be carried out. On the other hand, creating a bespoke database, using SPSS or a similar package, gives a researcher or organisation the scope to analyse data in any way they see fit – but is time-consuming to design and maintain, and may involve addressing copyright issues.

Using benchmarking and comparison groups

Practice-based outcome studies do not usually involve the use of comparison groups, such as clients on waiting lists, or those who have been randomly assigned to different treatment conditions. As a result, one of the limitations of this form of research is that it is open to the criticism that any changes in client problems that have been observed might have occurred in the absence of therapy. This issue can be addressed by comparing the outcomes recorded in a naturalistic pre-post comparison study with some kind of relevant *benchmark*. A benchmark consists of information about improvement rates that have been demonstrated in samples of the general population, or in clients who have received a form of therapy that is generally accepted (on the basis of RCT evidence) to be effective.

There have been many studies of the 'natural history' of psychological problems in the general population. In one well-known study, Jokela et al. (2011) tracked the mental health of 6,900 employees of the UK Civil Service over a 21-year period. These researchers found that self-reported psychological distress became more persistent over time, and was cumulative – prior distress increased the likelihood that the person would have a negative response to sources of stress later in their life. Fairburn et al. (2000) tracked the wellbeing of young women who had exhibited bulimia nervosa or binge eating disorder, and found that the majority of those who had been binge eaters tended to recover fully within a few years, while those with bulimia nervosa tended to oscillate between periods of healthy functioning and relapse. Wittchen and Fehm (2003) charted the natural course of untreated social fears and phobia, and found a tendency for these problems gradually to increase in intensity over the years, partly because of their negative impact on career progression. On the basis of these (and other) studies, those undertaking practice-based outcome studies may be able to argue that the clients in their study would have been unlikely to have improved in the absence of therapy. Some practice-based studies (Collins et al., 2012; Cooper and Sadri, 1991; Van Dierendonck et al., 1998) have sought to develop their own local estimates of the stability of problems by collecting information from individuals within their community who were not actively seeking help for psychological difficulties. This approach is potentially valuable, but runs the risk that the non-client sample may lack credibility if the sample size is too small or if there might be some potential bias in how participants have been recruited.

Although it is useful to refer to research into the natural course of a disorder, this strategy is not without its problems. For example, it is clear that at least some client groups have tendency to improve over time, such as the binge eaters in the Fairburn

et al. (2000) study. Also, it could reasonably be argued that those who seek counselling and psychotherapy represent a special subgroup of the population – the ones
who continue to get worse over the course of their lives are those who passively
accept their condition and do not seek help. Finally, being able to demonstrate that
people who might have become a bit worse have in fact got a bit better does not
take us very far – what most readers of research studies want to know is how the
levels of gain that have been recorded compare with gains associated with other
forms of therapy. For these reasons, it is useful to compare naturalistic pre-post data
with the findings of tightly controlled RCT studies.

The practice of benchmarking practice-based data against RCT findings is discussed in detail by Minami et al. (2007) and Weersing (2005). Making a credible
benchmark comparison involves taking account of a number of factors, such as
the demographic characteristics of clients, client diagnoses or presenting problems, the length of therapy, and the measures used. It is unlikely that an exact
match can be attained in which a community sample of clients seen in routine
practice could be precisely mapped on to a sample of clients from an RCT.
Nevertheless, it will usually be possible to make some kind of comparison that will
add to the generalisability of a practice-based study. An example of how this is
done can be found in Weersing and Weisz (2002), who compared the outcome
statistics obtained in relation to therapy with depressed young people who were
seen in their community therapy centre, with findings from RCT studies of CBT
for depression in similar samples. At the heart of this paper is a graph which
shows the trajectory of improvement in the community sample against the average
improvement in the RCT samples. It is very clear that the clients in the RCTs had
done considerably better. Weersing and Weisz (2002) were then able to discuss the
reasons why this difference had occurred, and identify ways in which their own
service might be improved. (By the way, the results obtained by Weersing and
Weisz (2002) should not be taken as a general reflection on the effectiveness of
routine treatment as against the kind of manualised evidence-based interventions
delivered in RCTs. For example, a benchmarking study of the effectiveness of
therapy for adult depression in routine practice, by Minami et al. (2008) found
that everyday 'ordinary' therapy was just as effective as treatment provided under
the special conditions of an RCT.)

When making comparisons between RCT findings and the results of practice-
based research, it is essential to take account of the ways in which outcome rates are
shaped and influenced by data collection procedures. Barkham et al. (2008) conducted a comparative review of the outcomes of RCT studies of therapy for
depression against findings from practice-based studies. This exercise showed that
improvement rates in RCTs were on average about 12% higher than in practice-
based studies. There would appear to be two main reasons for this difference. First,
the practice-based clients were more likely to have multiple problems (co-morbidity),
whereas the RCT clients were more likely to have a diagnosis of solely depression.
Second, perhaps as many as 10% of practice-based clients began therapy with scores
in or around the 'normal' range, and had no scope for improvement (at least,
improvement that could be measured by a symptom questionnaire). At this time, it is

not entirely clear how to interpret the fact that some people who turn up to therapy do not appear to have problems or be in distress. Such clients may be looking to get help to avoid problems emerging, or to consolidate what they have gained in previous therapy. On the other hand, it may be that they are experiencing significant current difficulties, but for some reason (denial, defensiveness, a lack of awareness) are not willing or able to disclose these difficulties through their answers to a questionnaire. It may then be that, for these clients, higher scores on a problem/symptom questionnaire may be an indication of positive change. This possibility raises difficult issues in relation to the use of self-report symptom measures in therapy research (McLeod, 2001), and underscores the importance of adopting a pluralistic stance in which, across the literature as a whole, the limitations of each methodology are balanced against the strengths of other research approaches.

A different type of methodological issue can arise when estimates of Effect Size (ES) are used to compare the outcomes of a practice-based naturalistic study against an RCT benchmark. The calculation of Effect Size is based on dividing the change between pre-therapy and post-therapy scores by the standard deviation (i.e., variability) of the sample. In a well-controlled RCT, the aim is to restrict the variability of the sample in relation to the outcome measure (e.g., scores on a depression scale) by using inclusion and exclusion criteria that mean only clients who score within a particular range are included in the study. By contrast, in routine practice a much wider range of clients is included. In some therapy agencies the only people who are excluded might be those who are extremely disturbed (e.g., psychotic). The implication of these differences in intake procedures means that an average change score in an RCT can yield a large ES (because it is divided by a smaller number), whereas the same average change score in a practice-based study will produce a lower ES. This issue is discussed in more detail by Lueger and Barkham (2010).

An alternative form of benchmarking consists of comparisons with other practice-based research. For example, outcome rates are available for very large samples of clients who have completed the CORE-OM (see for example Mullin et al., 2006). An example of how this type of benchmark data can be used is found in Armstrong (2010), who was able to identify differences between the outcomes obtained by the novice counsellors in his own study and the higher Effect Sizes reported in practice-based studies of the work of fully-trained and experienced counsellors. Mellor-Clark et al. (2013) provide a comprehensive review of benchmarking criteria associated with the use of the CORE outcome evaluation system in Employee Assistance Programmes (EAPs) and workplace counselling services.

One of the key principles of practice-based research is that data collection should involve the least possible disruption to the way therapy is routinely conducted. This means that a random assignment of clients to different treatment conditions is not possible. However, in some circumstances it may be possible to use clients as their own 'controls'. If they have been invited to complete a symptom measure at the time of their first contact with a service, and then perhaps have needed to wait to begin therapy, then the waiting period can be regarded as a 'baseline' that provides information on the stability of their problems prior to commencing therapy. Some practice-based studies have used a comparison between symptom measures administered at the start of this wait period, and then at the first therapy session, to provide a quasi-control group (Balfour and Lanman, 2012; Gibbard and Hanley, 2008).

In conclusion, careful use of benchmarking and comparison groups makes it possible to address, at least in part, the criticism that practice-based naturalistic studies lack meaningfulness because they do not provide any indication of what might have happened to clients if they had not received therapy. At the same time, it is clear that benchmarking is not a straightforward process, and is a methodological strategy that needs to be applied with care and thoughtfulness. A useful discussion of the issues associated with the use of therapy benchmarks can be found in Delgadillo et al. (2014).

Exercise 12.2   Power and control in practice-based outcome research

Knowledge is power. Within the practice-based outcome studies that you have read about, or the study that you are planning or carrying out, whose interests are best served by the data that are being collected, the way that these data are analysed, and the way that analysis is disseminated? In what ways might the power dynamics of practice-based research influence or compromise the results of such studies? What strategies might be deployed to change these power dynamics?

What can go wrong?

Practice-based outcome research almost certainly represents the domain of therapy research that is associated with the largest repository of un-analysed (or under-analysed) and un-published data. There are many counselling and psychotherapy services, around the world, that collect outcome data from clients, and then either publish a limited analysis of those data in annual reports or do nothing with the information that they accumulate. To some extent, this dissemination gap is due to the lack of resources within these organisations, in terms of the skills and knowledge needed to produce research articles. In some settings, there is also a reluctance to open up the work of an organisation to public scrutiny. However, it is also the case, once routine outcome statistics have been collected, that many therapy organisations quickly realise that the information that is available to them is virtually impossible to interpret because of missing data. It is very frustrating to put a lot of effort in collecting practice-based data, only to discover that end-of-therapy information has only been obtained for 50% of clients. It is not possible to have confidence in effectiveness estimates where information about a significant proportion of clients is lacking. For this reason, when designing a practice-based study, it is essential to implement as many as possible of the attrition-prevention strategies described in an earlier section of this chapter.

An area of weakness in some practice-based outcome studies has been the absence of contextual detail – information about who clients are, who therapists are, and what kind of organisation or institution it is that brings them together. The absence of such information undermines the basic philosophical rationale of this type of inquiry which is to analyse actual practices. To a large extent, this lack of attention given to contextual detail reflects the fact that the most influential studies in this field (e.g., Kraus et al., 2011; Stiles et al., 2006, 2008b) have been based on massive data-sets of thousands of clients from dozens of therapy services. In such projects it is hard to retain local detail, and so it is inevitable that there is tendency to concentrate on the common ground of client outcome scores.

Other options: variants on a basic practice-based outcome design

As with any type of research study, there are several ways in which practice-based outcome investigations can be extended and adapted. Some of the main variants are described in this section. For anyone embarking on a practice-based outcome study, I would urge extreme caution in respect of these options. This is an area of inquiry where it is wise not to try to do too much too soon. This is also an area in which the researcher has little control over the data collection process, and will need to rely on sustained and consistent efforts from others over a period of time. As a result, it is a real accomplishment, in practice-based research, to attain a sufficient sample of complete cases. Introducing additional data sources runs the risk of dilution of effort, leading to poor quality data and unpublishable or unconvincing findings. In most circumstances, it makes sense to start by establishing a basic outcome evaluation data collection and analysis system, and to add in other data collection elements later on.

Action research/quality enhancement. The most obvious way of extending a practice-based outcome study is to look at the results, consider how the service might be improved, introduce some strategies to enhance service quality, and use the next set of outcome data to evaluate whether these new ideas have had a positive effect. There are however few clear-cut examples of this type of project available. Buckroyd (2003) described a project in which client waiting time was identified as an issue, and the impact of new client contract procedures was assessed using analysis of practice-based data. Richardson and Reid (2006) used practice-based data in an action research cycle to develop a form of CBT that was tailored to the needs of older clients in a particular therapy service. One of the issues that is apparent in reading both these papers is the difficulty of doing justice, within the constraints of a journal article, to the kind of cycle of innovations and evaluation. Smith et al. (2010) have constructed guidelines for reporting action research projects. It would be good to see more of this kind of work being published. Action research/quality enhancement studies are relevant and motivating for practitioners, and have the potential to make a real difference to local services.

Client satisfaction studies. An alternative to collecting symptom or wellbeing measures from clients at the start and finish of therapy is to administer a one-off client satisfaction questionnaire at the end of therapy. This obviously saves a lot of time and bother. However, there are a number of important methodological limitations that have been found to be associated with this approach. Specifically, end-of-therapy satisfaction scales tend to produce implausibly high estimates of the value of therapy (e.g., 95% of clients satisfied with therapy) because of two factors: (i) less satisfied clients tend not to complete questionnaires, and (ii) a 'halo' effect resulting from client gratitude to the therapist for being a caring and empathic person. In general, client ratings of their overall satisfaction with therapy seem to be accessing something different from actual change. However, it is also important to acknowledge that being satisfied with therapy, while remaining troubled, may be an accurate representation of outcome for some clients. Nonetheless, the fact that clients tend to give very high ratings of overall satisfaction means that such scales do not differentiate very clearly between good and poor outcome cases. On the other hand, there is a lot of evidence that clients are much more discriminating when asked to rate their satisfaction with specific elements of therapy, such as waiting time, length of therapy, or the physical environment (Iwi et al., 1998; Macdonald et al., 1997; Philips, 2004; Rogers et al., 1995; Sloboda et al., 1993). This type of satisfaction question can be valuable as a means of supplementary data collected in pre- to post-therapy measures. It is the type of information that is crucial for as anyone undertaking an action research/quality enhancement project (see the earlier section). At the present time there are no particular satisfaction scales that have been validated or widely adopted. Instead, researchers using this technique have tended to borrow and adapt from existing scales to construct a scale that matches their own purposes.

Randomised Controlled Trials (RCTs). It is possible to build a randomised controlled trial around the routine collection of practice-based outcome data. Usually, an RCT that involved random assignment to different types of therapy intervention (e.g., psychodynamic *vs* cognitive-behavioural) would violate the principle that practice-based research should represent an effort to collect information about what happens in routine practice. However, it is possible that, within a large counselling service, there will be some therapists who offer (say) CBT and others who are psychodynamic. In such a situation it would also be possible, on assessment, to randomise those clients who did not state a preference for a particular approach. In a similar fashion, it might be possible to randomly allocate clients to a therapist of the same gender, or of the opposite gender. In services where there is a waiting list, clients could be randomly allocated either to receive therapy immediately or to wait for the (usual) period of three to six months. This creates a randomised trial in which the effects of therapy can be compared with the effect of a minimal intervention (being on a waiting list with regular calls or emails to check on whether the client had become an urgent case). However, this is a research design that tends to produce a certain amount of ethical unease in therapists. More widely used are practice-based RCT designs that involve the augmentation or enhancement of routine therapy. The most influential example of this approach can be found in a series of studies of client tracking/monitoring/feedback carried out by Michael Lambert and his colleagues (Lambert, 2007, 2010). In these studies, outcome data were collected along the lines of the practice-based studies described earlier in the chapter. In half of the cases information from measures was fed back to the therapist. In the other half of cases treatment continued as normal with no client feedback. A fascinating study along similar lines was conducted by Fluckiger and Holtforth (2008). These researchers were interested in the notion that outcomes might be improved if therapists paid more attention to the client's strengths. In their study, in half of the cases they saw, therapists spent a few minutes before the start of the session focusing on their client's strengths and how these might be relevant to the resolution of their problems. In the other cases therapists spent the same amount of time just reflecting on their clients with a specific emphasis on strengths. The results of this study were that the 'strengths' cases did better than the other cases. This kind of 'therapy enhancement' RCT has a lot of potential in organisations that have already established a robust system of practice-based data collection. It is also worth noting the kinds of objections that exist in relation to mainstream RCTs that compare therapy models, do not apply: an enhancement RCT remains close to everyday practice. There is a lot of information and training available within universities around how to conduct RCTs. A valuable starting point is a book by Nezu and Nezu (2007).

Practice surveys. Collecting data within a counselling or psychotherapy agency, for example by asking clients to complete measures at every session, represents just one way of gathering data on routine practice. An alternative approach, which has been seldom used, is to conduct a survey of therapists, and ask them to report on the clients seen on a specific day, or the most recent client, or on some other topic of interest. A study by Morrison, Bradley and Westen (2003, described in more detail on page 89, took this approach. In their study, Morrison et al. (2003) asked therapists in private practice to provide information on their most recent successful completed case of a patient with depression or anxiety. While the weakness of this model of data collection is that the researcher can never know about whether the cases reported by practitioners are being accurately described, it nevertheless provides plausible information in relation to research questions that cannot otherwise be pursued (or at least, not without enormous cost), and where the topic being explored is unlikely to be associated with informant defensiveness.

Analyses of personal cases. A further variant on practice-based outcome research is to analyse the outcomes associated with the work of a specific therapist. An early example of this type of study can be found in a paper by the pioneer of psychoanalysis in Norway, Harald Schjelderup, who published an analysis of the effectiveness of his treatment of clients with psychoneuroses (Schjelderup, 1955). This is in fact a remarkable piece of writing, one that is interesting, illuminating and honest. A similar project was published by the American psychologist Paul Clement, who analysed the characteristics and outcomes of 683 clients seen over a 26-year period of private practice (Clement, 1994). A brief update of results from the next fourteen years of practice is provided in Clement (2007).

Systematic case studies. Currently, there is renewed attention being given to the contribution that case study methods can make to the counselling and psychotherapy research literature (McLeod, 2010a, 2013c). The routine collection of practice-based data provides a basis for the strategic selection of cases for further scrutiny. If background information about the client and therapist, and weekly monitoring data, are available, then it is possible to conduct a systematic case study on the basis of an in-depth follow-up interview with the client. Cases can be selected on the grounds of theoretical and practical interest, for example comparison of good-outcome and poor-outcome cases, or closer examination of the experience of members of client groups who are under-represented.

Qualitative interviews. It is possible to use qualitative interviews to supplement findings from quantitative practice-based measures. Client accounts of what has been helpful or unhelpful about a service, or the ways in which they have been able to use counselling to move on in their lives, have the possibility to humanise practice-based data as well as making it possible to explain trends in the quantitative data. An example of how this can be done can be found in a study of a counselling service for individuals with visual impairment, published by Hodge et al. (2012). Some practice-based researchers have sought to incorporate qualitative data in the form of client written responses to open-ended items included in client satisfaction questionnaires distributed at the end of therapy. This strategy has its value, as a means of unearthing new ideas – it functions along the lines of the old-fashioned workplace 'suggestion box'. However, it is hard to evaluate the significance of a suggestion made by (say) one in one hundred clients. One of the functions of this type of brief qualitative data, and indeed also to some extent more detailed qualitative interviews, is to generate ideas that can then be explored in an action research cycle, or through further analysis of the existing quantitative practice-based data-set.

It may be useful to regard these variants on the basic practice-based evidence model as possibilities that can be activated as and when resources become available. For example, if a functioning set of routine data collection procedures is in place, it becomes possible to use short-term project workers, such as a student undertaking a Master's dissertation, to take responsibility for following through an action research cycle, or undertaking a batch of qualitative interviews. From the perspective of the student, such a task represents an opportunity to carry out research that has real-world impact, and to gain experience in collaborative working.

How to get published

Practice-based outcome studies have been published in many leading journals. As a result, there do not appear to be any barriers to publishing studies of this type as long as these are well-designed. It seems clear that the level of methodological sophistication of practice-based outcome studies has continued to rise, year-on-year, in response to the development of strategies such as benchmarking and techniques for estimating clinically significant and reliable change. It is therefore essential, when planning and writing a practice-based study, to look at recent papers. At the present time, unlike the situation in respect of reporting RCT findings (e.g., the widely used CONSORT guidelines) or the results of qualitative studies (Elliott, Fischer and Rennie, 1999), there do not exist any guidelines on how practice-based outcome study reports should be structured and what they should include. This means that there remains a considerable degree of variability in the quality of practice-based outcome articles, with some potentially interesting and valuable papers proving rather frustrating to read. It would be useful for both readers and authors if a consensus could be achieved around the reporting of practice-based outcome study investigations. My own personal preference is to go easy on figures and scatterplots. These methods for summarising complex data work well in conference and seminar presentations, where the presenter can talk the audience through what they mean and answer questions. By contrast, although one or two simple graphical representations of a change curve can work well in an article, more complex figures take up a lot of space in journal articles while leading to confusion in some readers. When deciding on a journal outlet for a practice-based outcome paper, it is important to keep in mind that the major international research journals, such as *Journal of Consulting* and *Clinical Psychology*, are only likely to publish large-sample studies that explore issues of general interest (e.g., sudden gains in therapy, the relative effectiveness of different therapists). Practice-based outcome articles that focus on evaluating and discussing the work of a particular therapy agency or clinic, are better sent to a national rather than international journal to make these more accessible to colleagues within a specific and local professional community.

Suggestions for further reading

When contemplating a practice-based study, it is essential to develop a close familiarity with published examples of this research genre in order to identify those elements of a research design that will be applicable to one's own situation. The chapter includes many references to interesting practice-based outcome studies. Other such studies can be located in reviews by Barkham et al. (2008), Cahill, Barkham and Stiles (2010), and McLeod (2010b).

More detailed understanding of the rationale for practice-based research, the development of this approach, and associated critical methodological issues, explained by leading figures within this movement, is available from:

Barkham, M., Hardy, G.E. and Mellor-Clark, J. (eds) (2010) *Developing and Delivering Practice-based Evidence: A Guide for the Psychological Therapies*. Chichester: Wiley-Blackwell.

Green, D. and Latchford, G. (2012) *Maximising the Benefits of Psychotherapy: A Practice-based Evidence Approach*. Oxford: Wiley-Blackwell.

Holmqvist, R., Philips, B. and Barkham, M. (forthcoming) Developing practice- based evidence: Benefits, challenges, and tensions. *Psychotherapy Research*.

Companion website material

The companion website (https://study.sagepub.com/mcleod) includes examples of practice-based research in a range of settings:

Hodge, S., Barr, W., Bowen, L. et al. (2012) Exploring the role of an emotional support and counselling service for people with visual impairments. *British Journal of Visual Impairment*, 31: 5–19.

Manthei, R. and Nourse, R. (2012) Evaluation of a counselling service for the elderly. *New Zealand Journal of Counselling*, 32: 29–53.

McNamara, J.R., Tamanini, K. and Pelletier-Walker, S. (2008) The impact of short-term counseling at a domestic violence shelter. *Research on Social Work Practice*, 18: 132–36.

13

Carrying out a Systematic Case Study

Introduction

The practice of counselling and psychotherapy involves working with 'cases'. A 'case' can be understood as comprising the entirety of an episode of therapy, from first contact with a service through to follow-up. From the earliest writings of Freud, Jung and their colleagues, case study knowledge has played a central role in the development of therapy theory, practice and training. The case study method provides an opportunity to explore the complex interactions between different aspects of the process of therapy, investigate the ways in which these processes unfold over time, and examine the links between specific processes and events in therapy and the eventual outcome of treatment. Case study research also makes it possible to consider the influence of contextual factors, such as the setting within which therapy takes place, and the cultural and social worlds of client and therapist. Case study knowledge makes sense to practitioners, and as a result this kind of research can make an important contribution to bridging the gap between research and practice.

In the context of the book, this chapter provides an introduction to mixed-methods research in which qualitative and quantitative data are combined in the same study. Earlier chapters have focused on the application of a single method within a study. In general, a mixed-methods study is not a sensible choice for a novice researcher. This is because qualitative and quantitative methodologies are associated with different validity criteria, may have different design requirements (for instance, in respect of sample size), and can be hard to write up. These methodological issues are resolvable; further information about viable strategies for mixed methods research can be found in Bergman (2008) and Hanson et al. (2005). The type of systematic case study inquiry that is described in the chapter represents a particular model of mixed-methods research that has been widely used within the counselling and psychotherapy research community in recent years.

My colleagues and I have previously written about the topics discussed in this chapter in a variety of places (McLeod, 2011; McLeod and Cooper, 2011; McLeod, Thurston and McLeod, 2014; Thurston, McLeod and McLeod, 2014). These sources offer alternative and expanded accounts of the issues explored below. Although every effort has been made to approach the topic in a fresh way, it is inevitable that some overlap will be apparent.

What is a systematic case study?

Traditionally, within the counselling and psychotherapy literature, case studies were written by the therapist in the case, based solely on his or her personal notes and reflections. While this type of 'clinical' case study has certainly produced a wealth of fascinating and informative case examples, it seems clear that this type of report struggles to achieve the standards of methodological rigour that have been established in other areas of therapy research. For example, it is highly likely that therapists are selective about what they write in their notes or recall about a case, and that they would have a tendency to interpret the process of a case in line with their pre-existing theoretical assumptions. As a result, there has emerged a general agreement within the field that it is not possible to regard traditional clinical case studies as reliable and valid forms of research-based 'evidence'.

The concept of a *systematic* case study is an attempt to hold on to the intrinsic value of case-based knowledge by finding ways to do case studies that can claim an acceptable degree of credibility. Systematic case study research is based on three key methodological principles. First, a 'rich case record' (Elliott, 2002) is compiled, which incorporates multiple sources of information on the case, for example from questionnaires, interviews and session transcripts as well as therapist notes. Second, the information collected on the case is analysed by a group or team of researchers, following a pre-determined set of procedures. This methodological strategy serves to overcome the possibility that the results of the case study will merely reflect the pre-existing theoretical ideas or beliefs of the therapist. Finally, the case is written up in accordance with a structure and guidelines that ensure the reader is fully informed about all relevant aspects of the treatment, and how the data were collected and analysed. This strategy is designed to prevent a selective reporting of findings.

A systematic case study involves the intensive analysis of multiple sources of information about a single case. The type of information that has been used in many recent systematic case study reports is well within the scope of most practitioners and students to collect. This type of case analysis can be employed to explore a wide spectrum of research questions within the field of counselling and psychotherapy.

Why would I want to do this kind of research?

Systematic case study research is an attractive option for novice researchers. It is possible to integrate this type of inquiry into routine practice. Analysing rich case data represents a good way of learning about the strengths and limitations of qualitative and quantitative methodologies. Case study research is ethically sensitive, because of the higher risk of disclosing the identity of participants, and so offers a good grounding in the handling of ethical issues. Working with a group of colleagues to analyse case data is generally an enjoyable and stimulating experience. Finally, the discipline of looking closely at what happens in an individual case inevitably leads to new understandings around the nature of the therapy process, and the links between theory and practice.

Exercise 13.1   Deciding to do a case study

If you are contemplating using case study methods in your research, it would be worthwhile reflecting on the implications of selecting this particular methodology. Given the research question that you are pursuing, what are the areas of knowledge and under-standing that you hope to achieve that would be harder to achieve (or impossible) with other methodologies? What are the areas of understanding that other methodologies might open up for you that would be less available in a case study inquiry? In what ways can you design your case study to maximise the distinctive strengths (and minimise the limitations) of this approach?

What kind of skills and support would I need?

Carrying out the kind of study described in this chapter requires familiarity with both qualitative and quantitative methods. However, case study research does not usually generate a sufficient volume of quantitative data to require analysis using a package such as SPSS. It is necessary to be able to draw on colleagues at various points in the process of conducting a systematic case study. For example, if the focus of the case study is your own work with a client, it would be essential for any fol-low-up interview(s) with that client to be carried out by another person. It is also necessary to be able to call on the inputs of other people during the phase of analys-ing data. It is valuable to be able to draw on experienced and informed supervision around ethical issues, and to receive general project supervision from someone who believes in the contribution of case-based methodology and has experience in using this approach.

Basic principles of systematic case-based inquiry

As with any form of research, it is necessary to find one's way into the appropriate mind-set. This is particularly important in relation to case study research, because it is probable that the researcher will have been exposed to various types of skepticism about the value of this approach. There are many experienced researchers in coun-selling/psychotherapy and allied disciplines who believe that case study research does not comprise a valid form of inquiry, and at best acts as a source for illustrative examples and teaching materials. The topics covered below provide a rationale for doing credible case study research that stands up as evidence and makes a meaning-ful contribution to knowledge.

Thinking like a case study researcher

To carry out a good piece of case study it is necessary to be clear about the potential role of case study inquiry within the overall range of methodologies that are currently available to therapy researchers. It is not sensible to operate on the assumption that case study research can answer every question and is all that we need to be doing. Instead, it is necessary to be able to understand the strengths and also the limitations of this approach. As mentioned earlier, case study research is particularly well-suited to (a) describing and analysing the complex interactions between different therapy processes; (b) understanding how change occurs over time; and (c) developing an understanding of how the process of therapy is influenced by contextual factors. In addition, case study research is also an effective means of: (d) identifying phenomena of theoretical and practical significance, that can then be investigated in a large-scale qualitative or quantitative study; and (e) developing new theoretical ideas. Case study research is not good at estimating the general effectiveness of therapy over a large sample of clients. There are also many research questions that address the relationship between a small number of factors/variables ('To what extent does early therapeutic alliance predict outcome?', 'How do clients respond to different types of therapist self-disclosure?') that are much easier to investigate by aggregating data across a large sample. In addition, there are many research questions that do not require data about a whole case, and can be explored perfectly well by collecting data at one point in time. The logic of case-based inquiry is explained in more detail by Fishman (1999), Flyvbjerg (2005) and McLeod (2010a).

Types of question that can be addressed using case study methodology

One of the pitfalls associated with case study research is that the researcher can easily find him- or herself overwhelmed by the amount of data accumulated, and ends up with a case report that does little more than describe what happened in the case. As with any type of study, it is necessary to define the research question in advance, collect data that are relevant to the task of answering the question, and write up the final report in a way that answers the question. There are basically four different types of research question that can be investigated using case study methods:

> *Outcome-oriented* case study research is concerned with one central question: 'How effective has therapy been in this case?'

> *Theory-oriented* case study research seeks to explore questions such as: 'How can the process of therapy in this case be understood in theoretical terms?' In a theory-oriented case study, data from a single case are used to test and refine an existing theoretical model or build a new theoretical framework.

> *Pragmatic* case studies address questions such as: 'What strategies and methods did the therapist use in this case?'; 'How were therapeutic methods adapted and practice that can be derived from this case?'; 'Which therapeutic strategies and interventions made a positive contribution to outcome, and which ones were harmful or hindering?' The primary goal of a pragmatic case study is to generate a detailed representation of how a specific therapy approach has been deployed with a specific client.

Experiential or narrative case studies aim to tell the story of the case, from the perspective of the client or therapist. These case studies explore questions such as: 'What was it like to be the client or therapist in this case?'; 'What was the meaning of this therapeutic encounter?'

It is possible to combine two questions or aims within one case study. For example, it is relatively straightforward to add a theory-building dimension to an outcome-oriented, pragmatic or narrative case study. However, it is still essential to be clear about what constitutes the primary goal of the study, and which question is of secondary importance. When writing up a case study, it is vital to be clear about the aims of the investigation, so that readers understand what the researcher was trying to achieve.

Ethical rigour

Ethical issues represent a major barrier to case study research. In an article reporting a research study that has collected quantitative data on 100 clients, it is virtually impossible to imagine any scenario in which the identity of any individual participant could be disclosed. By contrast, in a detailed report on a single case there are many ways in which the identity of the client and therapist might become apparent, particularly to people who already know them, such as colleagues and family members. There are also significant ethical issues associated with the experience of reading about one's own therapy, or reading about what one's own therapist truly thought and felt about you. It can be coercive to ask a client during therapy, or at the end of therapy, to give permission for their experiences to be used in a case study. There are also ethical risks around the possibility that a therapist might act differently if he or she believes that his or her work is going to be analysed in detail by a team of researchers.

These ethical issues act as a barrier to case study research because they can lead gatekeepers such as agency managers to refuse permission to collect case study data, and make clients reluctant to agree to taking part in such a study. A further barrier consists of the possibility that the client might withdraw permission to use the data at a late stage. Finally, some case study researchers can become paralysed by their moral responsibility toward the client or therapist, and avoid publishing their work.

There are a number of ethical procedures that can be applied to overcome these issues:

- An informed consent procedure that begins before the client ever meets the therapist.
- The therapist is not involved in negotiations around consent.
- Use of an independent advocate to represent the interests of the client.
- Process consent, in which agreement is checked out at each stage, up to the point of final publication.
- The client being able to read and approve what is written about him or her.
- Disguising any identifying information.

Further information about these procedures can be found in McLeod (2010a).

While recognising and being vigilant about these ethical issues, it is also important to acknowledge that some clients will welcome the opportunity to tell their story and will find it personally helpful and meaningful to take part in a case study project. Case study research has the potential to be ethically benign. However, it also has the potential to be an upsetting and unhelpful experience for some participants.

Choosing a case

There is a lot of work involved in collecting, analysing and writing up case study material, and there is no-one in the therapy world who has ever published more than a handful of cases. It is therefore necessary to choose cases for analysis in a purposeful manner. There are two broad case-selection strategies that can be used:

- *Typical cases* are of interest because they represent what 'usually' happens in a particular type of therapy. Some way of defining 'typicality' needs to be identified. For example, in a counselling agency where outcome data are collected on all clients, it may be possible to look at the whole range of clients and find a specific case that reflects the average severity score at intake and end of therapy, and has received the average number of clients. In many other research situations, there may be no evidence-based criteria that can be used to establish typicality. Sometimes the only option will be to start with the first client who agrees to take part in the project, and assume that what is observed in the therapy received by this person represents a reasonable approximation of typicality.
- *Theoretically-interesting cases* are of interest because they allow the researcher to focus attention on some aspect of therapy that is of particular relevance to their research question. For example, good-outcome cases provide opportunities to identify what happened when a specific form of therapy worked well. Poor-outcome cases create opportunities for understanding how a form of therapy might be improved. Unusual, surprising or anomalous cases also allow a researcher to test existing theories, and come up with new ideas. An important subtype of theoretically-interesting cases consists of cases in which a new approach to therapy is tried, or an established approach is used for the first time with a new client group.

Selecting cases for intensive case study research is not an exact science. Each case is likely to be typical in some respects and not typical in others. Inviting clients and therapists to take part in a case study before therapy has commenced means that it is not possible to know whether a case will end up with a good or poor outcome.

In practice, the issue of case selection is often handled by therapy researchers by collecting data on more cases than they will in the end be able to analyse. Many published therapy case studies are taken from the work of therapy agencies, research projects or individual practitioners, in which case data are collected on several cases with the choice being made at a later stage around which case or cases will be chosen for in-depth analysis. Other case studies are based on projects in which a student or practitioner has made a commitment to collect data on a limited series of cases.

In the end, it may be useful to keep in mind that any therapy case is potentially interesting because every person is interesting and every person's story is worth hearing. However, from a research point of view, when the aim is to use intensive single-case analysis to investigate a specific question, some cases may be more interesting than others.

Collecting data that enable generalisation

One of the most important characteristics of contemporary systematic case study research is the use of strategies to facilitate connections to be made between a specific case and the wider clinical population and world of practice. It is not logically possible to generalise from a single case. However, by the judicious recording and reporting of relevant information on a case, it is possible to make comparisons between that single case and other cases, or between a single case and findings from large-scale studies.

There are two main strategies that can be used to construct an argument around the generalisability of findings from a single case. The first is to collect and report standardised factual data that will allow the case to be positioned alongside other cases. This type of information can include demographic and biographical data on the client, such as age, gender, marital status, income, education, occupation, ethnicity, previous use of therapy, and previous/current use of medication. It can also include clinical case management data, such as number of sessions, number and occurrence of missed sessions, payment status, attributes and training of the therapist, and the therapy interventions that were used. Each of these pieces of information provides the reader with a point of connection with cases they have come across in their own practice, case studies they may have read, and the findings from other types of study.

The other strategy is to use theory as a means of building conceptual bridges between a specific case study and other cases and studies. For example, a researcher might be interested in what happens when a therapist makes use of a particular intervention or technique. Intensive analysis of the use of that intervention in a single case can be used to generate a model (or mini-theory) of how that technique was deployed by that therapist with that particular client. This model can then be tested by looking at whether it is confirmed in a subsequent case or in a different type of study such as interviews with clients who have received that intervention. Alternatively, there may be pre-existing studies that have generated guidelines for the use of that intervention. In such a scenario, the findings from the case study can be used to confirm the validity of these guidelines, or perhaps to contribute to the production of a more differentiated protocol. In any of these situations, some form of conceptualisation or model can be used to make connections between a single case and other sources of knowledge on a topic.

These forms of case study generalisation require advance planning. It is necessary to anticipate, at the planning stage of a study, possible points of connection that might be relevant at the analysis and write-up stage. The appropriate data can then be collected from the start.

Exercise 13.2   Imagining being the client

Imagine what it might be like to be a client in a case study investigation. This could either be a case study project that you are conducting yourself, or a published study that you have read about. What would worry you about taking part? What would excite you? In what ways might these meanings shape the course of therapy, and/or the type and quality of information that you contributed to the study?

Systematic interpretation of rich case data

Analysing case study data does not consist of the application of pre-determined procedures. Analysing data that have been collected using a questionnaire such as the Beck Depression Inventory means following a series of steps: adding up the score, comparing the score against published norms, and so on. The material collected in a systematic case study is fundamentally different from this, in that it comprises a combination of qualitative and quantitative data, gathered from a range of sources. Analysing case study data needs to be understood as an advanced pattern-recognition and hypothesis-testing task. Ultimately, case study data analysis is a process of *interpretation,* of finding meaning within a complex test.

In terms of the kind of approach that has been adopted by case study researchers in recent years, interpretation of case study data makes use of two analytic processes that occur within a cycle of inquiry. One aspect of this cycle of inquiry involves an individual attempt to make sense of the data. The other aspect involves sharing and comparing interpretations with other members of a team. This activity then feeds into a further turn of the cycle of inquiry, as each individual member of the team returns to the data and looks at these again, taking into account the ideas of colleagues.

At the level of the individual who is attempting to make sense of complex case study data, there are a number of strategies that can be helpful:

- Reading through the material slowly, and noting down any impressions and personal responses that arise.
- Summarising the content (the topics and issues explored) within each session.
- Identifying stages and significant turning points or events within the case (sometimes the turning points will be immediately apparent in quantitative data – for instance if the client's symptom score suddenly shifts between two sessions).

- Tracking a particular theme or process through the whole case (for instance there may be recurring metaphors and images that the client uses, or there may be weekly use of homework assignments).
- Looking for areas of convergence and divergence across various data sources.
- Checking that all of the information on the case has been taken into consideration.

These strategies provide ways of 'entering' the case and beginning to make sense of what it has to say. As with any interpretive activity, the researcher needs to possess some kind of conceptualisation or model of what he or she is looking for. At the same time, however, these ideas need to be held lightly, to allow new meaning to emerge and new learning to occur. Once patterns begin to emerge, it is important to pull these out by looking for counter-examples within the data and establishing the extent to which information from different sources 'triangulates' to provide the same conclusion.

At the level of a team of researchers working together, it is essential to establish a group culture that allows open dialogue rather than this being dominated by one or two powerful members. In practice, this is accomplished either by assembling a group of colleagues who know each other well enough to be honest with each other, or by adopting a structured way of working together. At the present time, there are three alternative models of group structure that have been adopted by teams of case study researchers:

1. The *quasi-judicial model* treats the data as if these were evidence in a court case, and divides the research team into subgroups who are given the task of developing and presenting competing interpretations of the case material. In principle, this strategy mirrors the use of 'prosecution' and 'defence' lawyers in a court case. In an outcome-oriented case study, for example, there may be an 'affirmative' team that argues the client has benefitted from therapy, and a 'sceptic' team that argues the opposite, that the case represents a poor outcome. The most fully developed version of this kind of quasi-judicial case analysis can be found in the *Hermeneutic Single Case Efficacy Design* (HSCED) approach that was devised by Elliott (2002) and which has been applied in many case study investigations. Other forms of quasi-judicial case-based inquiry are described in a special issue of the on-line journal, *Pragmatic Case Studies in Psychotherapy* (volume 7, module 1. 2011).
2. The well-known team-based qualitative research methodology known as *Consensual Qualitative Research* (CQR) has been adapted for use in case study research by Jackson, Chui and Hill (2012). This approach involves dividing up the task of data analysis between members of a research group, whose work is then audited by an external expert.
3. The *Ward method* (Schielke et al., 2009) is a structured form of group decision making and problem solving, which forces each member of the group to listen closely to the ideas of other members in preparation for incorporating these ideas into their own analysis of the data. The Ward method is based on an assumption that the ideas of the group will converge within three or four such cycles of co-consultation. An example of how the Ward method can be used in case study research can be found in Smith et al. (2014).

These group-centred approaches to data analysis and interpretation are informed by a belief that each member of a group will be able to contribute valuable ideas and insights, but that the ideas of any particular individual in the group are likely to be incomplete or biased in some fashion. The benefits of working together in a group are that each member is motivated to do the best they can, and will be able to point out the shortcomings of at least some of the ideas generated by other members.

In some systematic case study articles, limitations of space will mean that the individual and group-based analytic procedures that have been followed may not be explained in detail (or may not be explained at all). However, the majority of recent case study articles have made use of the kind of analytic strategies that are outlined above.

A step-by-step guide to carrying out a systematic case study

The planning process for a piece of case study research needs to take account of the time that will elapse while therapy is on-going. In some situations, for example in a service that only offers time-limited therapy, it will be possible to anticipate how long this will be. In other situations the length of therapy may be indeterminate.

As with any other form of research, it is necessary to start with a question. An intention to just 'do a case study' is unlikely to lead to a satisfactory research product. Ideally, the research aim or question then translates into a specification of the type of data that will be collected. If the research is being conducted in a therapy service where certain forms of data are already being collected, with no scope for negotiation or extension of the data protocol, then consideration needs to be given to the extent to which the intended aim or question can in fact be addressed in a satisfactory manner with the data available.

An absolutely crucial aspect of case study planning is to construct a research situation in which client, therapist and organisation feel comfortable about taking part, and are able to withdraw consent at any stage. By contrast, a research situation in which there is pressure on participants to take part, or to continue to take part, is both ethically unsound and likely to result in data that lack meaningfulness. In practice, one of the ways in which a congenial research relationship can be established is to collect data on many more cases than will ever be analysed. In that kind of scenario, it will not be a problem if a client decides to withdraw their involvement, even at the last moment. A high proportion of the systematic case studies that have been published in recent years have emerged from projects in which all clients starting therapy at an agency are invited to contribute data. Then, at a later point, it is possible to select cases for detailed analysis based on a combination of client willingness to continue their involvement, and an informed judgement around the theoretical or practical value of the case as a piece of research.

Building this kind of climate of care involves paying a lot of attention to the process of explaining and receiving informed ethical consent. For example, if possible clients should be asked about their 'in-principle' willingness to take part in a case study before they ever meet their therapist. The therapist should not be involved in doing the asking at any stage. A client needs to know that they can withdraw consent at any point, without any cost to them. All of this needs to be explained clearly, both verbally and in writing. It is good for clients to know that they are doing something altruistic and worthwhile, and that researchers are fully committed to taking care of them.

Typically, a systematic case study will be built around the collection of multiple sources of data, such as:

- a pre-therapy interview (or assessment notes);
- outcome measures administered on a regular basis;
- information about the process of therapy, such as client descriptions of significant events, or completion of an alliance scale;
- therapist notes;
- session recordings;
- end of therapy or the follow-up interview.

In many counselling and psychotherapy centres and clinics, much of this information will be collected on a routine basis, and it may be possible to carry out a systematic case study on virtually any client, as long as that person is willing to take part, and also willing to come back on a further occasion for a lengthy follow-up interview.

Information about instruments and measures that can be used to collect case data can be found in Chapter 9, and in McLeod (2010a). It will also be helpful to look at the types of data that have been used in exemplar published studies. One of the key choice-points, in case study research, regards the decision of whether or not to record sessions, and then transcribe some or all of these sessions. Transcribing is very time-consuming, but has the potential to yield research insights that are not accessible using other techniques. A useful compromise would be to transcribe selected sessions. For example, the first session is always interesting. The client or therapist may be able to identify certain sessions that were turning-points, and are worth looking at more closely.

It is not sensible for the researcher to analyse or think about the data while these are coming in, to avoid any temptation to influence the process of therapy. The exception to this rule occurs when the therapist is the main researcher, and some of the data are being used within therapy to track client progress. However, it is important for someone to scan or review the data as these are collected, in case the client is using questionnaires to try to communicate an intention to self-harm or engage in other forms of risky conduct.

Once the data are in, it will be helpful to gather these up in a 'case book' that can then be used as the definitive data-set for the ensuing case analysis. It would be a good idea, when preparing the case book, to carry out an initial screen of the data to alter identities and change names.

It will then be necessary to assemble a research team to analyse the data, and perhaps also be involved in writing parts of the final report or article. Various models for how such a case study analysis team were introduced earlier in the chapter. It is usually a good idea if the therapist is included in the team, and there is at least one other member of the team who has actually met the client face-to-face (for example, through conducting the follow-up interview). Although there are many examples of good-quality case studies that have not made direct use of the therapist in the analysis stage, the involvement of the therapist has the potential to add depth to the study. The golden rule, however, is not to allow their view of the case to dominate the analysis.

The final stage of a case study project is to write the article. It can be helpful if the client is willing to read a draft of the analysis and offer comments. Sometimes a client can clarify aspects of the case that were hard for outsider members of the research team to understand. Also, receiving the approval of the client can give a research team a valuable morale boost at a point when their energy for the project may be flagging. Being able to report in a paper that the client basically agreed with the analysis of the case can make the whole study more plausible to readers. However, it is always important to be mindful of the potential impact on the client of reading about their own therapy.

The experience of working in a small research team to plan, collect and analyse case study data tends to be enjoyable and rewarding for participants, in terms of learning about themselves, learning about therapy, and forming supportive relationships with colleagues. This kind of research can offer practitioners and students a satisfying blend of research participation and professional development.

What can go wrong?

There are a few things that can go wrong with case study projects. One of the pitfalls is to lack clarity about the question that is being asked, or about what it is that was found. This can lead to a case report that consists of a somewhat shapeless accumulation of descriptive information about what happened, which leaves the reader with the task of making some sense of it all. Another reason why some case studies never get completed is that the client withdraws, or there are unresolved dilemmas around ethical issues that mean the researcher is uncertain about his or her right to publish. A further difficulty in producing a published case study occurs when the author of the study does not find the right tone or stance in his or her writing. For example, people do not want to read case studies that claim too much in terms of generalisable conclusions, or that come across as public relations vehicles for a particular type of therapy. Well-written case studies are grounded in a sufficient degree of confidence that there is something worth saying, accompanied by a sufficient sense of being open to new learning. Compared to other forms of research, a case study gets closer to (or seeks to get closer to) the complex lived reality of how a therapeutic relationship plays out over time. To then write up the case as if everything that occurred was entirely in line with a specific model of therapy will then result in case study reports that come across as false and implausible.

Exemplar studies

Year-on-year, an increasing number of good quality therapy case studies are being published. A detailed account and discussion of some of these studies can be found in McLeod (2010a). Particularly recommended, as examples of different styles of using a case study research team, are the case study articles by Elliott et al. (2009), Hill et al. (2008), Kasper et al. (2008), Råbu et al. (2011), and Smith et al. (2014). A case study produced by Stinckens and Elliott (2014) is of particular interest here because it is possible to access a detailed, separate account of the thinking that went in to the broader project from which it was derived (Stinckens, Elliott and Leijssen, 2009).

Variants

In some research situations it will be relevant, and indeed possible, to carry out a series of case studies. This strategy has the advantage of making this type of research less ethically sensitive – within a series of five or six cases, each individual client will be less identifiable. Another strategy, when there are multiple cases, is to compare good-outcome and poor-outcome cases, as a means of looking at the elements of therapy that seem to contribute to success and failure. It is also possible to conduct meta-analyses of sets of case studies on the same client group. These variants are discussed in more detail in McLeod (2010a) and McLeod (2013c).

How to get published

Several leading research journals that are open to systematic case study articles, including *Counselling and Psychotherapy Research*, *Person-Centered and Experiential Psychotherapies,* and *Psychotherapy*. There is a strong tradition of publishing case studies within CBT journals. There are two journals that specialise in case study reports: *Clinical Case Studies,* and *Pragmatic Case Studies in Psychotherapy.*

Suggestions for further reading

Key further reading, which explores all of the issues raised in the present chapter in more depth, is McLeod, J. (2010a) *Case Study Research in Counselling and Psychotherapy.* London: Sage.

The on-line journal *Pragmatic Case Studies in Psychotherapy* publishes interesting cases, and also cutting-edge articles on case study methodology.

Companion website material

There are several case-study papers on the companion website (https://study.sage-pub.com/mcleod) for this book:

1. Articles on principles of case study methodology

Bohart, A.C., Tallman, K.L., Byock, G. et al. (2011) The "Research Jury" Method: The application of the jury trial model to evaluating the validity of descriptive and causal statements about psychotherapy process and outcome. *Pragmatic Case Studies in Psychotherapy,* 7(1): 101–44.

Flyvbjerg, B. (2006) Five misunderstandings about case-study research. *Qualitative Inquiry,* 12: 219–45. (essential reading)

Foster, L.H. (2010) A best kept secret: single-subject research design in counseling. *Counseling Outcome Research and Evaluation,* 1: 30–9.

McLeod, J. (2013) Increasing the rigor of case study evidence in therapy research. *Pragmatic Case Studies in Psychotherapy,* 9: 382–402.

Miller, R.B. (2011) Real Clinical Trials (RCT) – Panels of Psychological Inquiry for Transforming Anecdotal Data into Clinical Facts and Validated Judgments: Introduction to a Pilot Test with the Case of "Anna". *Pragmatic Case Studies in Psychotherapy,* 7(1): 6–36.

Stephen, S. and Elliott, R. (2011) Developing the Adjudicated Case Study Method. *Pragmatic Case Studies in Psychotherapy,* 7(1): 230–41.

2. Examples of case study research in action

Kramer, U. (2009) Between manualized treatments and principle-guided psychotherapy: illustration in the case of Caroline. *Pragmatic Case Studies in Psychotherapy,* 5(2): 45–51. http://hdl.rutgers.edu/1782.1/pcsp_journal

McLeod, J. (2013c) Transactional Analysis psychotherapy with a woman suffering from Multiple Sclerosis: a systematic case study. *Transactional Analysis Journal,* 43: 212–23.

Powell, M.L. and Newgent, R.A. (2010) Improving the empirical credibility of cinematherapy: a single-subject interrupted time-series design. *Counseling Outcome Research and Evaluation,* 1: 40–9.

Widdowson, M. (2012) TA treatment of depression - A Hermeneutic Single-Case Efficacy Design study – "Peter". *International Journal of Transactional Analysis Research,* 3: 3–13.

14

Using Personal Experience as a Basis for Research

Introduction

Within the field of research in counselling and psychotherapy research, there has been a growing willingness in recent years to regard the personal experience of the researcher as a potentially valuable and valid source of evidence. Within this general approach to inquiry, it is possible to identify a number of different sub-traditions. There have been many useful contributions to knowledge that have consisted of therapists and clients merely writing about their own lives, or their experience of specific events, without positioning their work within a specific methodological tradition. Historically, the use of personal experience as a source of psychological data has been described as *introspection,* which was the basis for early research into processes of memory and learning. In the 1970s a whole range of new genres of personal experience research began to emerge: mindful inquiry (Bentz and Shapiro, 1998), reflexive action research (Lees, 2001), transpersonal research (Braud and Anderson, 1998), dialogal research (Halling, Leifer and Roe, 2006); heuristic inquiry (Douglass and Moustakas, 1985; Moustakas, 1990); narrative inquiry (Etherington, 2000, 2002; Speedy, 2008). Currently, *autoethnography* represents the most influential and widely-used methodology within this tradition (Ellis, 2004).

What is a personal experience study?

Personal experience research involves the researcher (or each member of a group of researchers) making a systematic effort to document, analyse and communicate their own personal or subjective experience of a topic or phenomenon. The main rationale for this approach is that an individual who is undertaking research of this kind will be better able to produce an account that is more comprehensive, honest and profound than anything that would emerge from interviews, questionnaires, or other mainstream data collection strategies. In addition, a personal experience study may be carried out in situations in which data would otherwise be hard to collect.

The concept of 'autoethnography' represents a fusion of two different knowledge traditions: autobiography and ethnography. In an autobiography, a person seeks to contribute to knowledge by recounting the story of their own life. By contrast, ethnography can be understood as the use of participant observation, initially employed by social anthropologists, as a means of leaning about the 'way of life' of a culture or group of people. Although these traditions can be viewed as distinct from each other, it is also clear that these overlap in many ways. An autobiography may focus on a person, but that individual story always conveys important insights into the culture or cultures within which that person has lived. Similarly, an ethnographic study of culture needs to be informed by an appreciation of the life-trajectories (biographies) of members of that culture. In addition, the experience of engagement in studying another culture becomes an episode (sometimes a dramatic, vivid and life-changing episode) in the autobiography of the researcher. Autoethnography, as an approach to knowledge, has grown and developed in that intersecting space between autobiography and ethnography.

Why would I want to do this kind of research?

There are several reasons why it is desirable for novice researchers to undertake this kind of research. First, it is possible to use this approach to generate practically useful knowledge – several examples of practice-oriented personal experience studies are provided later in this chapter. Second, the experience of conducting an autoethnography, or similar studies, represents a good way to learn about the limitations of mainstream methodologies such as interview-based qualitative research or the use of measures: it becomes pretty obvious, quite quickly, that there exist levels of awareness and knowing that are not tapped by standard approaches. Third, most people who undertake personal experience research report that there is a great deal of personal learning and development arising from this kind of work (see, for example, Etherington, 2004b). Fourth, there is an aesthetic and creative dimension to personal experience research that can be highly satisfying.

Exercise 14.1   Choosing a topic

If you are thinking about undertaking an autoethnographic study, then what aspect or episode from your life would you wish to explore? What might be the effect on you, and those around you, of systematically analysing and writing about that issue?

What kind of skills and support would I need?

In the end, the success of an autoethnographic study will depend to a large extent on the capacity of the researcher to write about his or her experience in a direct and authentic manner. As a result, anyone who has difficulty in outing their feelings into words, or who becomes anxious or emotionally incapacitated at the prospect of undertaking a sustained piece of writing, might want to think carefully before committing themself to a mainly autoethnographic dissertation or thesis. Similarly, doing an autoethnography requires a willingness to be known, at a personal level, which may not be congenial to some people. It is also important to take account of the potential implications of an autoethnographic inquiry for other people who might be part of the author's personal story. For example, writing about one's personal experience of therapy involves describing one's therapist. It is only sensible to embark on such a study if one has confidence in being able to approach the therapist (or others who might be mentioned in the study) for their approval.

Autoethnography is probably the form of therapy research that most heavily depends on the establishment of a strong supportive relationship between the researcher and research supervisor (or equivalent mentor or consultant if the study is not being conducted in an academic context). Good autoethnographic research is somewhat risky, and requires courage, and it is important to have someone who is close to the process who can be trusted. Analysing or making sense of material that is generated in an autoethnographic project (such as personal diaries, artefacts, or descriptions of events) involves the rational part of the researcher observing and interpreting the emotional or spontaneous side of his or her way of being. This can be a hard thing to accomplish, and it would be useful to have someone else who is able to function as an external reference point. This is particularly necessary when the focus of the research is concerned with highly sensitive or upsetting experiences. Finally, there are many moral and ethical complexities associated with autoethnographic research arising from the depth of disclosure that can occur. As in any area of research, good practice in ethical problem solving involves consulting others and looking at the issue from a range of perspectives.

A step-by-step guide to conducting a personal experience study

Before beginning an autoethnographic study, or indeed in advance of deciding to use this methodology at all, it will be necessary to do some reading on the background to the approach, the underlying methodological principles that inform this kind of work, and the ways in which personal experience research differs from other types of qualitative inquiry. The items listed in the *further reading* section at the end of this chapter provide a good starting point for entry into this literature.

The practical reality of conducting a personal experience study can be divided into four broad stages: deciding on a question or focus; addressing ethical issues; generating data; and writing.

Deciding on a question or focus. As with any research study, an autoethnographic study needs to be organised around a question that is being explored or answered. Ultimately, the aim of autoethnographic or personal experience research will be to *describe* an episode or area of experience in a person's life. Some examples of autoethnographic studies are outlined below. It can be seen that, although they address different topics, all of them were trying to answer the question of 'What was it like to … ?' Philosophically, autoethnographic research is a *phenomenological* approach to knowledge, which seeks to establish the essential structure or features of an area of experience. An appreciation of this philosophical stance is helpful as a way of recognising the strength of autoethnography, compared to other qualitative methods such as interviewing. When interviewing another person, the researcher can only push so far – it is difficult or impossible to know if the informant has more to give, or what might be required to encourage them to go further. By contrast, when the subject of inquiry is one's own personal experience, or personal story, the researcher has the capability, if they are willing, to take the question as far as it will go. The level of disclosure required in autoethnographic research tends to shape the question that the researcher selects for investigation. The research topic needs to be something around which the researcher has a meaningful and detailed story to tell. At the same time, it has to be a topic where the researcher can live with the fact that others will learn about previously hidden, and possibly embarrassing, aspects of their experience. Another factor to take into consideration, when choosing a topic for autoethnographic research, is the issue of whether there is an existing literature on that theme. It may be informative to construct a free-standing account of personal experience that does not connect up with any published theory or research studies. However, such an account would usually be classified as an autobiography, short story, or novel. To be classified as a piece of research, links need to be made with the research literature. This is not an argument that research is 'better' or 'worse', or more or less useful, than art. It can all be useful (or otherwise) – it is just that these are different genres of writing.

Addressing ethical issues. The routine ethical issues that arise in all research have been discussed in Chapter 5. Autoethnography raises additional ethical issues because the subject of the research is being overtly identified through the name of the author. This means that the usual procedures to maintain confidentiality are not applicable. There are two areas of risk – to researchers, and to other people (e.g., family members or colleagues) mentioned in autoethnographic reports. The risks to authors are that they may not know what they are letting themselves in for, in publishing their story. What may seem a brave and authentic piece of writing, within the safe environment of a university department, may over time become a source of regret, as readers of the research find meaning that the author had not consciously intended. Another risk to researchers can occur in the later stages of projects, when they become aware of the personal sensitivity of the material, but are under pressure to complete a study. The risk to other people is that it is very easy for a family member, colleague, therapist, or whoever else was part of the drama of a writer's life, to recognise themselves in the eventual dissertation or article. While it is possible, and desirable, to collect formal consent from such participants, there is relatively little scope to disguise what is written about them. As a consequence, there are many possibilities for upsetting people. The nature of these ethical issues, and strategies for dealing with them, are thoroughly examined in Tolich (2010) and Sieber and Tolich (2013), which comprise essential reading for anyone planning to undertake an autoethnographic study.

Generating data. The most interesting and rewarding part of an autoethnographic project tends to be the stage of generating data or compiling a text. This phase of the study takes the form of a journey of systematic self-exploration. Most autoethnographic research is grounded in a period of sustained writing, during which the researcher captures in words as much of the target experience as they can. Writing can take place in diaries and journals, scraps of paper, participation in writing workshops, or through using writing exercises such as those in Bolton (2013), Cameron (1994), Hunt (2000) and other sources. Many personal experience researchers will use techniques to augment their awareness of events, such as writing poetry, generating images and metaphors, recording dreams, and meditation. Some researchers will invite other people to interview them. There are several creative ways of using artefacts such as photographs, music, documents and objects. These artefacts can represent or symbolise something that happened at the time of the original experience, or can be used to trigger memories of that experience. As with any form of qualitative research, the aim is to assemble a text that forms the basis for analysis and interpretation.

Writing. The hardest part of an autoethnographic study is writing the paper or dissertation. Good personal experience writing has an aesthetic quality to it, is vivid and memorable, and has an emotional impact. One of the ways in which these objectives are accomplished is to use writing to 'show' as well as to 'tell'. Other than producing a screenplay or theatre script, any form of writing will always include a significant amount of reporting or telling. Autoethnographic writing tries to minimise the amount of explanatory writing, in order to give more space to passages that convey the here-and-now 'lived experience' of key aspects of the topic being studied. This can be quite challenging for students or therapists who have been trained and socialised in the use of 'prosaic' and scientific modes of professional communication. Many autoethnographic articles use photographs or poetry as a contrast to prosaic writing. A further challenge is that an autoethnographic article or dissertation tends to move back and forward between lived experience, reflection, and theory. This means that this type of article is unlikely to conform to the normal structure of a journal research article. Authors will also often use different fonts, areas of the page, columns and colours to mark out the distinct 'voices' or positions being conveyed in a study. Done well, autoethnographic writing is powerful and memorable. Done not so well, it can be hard to follow.

Compared to other research methodologies, there are fewer rules or guidelines associated with autoethnography and other personal experience approaches. Nevertheless, as with any research writing, or indeed any successful professional writing, it helps to develop a routine or discipline, reflected in such factors as setting aside specific blocks of time for writing and finding or creating the right kind of writing environment.

Exercise 14.2   Autoethnographic techniques

What are the autoethnographic activities that would help you to explore your story? What are the activities that would be less helpful? As you read articles that have used these methods, which inquiry strategies are you particularly drawn to?

Examples of personal experience research

The best way to develop an appreciation of the possibilities of autoethnographic research is to read actual studies that have used this approach. The following sections provide brief summaries of some autoethnographic studies that are particularly relevant to the field of counselling and psychotherapy. These fall into two broad categories – studies of professional identity issues, and studies of the experience of problems and treatments.

Autoethnographic research into professional identity issues

Double Bind: An Essay on Counselling Training (Fetherston, 2002). An exploration of some of the tensions and contradictions associated with training as a counsellor. A notable feature of this article is the creative use of page layout, with competing perspectives on the training experience being displayed in side-by-side columns. The report is anchored in the text of an essay written for the training course.

In Search of Professional Esteem (Leitch, 2006). A ruthlessly honest account of the career development of a successful woman academic. An example of an autoethnographic account that describes emotional aspects of personal experience that are usually hidden.

Implementing a Client-centred Approach in Rehabilitation (Bright et al., 2012). This study reports on a group autoethnographic study, in which three practitioners worked together to explore their experience and learning in relation to developing new ways of working with clients. Each member of the group wrote their own individual autoethnographic account, which was then discussed in the group. A detailed account is given of the methodological procedures that were used to collect and analyse data.

Psychiatric Nursing Liaison in a Combat Zone (Whybrow, 2013). An autoethnographic exploration of the experience of a psychiatric nurse attached to front-line units in the British army in Afghanistan. Personal experience material was collected using a journal that was kept during the period of employment, which was then subjected to thematic analysis.

Autoethnographic research into the experience of problems and treatments

The Search for Meaning after Pregnancy Loss (Sheach Leith, 2009). A classic autoethnographic study, which uses photographs, documents and vivid accounts of key moments, to describe and evoke the experience of multiple pregnancy losses over a period of years. This study represents a good example of how highly personal material can be interwoven with theoretical analysis of health and social policy issues.

Reflective Journaling and Meditation to Cope with Life-threatening Breast Cancer (Sealy, 2012). The story of how one woman was affected by breast cancer, and how she coped with the emotional turmoil associated with her illness. This study makes a valuable contribution to an understanding of psychotherapeutic support in long-term health conditions, by analysing the positive contribution, and also limitations, of journal writing.

Reflecting on Growth through Trauma (Borawski, 2007). This article mainly consists of a vivid and detailed account of a day in the life of the author, when she was attacked and robbed, and the long-term effect of this event on her wellbeing and personal development. The personal narrative is accompanied by some effective and thoughtful links to the literature on post-traumatic growth.

Mental Illness in the Workplace (Kidd and Finlayson, 2010). A collective autoethnography, in which 19 nurses wrote individual accounts of their personal experience of mental health issues in the nursing workplace. These accounts were analysed thematically, with excerpts from individual stories used to illustrate each theme. The article includes information about how the data were collected and analysed, and makes links to a range of issues around workplace stress.

A Personal Battle against Obsessive-Compulsive Disorder (Brooks, 2011). A detailed first-person narrative of the inner experience of OCD, and what it was like to undergo various forms of treatment, including CBT.

The Meaning of Therapy (Borck, 2011). There are relatively few autoethnographic studies of the experience of psychotherapy. This study provides a brief, but sharp, account of the author's experience in therapy (2011: 407). The article also provides an example of how a limited amount of carefully-selected autoethnographic material can serve as the basis for valuable and insightful theoretical exploration and analysis.

The Abyss: Exploring Depression through a Narrative of the Self (Smith, 1999). A powerful, moving, and technically very skilful account of the author's experience of severe long-term depression and fragments of therapy. Includes a comparison between themes arising in the autoethnography, and other non-autoethnographic studies of the experience and meaning of depression.

Fathers and Sons (Sparkes, 2012). An outstanding achievement, which demonstrates the potential of an autoethnographic approach to knowing. The author uses poetry and accounts of significant events to draw out the interconnectedness of his relationships with his father and his own son.

These studies have been selected to offer an introduction to the diverse territory of autoethnographic research. Each of these makes a meaningful contribution to knowledge, by using individual cases and lives to illustrate shared aspects of the experience of being a person. These studies also exemplify the many different ways in which autoethnographic studies can be carried out and written up. Most of these are based on the experiences of the author alone, while others make use of a group of co-researchers. Studies also differ in the extent to which the method is explained, and connections to theory and previous research are discussed.

Exercise 14.3 Writing about personal experience

Once you have read a few of the studies listed in the preceding sections, take some time to reflect on how they came across to you as a reader. What were the writing strategies that seemed more or less effective? What were the writing styles that you could imagine using within your own study?

What can go wrong?

The things that can go wrong in autoethnography and other forms of personal experience inquiry are rather different from the things that tend to go wrong in other types of research. Generally, research projects do not work out because of missing data and a breakdown in co-operation between the researcher and potential informants or research sites. These problems do not arise in autoethnography because the researcher is completely in charge of the data. What goes wrong instead is that sometimes the researcher gets stuck because it becomes too emotionally painful or revealing to proceed with the study. Another way in which autoethnography can go wrong arises from difficulty in finding the right tone and style in the ultimate written dissertation or article. Effective autoethnographic reports will seem effortless – they flow, are easy to read, and carry impact. But a lot of work needs to go on behind the scenes to allow this to happen.

Variants on a standard autoethnographic study

The examples and discussion in this chapter have focused on autoethnographic studies that have led to a particular kind of product – a written report of some kind. It is obvious, to anyone who has reflected on the nature of autoethnography and other personal experience methodologies, that written reports in fact represent rather limited and restricted ways to communicate the kind of insight and understanding that can be generated by this form of inquiry. As a result, some autoethnographers have followed the example of performance artists in attempting to find ways to present their work in formats such as objects, pictures and displays, videos and theatrical enactments. It is difficult to direct readers to accessible examples of such outputs, which tend to be ephemeral. However, it is likely that in future more of this kind of output will be available on the internet.

Another key variant in autoethnographic inquiry is just to write about the experience of being a therapist, without labelling the piece as autoethnography or as following any particular methodological tradition at all. The counselling and psychotherapy literature includes many fascinating first-person accounts of the experience of having a career as a therapist (Comas-Dias, 2010; Dryden and Spurling, 1989; Haldeman, 2010; Marzillier, 2010), the experience of receiving personal therapy (Anonymous, 2011; Curtis, 2011; Freeman, 2011; Geller et al., 2005) and the experience of specific events in therapy (Callahan and Ditloff, 2007; Kottler and Carlson, 2005). Most of these books, articles and chapters could 'pass' as autoethnographic studies.

A further direction that is inevitable within autoethnography and personal experience research is the development of efforts to use this kind of research within meta-analyses and literature reviews. At the present time relatively few autoethnographic studies have been published, so there is probably only one such study that looks at OCD (Brooks, 2011) or depression (Smith, 1999). As time goes on, it is certain that multiple personal experience accounts of a whole range of therapy-relevant issues will be produced, and it will be possible to look at the extent to which these studies support and confirm findings from other types of research, and the degree to which these challenge and extend the conclusions of mainstream research.

How to get published

In relation to publishing an autoethnographic study, or similar type of investigation, it is important to be aware that some academic researchers, journal editors and reviewers are quite strongly opposed to this approach to research. One of the leading British autoethnographers, Andrew Sparkes, has written about how, at various points in his (very successful) academic career, he has had to respond to accusations that the research carried out by his students and himself was 'self-indulgent' (Sparkes, 2002, 2013). Relatively few of these critical positions find their way into print. An interesting and instructive exception can be found in a paper by Delamont (2009), who characterises autoethnography as 'narcissistic' and 'self-obsessional'. This article is particularly valuable because it is very clear that Delamont (2009) is not a 'positivist' researcher who believes that the only phenomena worth studying are those that are measurable. On the contrary, Delamont (2009) passionately believes in the central role of researcher reflexivity, but argues that this kind of self-awareness should be used to produce more in-depth understandings of the cultural groups or individuals who are being studied (i.e., other people) rather than as a basis for the researcher to write about him- or herself.

It is essential for therapy researchers who use autoethnographic and other personal experience methodologies to take account of the ways in which their research might be perceived by others. This is all the more important because it is often the case that personal experience research is supervised by tutors who strongly identify with the approach, and have assembled a team of colleagues and students who hold similar views. In this kind of situation, there can be a tendency to regard critics as ill-informed or lacking in awareness. Clearly, some critics may well be ill-informed, but others, such as Delamont (2009), are not. One of the difficult methodological issues that autoethnographic researchers struggle to address is that this kind of research is almost entirely carried out by middle-class professional people, with the consequence that it cannot adequately reflect the experiences of oppressed and less articulate members of society. The key point here is that the production of knowledge always involves a process of critical debate and dialogue, and personal experience inquiry is no different from any other methodology in this respect.

In light of the experimental nature of personal experience research, it is necessary to be realistic and strategic about how prospective articles are written and where they are submitted. The studies that are referenced in this chapter represent possible publication outlets for autoethnographic research. Many of the leading counselling and psychotherapy journals, such as *Counselling Psychology Quarterly, Journal of Counseling Psychology, Psychotherapy, Psychology and Psychotherapy*, and *Psychotherapy Research*, have never (to my knowledge) published an autoethnographic paper. Each of these journals has published many well-received qualitative studies, so they are not hostile to non-quantitative research. But at least until now, autoethnography has been a step too far.

Suggestions for further reading

An overview of how autoethnographic and other personal experience methodologies have been used in research in counselling and psychotherapy (with different examples from those highlighted in the chapter) can be found in Chapter 10 of McLeod, J. (2011) *Qualitative Research in Counselling and Psychotherapy* (2nd edn). London: Sage.

Companion website material

The companion website (https://study.sagepub.com/mcleod) offers access to a number of key papers:

Brooks, C.F. (2011) Social performance and secret ritual: battling against Obsessive-Compulsive Disorder. *Qualitative Health Research*, 21: 249–61.

Douglass, B.G. and Moustakas, C. (1985) Heuristic inquiry: the internal search to know, *Journal of Humanistic Psychology*, 25: 39–55.

Leitch, R. (2006) Outside the spoon drawer, naked and skinless in search of my professional esteem. The tale of an "academic pro". *Qualitative Inquiry*, 12: 353–64.

Muncey, T. (2005) Doing autoethnography. *International Journal of Qualitative Methods*, 4: 69–86.

Tolich, M. (2010) A critique of current practice: ten foundational guidelines for autoethnographers. *Qualitative Health Research*, 20: 1599–610.

Smith, B. (1999) The abyss: exploring depression through a narrative of the self. *Qualitative Inquiry*, 5: 264–79.

Sparkes, A.P. (2012) Fathers and sons: in bits and pieces. *Qualitative Inquiry*, 18: 174–85.

Wall, S. (2006) An autoethnography on learning about autoethnography. *International Journal of Qualitative Methods*, 5: 146–60.

Wall, S. (2008) Easier said than done: writing an autoethnography. *International Journal of Qualitative Methods*, 7: 38–53.

15

Disseminating the Findings of your Research Study

Introduction

One of the fundamental differences between formal research and the kind of informal personal reflection on practice that is part of supervision and training is that the products of research are disseminated and become part of a general stock of knowledge and understanding. Usually, the findings of research are disseminated in written form. Although some researchers are beginning to experiment with other media such as video and live performance, or are publishing their work on the internet, the main way of passing on research is through written articles, chapters, reports and books. The aim of these notes is to offer some guidelines for getting into print. Many counsellors who do research do so in the context of studying for a degree, and initially write up their results in a Master's or doctoral dissertation. Other counsellors carry out research as part of the audit and evaluation function of their agency or clinic, and their work remains hidden within internal memos and reports. It is important for counsellors who wish to continue their professional development to the stage of making an impact on their peers, of claiming their own authority and professional voice, to go beyond this and publish in the public realm. Here is how to do it.

There are four main types of publication outlet: journals, conferences, books and monographs. These are discussed in turn.

Exercise 15.1   Formulating a dissemination strategy

It is important to think about what you want to accomplish, through disseminating your work. The following sections of this chapter introduce a range of alternative publishing outlets. Before reading these sections, take some time to reflect on your hopes, fears and goals around publication. Who will be your audience? What do you want for yourself? In what ways might publication serve to further the interests of your research participants?

Publishing in journals

There is a huge international journals industry which is largely invisible to those outside the academic world. Advances in desktop publishing and printing have made it much cheaper to produce journals. Whereas commercial magazines need to pay authors for every word that they publish, the contributors to professional and academic journals do not usually get paid, and in many journals the editor will receive an honorarium rather than a salary. Moreover, many journals enjoy fixed subscriptions tied in to the membership of professional bodies. For example, all 30,000 members of the British Association for Counselling and Psychotherapy receive the journals *Therapy Today* (a professional journal) and *Counselling and Psychotherapy Research* (a peer-reviewed international research journal), paid for out of their membership dues. Professional and academic journals can survive with quite limited subscription bases (around 1,000 would appear to be sufficient for a viable journal). Publishing companies therefore like publishing journals, which provide a steady income, low outgoings, and a vehicle for promoting their book sales.

The economics of the journals publishing industry have a number of implications for anyone wishing to get into print:

- There are *lots* of journals. If you cannot get your article accepted by a mainstream journal there will be some other niche journal, somewhere, that will in all likelihood be glad to have it.
- Most journals are run on a shoestring. People who review articles for journals are not paid. There is no one paid to have the time to polish up your grammar, spelling and use of references, or to give you general advice. You also have to meet their deadlines (e.g., for proof reading) and follow their instructions.
- You must only submit your article to one journal at a time. If everyone were to submit their stuff to three or four journals simultaneously, the editing and reviewing system would collapse under the strain.
- You will not be paid. Normally, if you have an article accepted in a journal you will get a free copy of the journal (the one with your paper in it) and access to a pdf copy of your paper.

A broad distinction can be made between *professional* and *research/academic* journals, although there are also some journals which straddle this divide. Professional journals are mainly concerned with publishing articles about professional issues. In the counselling and psychotherapy world such journals include *Therapy Today*, the *Journal of Counseling and Development*, *The Counseling Psychologist*, *American Psychologist* and *The Psychologist*. These journals are the official organs of professional associations. Although they may include excellent learned articles on theory and practice, they seldom carry original research, and they also tend to include fairly lengthy sections on announcements, meetings of professional committees, and general professional business. In addition, they carry a lot of advertising for courses and conferences. By contrast, academic journals such as *Counselling and Psychotherapy Research*, *British Journal of Guidance and Counselling*, *Counselling Psychology Quarterly*, *Journal of Counseling Psychology*, and *Psychology and Psychotherapy* will carry mainly research reports, reviews of the research literature, and articles on theory and methodology. These do not cover professional business, and include only limited advertising. Some of the differences between the publication policies of these different types of journal are outlined in Box 15.1.

Box 15.1   Publication policies of professional and academic journals

Professional journals

Publication criteria weighted toward topicality, interest value, readability.

May commission articles.

Decision to publish often made by the editor.

Broad readership.

More flexibility over writing.

National readership.

Academic journals

Publication criteria weighted toward research rigour.

Publication almost wholly responsive to submissions sent in.

Decision to publish always arrived at through peer review.

Limited circulation but more likely to be held in libraries as a permanent record.

Likely to be available on-line.

Abstracted in databases.

Strict writing style conventions and format.

International readership.

In deciding which journal to submit work to, it is essential to get hold of an actual copy of the journal. Look at the kind of articles that are published in the journal, and choose one which carries articles that are similar in style and content to the one you intend to write. Inside the cover of every journal it is possible to find some sort of 'mission statement' describing the type of papers the journal would like to receive. Sometimes this statement can be misleading, because editorial policies can outgrow the original journal remit, so it is always important to look at a few recent issues to get a feel for the territory which the journal has carved out for itself. Inside the front or back cover there will usually be other vital information, including:

- the minimum and maximum length for articles;
- guidelines for preparing articles, for example referencing conventions, policy on sexist language, ethical waivers, and perhaps even rules on the use of subheadings, notes, tables, diagrams, photographs and figures: most journals will require that articles are submitted with the author's name and address on a separate page (to facilitate anonymous reviewing);
- who to send the articles to, if paper copies, then how many copies (which are not returned) and how to print it (typically 1.5 or double spaced on one side of the page);
- publication dates and deadlines, acceptance rates.

It is essential to follow these instructions as far as you can. A paper which at least *looks* as though it has been carefully prepared in accordance with the guidelines laid down by a journal will be viewed more favourably. One of the hardest things is ensuring that references are laid out exactly according to the requirements of a particular journal. There are many referencing formats in use, some of which may differ only in their use of full stops and capital letters. Bibliographic software packages such as *Endnote* can be invaluable in constructing reference lists, because they can transform a set of references from one format to another.

There are other aspects of the 'house style' of a journal that tend not to be explained in their instructions for authors sections, and can only be discovered by looking at articles published in the journal itself. Most research journals expect articles to be structured around a series of subheaded sections: Abstract; Introduction (including a brief literature review) leading into a statement of the research question(s) or hypothesis; Methods/Procedures; Results; Discussion; References (see Box 15.2). However, specific journals may deviate from this structure slightly or use different terminology. Qualitative studies are notoriously difficult to fit into this kind of linear format, and it is worth looking at how your particular target journal handles qualitative material.

Box 15.2   The structure of a typical research paper

1. Title of the article.
2. Names and contact details of authors.
3. Abstract (brief summary of the paper) – typically no more than 300 words.
4. Keywords (in alphabetical order).
5. Introductory section, which usually includes:

   i. the 'hook': an opening statement on the general interest and significance of the topic;
   ii. the literature review: placing the study in the context of previous research, theory and policy debates;
   iii. a statement showing the aims of the present study, and sometimes also a brief summary of the design of the study.

Note here that the Introduction follows a logical progression, and tells a story that starts with a general statement of the topic, narrowing this down to specific research that has been carried out in relation to the topic, drawing some conclusions about the gaps in the literature, explaining what kind of further research is now required, and introducing the aims of the current study, which has been designed to fill some of these gaps. The Introduction is mainly written in the present tense (apart from the aims bit at the end) to reflect the fact that it is a statement of established fact.

6. Methods section, which usually includes a series of sections with subtitles such as:

   i. participants: those who took part in the study;
   ii. measures/instruments: the techniques by which the data were collected;
   iii. procedures: how the participants were recruited, what happened to them during the study;
   iv. ethical issues and how they were addressed; ethical consent procedures; source of ethical approval;

    v. the researchers: sometimes in qualitative studies there is a brief paragraph describing the background and expectations of the researchers;

    vi. analysis: the procedures/strategy for analysing the data (mainly found in qualitative studies).

Note that the Methods section is usually written in the past tense – 'This is what we did'.

7. Results section. Here the factual findings of the study are presented, with no interpretation or explanation. If quantitative/statistical data are reported, there will always be a corresponding written statement that states what the numbers actually mean. This is also written in the past tense: 'This is what we found'.

8. Discussion. This section usually includes:

    i. a brief statement on what the study aimed to do, and what it has claimed to find;

    ii. a rehearsal of the strengths and weaknesses of the study;

    iii. careful comparison of the results of the study in contrast to the results of previous studies (i.e., those mentioned earlier in the literature review – no new literature is introduced here), along with an interpretation of any contradictory findings (e.g., 'Our results contradict those of Smith and Jones (2002) because ....')

    iv. discussion of the implications of the findings for theory, further research, and practice.

9. References.

10. Appendices – e.g., a copy of the questionnaire that was used.

11. Some journals make supplementary material available on-line, at the journal website.

Note that footnotes and endnotes are rarely used in journals that publish counselling and psychotherapy research papers. Consult recent issues of journals that are of interest to you for examples of permitted usage of footnotes and endnotes.

The length of a research paper can be between 2,000 and 7,000 words. It is essential to check the recommended word limit imposed in a target journal before submitting your paper to it. Journal editors usually have many papers waiting to be published, and only have a fixed number of pages/words that they can use in each issue. They are therefore unlikely to accept articles that are unnecessarily long (i.e., padded out). If you have carried out a small-scale study, editors will like it if you send in a brief paper, perhaps titled as an 'exploratory study' or 'early returns from ... ', etc.

So why are research papers structured in this kind of standard template? The advantage of a standard structure is that it allows busy people to read a paper quickly. Studies carried out on the reading strategies of experienced researchers have found that they rarely read a research paper straight through from start to finish. First, they use the title, author list (what are these people up to?) and abstract to decide whether the paper is

                                                                   (Continued)

(Continued)

of interest. Then, if the paper is potentially relevant to them, they sample the aims statement, the method and the start of the discussion, to assess the 'guts' of the argument. Only if there is anything puzzling or unexpected about the findings will they read the paper all the way through from the start, for example to check whether the literature review has missed anything or is biased, if the procedures or sample were unusual in some way, or whether the authors might have missed something in the analysis.

The structure of a research paper can be thought of as similar to an egg-timer shape: it starts off broad (with a general statement of interest), narrows down to very specific details in the middle, and finally broadens out again to conclude with a general statement.

The normal procedure is to send in your article with a short covering letter. Almost all journals make use of on-line submission portals for articles. Fairly soon there usually follows a brief acknowledgement of receipt of the article. Very occasionally editors may return an article at this point if it is clearly inappropriate for the journal, too long, or otherwise unsuitable. However, most articles will be sent off at this point for independent peer review. This means that anything that identifies the author(s) needs to have been deleted from the paper, which is reviewed by three experts nominated by the editor. Reviewers are customarily given three to four weeks to prepare their (anonymous) reports, although it is not uncommon for them to take much longer. The standard practice is for reviewers to make ratings on the overall quality of the paper and its suitability for the journal. They will also write a brief report on the paper, which may be quite brief (five or six lines) or more lengthy (two or three pages in some cases). The ratings may or may not be sent to the author(s), depending on journal policy, but the report will almost always be sent on, accompanied by a covering letter (email) from the editor. This letter will either reject the paper, perhaps recommending other journals which might consider it, or will suggest alterations that need to be carried out. It is unusual for papers to be accepted for publication without any rewriting at all.

At this point many would-be authors can become dispirited. Having opened their letter from the journal, they are faced with three critical and cryptic sets of anonymous comments, some of which may contradict each other. This experience can seem like an invitation to low self-esteem, frustrated rage and depression. Personally, I have often had to banish such reports to the outer reaches of my office for several days (or longer!) before being able to read them in a balanced and constructive fashion. It is helpful to remind oneself of what is happening in these circumstances. Reviewers are not being asked to be therapeutic or supportive, but to help the editor produce the best quality work for his or her journal. If an editor does not want to publish a paper at this stage, he or she will say so very clearly. Therefore, any invitation to resubmit a paper is an acknowledgement that it has the potential to make the grade.

Once the rewriting has been done (which may take months) it is usual to send it in along with a covering letter which explains briefly how the main points made by reviewers have been addressed. It may be necessary to explain why some of these points have *not* been addressed – reviewers can be wrong! Again, there will be a waiting period while the paper is being considered. Some journals may permit further rounds of revisions. Once the paper has been accepted there will be yet another delay while it takes its place in the queue of articles for publication. Some prestigious journals have publication delays of over 12 months.

It is clear that this whole process takes time. It is common for at least 18 months to elapse between submitting an article to an academic journal and seeing it in print. Some professional journals do not employ such elaborate review procedures, and can turn round articles more quickly. Less popular or new journals may not receive many papers and thus may be in a position to put an article straight into the next edition. Increasingly, journals are publishing articles on line as soon as they have been accepted, even if they do not appear in print until several months have elapsed.

It is sensible to be on the alert for upcoming special issues of journals. Editors or the editorial boards of many journals like to reserve one or two editions each year for symposia or collections of articles on specific topics. Notification of these special issues is usually advertised in the journal about two years ahead, with a deadline for submission of articles around 12 months ahead of the eventual publication date. Note that it can be easier to get an article accepted for a special edition (there is less competition) and once published it will receive more attention, since anyone interested in the topic will seek out the journal, even if they do not normally read it.

Which journal to choose? The politics of academic publishing

At the present time, counselling and psychotherapy research papers are published in a very wide range of journals. A list of therapy research journals is available in McLeod (2013b: 57–8). It can be hard to know which journal to approach. To some extent the decision may be influenced by the topic of your research – for example, if you have carried out a study of counselling for people with eating disorders there are specialist eating disorders journals that may be keen to publish your work. On the other hand, there are many generalist journals that would also publish a paper on counselling for people with eating disorders

In deciding which journal might represent the best outlet for your research, it is helpful to know a bit about the politics of academic publishing. Governments in most countries are committed to promoting academic excellence. They also tend to spend a lot of money on supporting universities, and are understandably keen to have evidence that their investment is resulting in some kind of measurable pay-off. There are many metrics that can be used to evaluate the productivity and quality of work of academic departments and individual faculty members, for example, research and consultancy income, number of PhD students who have completed, number of books and papers published each year, and the social and economic impact of research (e.g., in the form of patents, inventions and spin-off companies and other forms of 'knowledge transfer'). One of the most important indices that is used is the 'impact factor': this is the number of times within a given period that a particular article is referenced in other articles. Impact can be assessed in terms of specific articles, or the output of an individual researcher, or a journal as a whole. Impact measures are important for anyone interested in developing an academic career, because most universities will look closely at the impact of a person's publications when considering him or her for a permanent (tenured) position, or for promotion to a senior position. It is therefore crucial for aspiring academics to publish their work in journals that are edited, read, and cited by leading figures in the field. In the world of counselling and psychotherapy, the high impact factor journals are:

- *American Journal of Psychiatry*
- *British Journal of Clinical Psychology*
- *Clinical Psychology: Science and Practice*
- *Counseling Psychologist*
- *Counselling Psychology Quarterly*
- *Journal of Clinical Psychology*
- *Journal of Consulting and Clinical Psychology*
- *Journal of Counseling Psychology*
- *Psychological Medicine*
- *Psychology and Psychotherapy*
- *Psychotherapy*
- *Psychotherapy Research.*

The implications for authors of this kind of 'league table' are that it is tough to get a paper published in one of these journals – there is a lot of competition, articles need to attain high standards of technical excellence, reviewers are often fairly brutal, rejection rates are high, and there is a long waiting time between acceptance of an article and its eventual publication. It is therefore a high risk strategy to submit a paper to one of these journals, as you may wait for several months to learn that your paper has not been accepted, and then will need to start again with a lower-impact journal. Papers in high-impact journals that report on work carried out by new researchers are usually co-written with more experienced researchers (e.g., a PhD supervisor) who have a prior track record of having had their papers accepted by that journal.

The concept of 'impact factor' refers to the global politics of academic publishing. There is another level of micro-politics that also needs to be taken into account. Most academics are passionate about their work, and are motivated to guard their reputations, defend themselves against attacks on their ideas, and promote the work of their students in a quasi-parental manner. The people who edit journals are members of editorial boards of journals and the reviewers who are likely to have most influence on eventual accept/reject decisions: they are also experienced academics who are driven by these passions and motives. When considering submitting an article to a journal, it is therefore wise to do some research on the people who run that journal. Who is the editor? What are his or her interests? What are his or her positions on key issues, such as the role of qualitative *vs* quantitative methods? Similarly – who is on the editorial board of the journal, who publishes a lot in the journal, who seems to do a lot of reviewing (most journals will publish an annual list of reviewers to acknowledge their efforts)? In carrying out this kind of intelligence work, it is important to be alert for changes of editor. The kind of papers accepted by a journal can shift quite markedly following the appointment of a new editor. (This shift may not be immediately apparent, because an incoming editor will initially be processing papers that have been accepted under the regime of the previous editor.) An invaluable source of information on these matters is informal consultation with experienced academics, who are often happy to advise on which journal, right now, might want to publish your work.

Handling the micro-politics of academic publishing goes further than just selecting the most suitable journal. It also incorporates the deployment of writing strategies that will avoid antagonising reviewers. Most reviewers are fair-minded, and willing to recommend acceptance of articles that challenge their beliefs, or the results of their own research. At the same time, anyone seeking to publish an article that challenges existing knowledge needs to be aware that reviewers will inevitably pay special attention to such articles, in terms of looking for methodological flaws and unsupported conclusions. There are two attributes of research papers that tend to trigger a 'rejection response' in reviewers and editors. The first attribute consists of failure on the part of an author to reference, acknowledge and discuss relevant sources. For example, speaking personally, I have published fairly widely (in accessible sources) around the area of workplace counselling, including reviews of relevant studies and discussion on key methodological issues. If a journal editor sends me an article to review, that consists of a study of workplace counselling, which seems to have been written in ignorance of the issues I have spent many months working on, then obviously I will experience strong feelings of despair and irritation. By contrast, if that author had acknowledged those issues, and had then challenged my position on them, I would be interested and delighted – here is someone who is taking the research conversation forward.

A second attribute of politically-insensitive writing is to make over-exaggerated claims in the discussion and conclusion section of a paper. There is a delicate balancing act here. On the whole, editors will want to publish articles that say something new. On the other hand, it is extremely unlikely that a single research study will arrive at findings that fundamentally change the landscape of knowledge in respect of a particular topic. Well-written discussion and conclusion sections in research articles therefore need to do two things – acknowledge the extent to which the findings reinforce and support existing knowledge, and then tentatively outline some ways in which the findings *extend* that knowledge or open up possibilities that need to be further explored in subsequent research. In pointing out these possible new insights, it is always necessary to place the discussion within the context of an appreciation of the limitations of your study (see Box 15.2 on page 222).

As with any area of life, academic publishing has its own power structure and power struggles. Many academics regard conflict and argument as intrinsic to good academic work, on the grounds that the ideas and methods that have most validity are the ones that have survived a process of rigorous critical scrutiny. This commitment to challenge and debate is alien to many people within the world of counselling and psychotherapy, which generally places more value on acceptance, consensus and empathy rather than robust dissent. Any political structure also creates insiders and outsiders. In order to get work published it is necessary to learn to be an insider, which requires becoming familiar with the rules of the academic game. The best way to do this is through meeting, talking to, and knowing experienced people who are already inside the system. This can be achieved by being a student and engaging in conversations with tutors. Another strategy is to attend research conferences where groups of 'insiders' can be found in one place at one time.

Conference proceedings

For many researchers, giving a paper at a conference represents a good way to get started in their writing career. The dates and venues of conferences are advertised about nine months in advance in relevant professional journals, or on the internet, along with a call for papers. For most conferences, the act of submitting a paper merely involves writing an abstract (i.e., a 300-word summary). A few conferences will demand to see the whole of the paper at the submission point, but this is rare. When the time for the conference comes round, a formal paper may or may not need to be written. Some people at conferences will actually read out papers, but this form of presentation is almost always boring and static. Presentations where the speaker talks freely around overhead projector headings tend to be better received. At a conference, ordinary speakers will have 20 minutes for their talk, plus 10 minutes for questions (keynote or megastar speakers are allowed longer), which puts pressure on the presenter to express his or her ideas crisply and succinctly – a good discipline. Following the conference, the journal of the professional association responsible for the event will publish the title (and sometimes also the abstract) of each paper, along with the name and address of the presenter. It is quite common to receive several requests for copies of a conference paper. The people who want to read the paper are likely to be interested enough in it to give feedback if asked. Useful feedback can also be received during the conference itself, either through formal questions asked after the paper, or less formally in the bar or round the dinner table. If you have actually written a paper in advance of a conference, it would be useful to take 10–20 copies to the event to distribute to people interested in your work. Another format that is increasingly employed at conferences is the *poster* presentation. Researchers will display their work on a poster, and during a session of the conference will stand beside this to answer questions. This can be a very rewarding way of meeting other people with similar research interests. It can also be less terrifying than standing up and delivering a paper. Contributing a paper or poster at a conference can be a useful way of achieving some degree of dissemination of research, and getting the material into the public domain. It is also an excellent way to rehearse ideas that can be later worked up into a published article.

Publishing a book

Most journal articles are between 2,500 and 7,000 words in length. A book can be anything between 50,000 and 100,000 words. There is therefore much more work entailed in writing a book, compared to writing a paper. Also, it is unusual, nowadays, to see book-length research reports in the field of counselling and psychotherapy. Nevertheless, there may be situations where the only way to do justice to a piece of research is to give it the space made possible by a book. Examples of some widely read counselling and psychotherapy research books which have appeared in recent years are listed at the end of this section.

Unlike a research paper, which is written and then sent off to a journal, no one in their right mind would ever write a research book and send it off cold to a publisher. The procedure is to submit a proposal to the publisher, which is then reviewed by two or three academic referees. Just as in deciding on which journal to approach with an article, it is important to investigate the previous work published by an imprint. A book proposal is more likely to be accepted if it fits into the publisher's existing portfolio. A good proposal will include the following information:

- A title and general outline or aims.
- A synopsis of each chapter.
- Information about the previous writing experience of the author(s). If they have limited experience, then a sample chapter should be included.
- The anticipated readership for the book.
- How the book compares with other texts in the same field.
- Some indication of the timescale for finishing the manuscript.

As with journal article submissions, the process of getting a book proposal accepted may take some time and involve changes to the original conception. Once a publisher accepts a proposal, they will issue a contract and may pay a small advance on future royalties. (It is perhaps important to stress here that the earnings from academic or research books are meagre.) The publisher will allocate an editor to the book, who can be treated as an ally. Book editors cajole and encourage their authors, and are willing to discuss the project quite openly. Editors also put a great deal of work into ensuring that the final copy of the book is as near perfect as it can be.

One of the crucial factors that needs to be understood in relation to book publishing is that publishers are partly interested in the quality of a book but are much more interested in whether it will *sell*. As explained earlier, the economics of journal publishing are fairly stable. Books, on the other hand, are more hit or miss. It is not unusual for academic or research-focused books to struggle to break even. Publishers continually seek to be reassured that there is a market for a proposed book. The idea that a book will be bought by large numbers of students on courses in different colleges and universities (preferably all around the globe) is the kind of thing that publishers like to hear.

It is worth noting that publishers are traditionally cautious about edited collections, conference proceedings or unreconstituted doctoral dissertations. The latter are often far too dry and technical to work in book form, and multi-author edited books can be fragmented and inconsistent. Obviously many edited books are published every year in the counselling and psychotherapy domain, but many of these are put together by highly experienced academic editors. For example, in Britain, Professor Windy Dryden has edited many counselling books. Close examination of these books will reveal the extent to which he has provided a clear structure and aims for the authors he has included.

Being invited to contribute to an edited book is a good way of getting published for the first time. One of the ways of being asked to write a book chapter is to become known, for example by giving talks and conference papers.

Here are some examples of book-length research reports:

Dreier, O. (2008) *Psychotherapy in Everyday Life*. New York: Cambridge University Press.
Etherington, K. (2000) *Narrative Approaches to Working with Adult Male Survivors of Child Sexual Abuse: The Client's, the Counsellor's and the Researcher's Story*. London: Jessica Kingsley.
Gubrium, J.F. (1992) *Out of Control, Family Therapy and Domestic Disorder*. Thousand Oaks, CA: Sage.
Hill, C.E. (1989) *Therapist Techniques and Client Outcomes: Eight Cases of Brief Psychotherapy*. Thousand Oaks, CA: Sage.
Howe, D. (1989) *The Consumer's View of Family Therapy*. Aldershot: Gower.
O'Neill, P. (1998) *Negotiating Consent in Psychotherapy*. New York: New York University Press.
Waldram, J.B. (2012) *Hound Pound Narrative: Sexual Offender Habilitation and the Anthropology of Therapeutic Intervention*. Berkeley: University of California Press.
Wallerstein, R.S. (1986) *Forty-two Lives in Treatment: A Study of Psychoanalysis and Psychotherapy*. New York: Guilford.

It is important to note that these authors were all experienced researchers, who had published standard research papers before they wrote these book-length reports.

Publishing a monograph

A monograph can be defined as an academic text that is shorter than a book (around 30,000 words), and is not usually published by a commercial company.

Many university departments support their own monograph series, as do some voluntary and public sector agencies. Indeed, with the ready availability of desktop publishing and printing, any individual or group can produce their own monograph-length reports. There are many research projects which produce substantial reports, for example an end-of-project report to a funding body, which do not translate easily into journal articles. If such monographs are advertised in the appropriate professional journals, they can easily generate sales that are sufficient to cover costs. It is not difficult to get an ISBN number which will ensure that the monograph eventually finds its way into bibliographic listings. The people who are interested enough in a subject to seek out a monograph tend not to be particularly concerned about how 'glossy' the product is, as long as it is accurate and well edited. To some extent, a degree of unglossiness can help to give a monograph an aura of authenticity. A good example of a locally published monograph series has been the *Dulwich Centre* series, which has presented much of the work of narrative therapists Michael White and David Epston and their colleagues. This set of writings has been enormously influential, without any involvement or support from international publishing houses.

Internet and Kindle publishing

A growing number of academics and researchers are self-publishing their work on Kindle and similar on-line platforms. Detailed information on how to prepare copy for on-line publication is available on these sites. There are also a variety of support groups for self-publishing authors. Compared to paper copies, e-books remain somewhat restricted in terms of what is possible in relation to layout and formatting. Compared to publishing in journal articles, there is an absence of pre-publication quality control through peer reviewing. On the other hand, much more open reviewing and dialogue take place within the comment and feedback sections of on-line publishers.

Writing practitioner research

A central theme within my own work has been to emphasise the distinctiveness of practitioner research in counselling. To do justice to the principles of practitioner research, for example a commitment to critical reflexivity and to the goal of producing knowledge in context, it is necessary to write more creatively and personally than is usually the case in the psychological and social scientific literature. Some of the ways in which practitioner writing may differ from conventional research writing are as follows:

- *A greater willingness to write in the first person where appropriate.* It can be very hard for people who have been trained to be detached, scientific 'observers' to use the word 'I' in work that is to be publicly disseminated. The use of first-person writing is essential if the study is to be 'owned' and grounded in a context. At the same time, over-use of the first person can be a distraction. Beginning every sentence with 'I believe ... ' in the end diminishes the impact of use of a personal voice.
- *Including the voices of other people.* As counsellors, we do not regard our clients as 'subjects' (or objects). Why, then, in research, are participants or informants written about as if they were passive 'response-machines' or specimens? Any attempt to engage in dialogical, collaborative research will mean that other people have the right to see their own words in the final article or report.
- *More space given to ethical and moral considerations.* In mainstream research it is generally assumed that ethical issues have been dealt with as part of the general methodological competence of the researcher, and as a result do not require detailed discussion. In practitioner research the closeness of the research to practice, and the over-riding priority given to positive empowerment and enhancing the wellbeing of participants, will often mean that ethical and moral issues are more complex and less resolved, and will therefore call for more in-depth discussion.
- *Using various forms of writing to represent experience.* Conventional social scientific writing adopts a highly detached and distanced perspective on experience, and does not allow the reader to 'dwell in' (Mair, 1989) the world of those being written about. In recent years, some social scientists have started to experiment with different approaches to writing, drawing on drama, fiction and poetry. Gergen (1997) provides a very useful discussion of the implications of different forms of writing.
- *Writing about the implications for practice.* If you carry out a piece of practitioner research and write it up, then what readers will want to know is the impact that research made on your practice. In practitioner research papers it is important to give examples of the implications for practice, or to devote a section of the paper to this theme.

As a result of these considerations, practitioner research articles are likely to look somewhat different from the kinds of research articles that can be found in the current literature. There are likely to be additional sections giving reflexive and contextual information. There will be a section explicitly examining implications for practice. There may be more space given to ethical issues and the whole thing may be structured and written from a more dialogical standpoint. One of the implications that arises from these considerations is that it may be hard to publish practitioner research in mainstream journals, or it might be necessary to make compromises to enable your work to be accepted. Alternatively, it could be necessary to select 'niche' journals that are open to your approach. Journals that are particularly open to more personal forms of writing include:

- *Canadian Journal of Counselling and Psychotherapy.*
- *Family Process.*
- *Journal of Constructivist Psychology.*

- *Journal of Critical Psychology, Counselling and Psychotherapy.*
- *Journal of Humanistic Psychology.*
- *Journal of Systemic Therapies.*
- *New Zealand Journal of Counselling.*
- *Psychodynamic Practice.*
- *Qualitative Inquiry.*
- *Qualitative Reports.*
- *Qualitative Research in Psychology.*

An interesting example of how one author adapted her writing style to meet the requirements of different publication outlets can be found in the work of Susan Morrow (see Box 15.3).

Box 15.3   Contrasting ways of reporting the same research study

Morrow, S.L. and Smith, M.L. (1995) Constructions of survival and coping by women who have survived childhood sexual abuse, *Journal of Counseling Psychology*, 42: 4–33.

Morrow, S.L. (2006) 'Honor and respect: feminist collaborative research with sexually abused women', in C.T. Fischer (ed.), *Qualitative Research Methods for Psychologists: Introduction through Empirical Examples*. New York: Academic Press.

Morrow, S.L. (2009) 'A journey into survival and coping by women survivors of childhood sexual abuse', in L. Finlay and K. Evans (eds), *Relational-centred Research for Psychotherapists: Exploring Meanings and Experiences*. Chichester: Wiley-Blackwell.

These publications tell a chronological story: the most 'technical' version of the study can be found in Morrow and Smith (1995) and the most personal version in Morrow (2009). Note how long it took Susan Morrow to write the article she had always wanted to write.

Doing the writing

It is all very well to outline the various kinds of publication outlet that are available and how they operate. For some people reading this, the main hurdle comes long before even starting to think about which journal to approach with a paper. That hurdle is writing. It is possible to be a gifted researcher and yet experience writing as an activity that is utterly painful and frustrating. There is no easy way round this. It may be helpful, however, to consider three propositions:

1. Writing is a skill. Everyone who writes can write better. There are ways of learning how to write more effectively.
2. Everyone can write when they are sufficiently in tune with what they are writing, when they have found their own 'voice' or 'author-ity'. If you are stuck with your writing, approach the problem as a counsellor. What do you *really* want to say?
3. The kind of writing that tends to be expected in research publications is linear, abstract, middle-class, western white male kind of stuff. There are other ways of communicating.

If you find writing difficult, my suggestion is that you study writing. Dig out the work of writers in your field whom you admire. How do *they* do it, how do they structure sentences, paragraphs, chapters and even whole books? There are also several books which give good advice on how to write and how to create the conditions for writing (see the reading list below).

When looking at published work from a perspective of wondering 'How was this written?', it is useful to develop a sensitivity to the way that articles are structured. One of the most terrifying experiences is to sit down with a blank sheet of paper or empty word-processor file in hopes of being able to grind out an article or chapter. It is much better to already have a structure or template around which one's words and ideas can be woven. Box 15.4 provides some hints for constructing writing templates. These are not hard and fast rules. Many excellent social science writers have developed alternative ways of structuring their written output. To some extent the structure may be dictated by the requirements of a journal or book editor. But the point is that, virtually always, good writing involves having a clear structure which allows the reader to follow the thread(s) of the argument through from beginning to end. Poor writing occurs when this does not happen, when the author has 'lost the plot'.

Box 15.4   Some basic rules for structuring a paper, article or chapter

Anchor the beginning and the end. There should normally be some kind of introduction, which tells the reader why this is an important topic, outlines the aims of the paper, and may also briefly describe how the article is structured (i.e., what follows). There should also normally be a conclusion, which summarises the main argument and draws out implications for the future (e.g., implications for practice, for further research, for theory-building, etc.). Omitting a conventional introduction or conclusion can have great dramatic effect and impact, but also runs the risk of making your piece incomprehensible.

Use subheadings and sections. It is difficult to write good stuff that flows on and on without any breaks. These breaks can be indicated by subheadings, section numbering, or even by lines or asterisks in the middle of the page. Each section should be brought to a close with a brief summary or conclusion, and then there should be a brief statement at the beginning of the next section introducing the new theme or sub-topic. Look at published books and articles. There are many different levels of subheading that can be used, for example major subheadings (in bold) and minor sub-headings (in italics). In a few places there could also be subsidiary divisions marked by the first word or phrase of a section being italicised. It is seldom effective to go beyond two or three levels of subheading, except in very technical writing, or to use complex systems of numbering (e.g., section 1.2, 1.2.1, etc.).

Use quotations for special effect, not to carry the main argument. As a rock fan, I tend to think about a piece of writing as similar to recording a music track. First the basic track is laid down quite simply, often with just the voice and a guitar or piano. Later, added musical layers are dubbed on, backing vocals, a full rhythm section, solos, etc. Applying this metaphor to writing, it can be seen that a quote is the same embellishment as a guitar or saxophone solo. If you write a piece that comprises a series of quotes (whether from published authors or from your research informants) it will be very difficult for readers to follow the direction of the argument. You need to learn to rely first and foremost on your own 'voice' and then bring in other voices to provide emphasis or contrast.

Don't use the good stuff too early on. In any paper or chapter there will perhaps be two or three really good ideas and a lot of padding. If this is the case, then it is not sensible to include any glittering moments before more mundane material. It is better to work up to the more interesting ideas, and then use these to critique and illuminate the background material.

Do not use pie charts or histograms. Be sparing with the use of diagrams and images. Be very sparing indeed with your use of poetry. These are devices that can be very effective in the context of oral presentations, but can tend to make research papers seem cluttered (e.g., 'Why is the author using a pie chart where the same information could be provided in two lines of text?') or trying too hard to be persuasive.

Most sane and sensible people do not enjoy writing. Sitting on one's own for hours at a time, struggling to produce something that may well be rejected or need to be significantly modified in the light of feedback (at some indeterminate future date), is not a particularly rewarding experience. Box 15.5 offers some ideas about how to ease the pain of writing, and Box 15.6 describes a self-exploration exercise that may help you to become more aware of your own strengths and issues around the act of writing.

Box 15.5   Easing the pain of writing

Here are some 'writing rules' that may be helpful:

1. Decide on a regular time and place where you will do your writing. This can be very different for different writers – for example, first thing in the morning, last thing at night, in a room with no distractions, in a café (J.K. Rowling), etc.
2. During that time, just write. It does not matter what you write, just get some words onto paper/into the laptop. Writing is a job. Keep at it. Some days it will flow, other days it will seem impossible. That doesn't matter – just focus on writing.
3. Keep a notebook with you at all times, and jot down ideas that come to you. Your best ideas will probably not come to you as you write (that's the time when you

(Continued)

(Continued)

        must turn the ideas into sentences and paragraphs). You have to learn to harvest the products of your imagination/unconscious whenever they reveal themselves to you.

4. Every piece of writing, no matter how long, can be broken down into a series of 'scenes' or sections. For example, a typical research paper (see Box 15.2) consists of a sequence of 200-word 'bits'.

5. Become interested in how other people write. How do good writers structure sentences and paragraphs. How do they capture and retain your interest? How do they succinctly report detailed information? How do they handle such difficult writing challenges as reporting their own involvement in the research (reflexivity)? At the start of your writing career, do not try to be original. Instead, be willing to copy and learn from others.

6. Write a lot and edit this savagely. As a practice exercise, take something you have written and continuously delete more and more bits of it. You will find that the more you edit, the tighter and more readable it will become.

7. Find someone who will read your final draft and be completely honest with you. If that person (i.e., a well-informed and sympathetic reader) cannot understand a word, phrase or passage, or gets confused by the structure and flow of your argument, then this needs to be changed. It does not matter if you understand what you have written – you will not be there to explain to readers what it means.

8. Find your audience and your voice. This takes time. It is valuable to give talks about your work at conferences and meetings, or teach it to your students. The more you are able to access an inner voice that is speaking to a specific audience, the easier it will be to write.

Exercise 15.2   How do you write?

The aims of this exercise are:

- to give you a chance to reflect on your writing practices;
- to hear about how other people tackle the same issues;
- to get feedback from others.

You are invited to spend around 20 minutes writing your responses to the questions listed below. You should then share what you have written (or those bits of it you choose to share) with a small group of colleagues, or with individuals who are supportive of you (e.g., your research supervisor, your therapist, etc.).

The way I prepare for writing is to ...

My preferred medium for writing is ...

The place I use for writing is ...

The time I use for writing is ...

My favourite writers (academic and other) are ...

What I have learned from them is ...

What helps my writing is ...

What holds back my writing is ...

The biggest problem I have in writing is ...

The best thing I ever wrote was ...

What would help me to write more effectively is ...

It can be valuable to document what you have written in a personal journal to enable you to reflect at some future date on how your writing skills and strategies have developed.

Other ways of getting the message across

Because of the domination of research by academics, it is natural to assume that research outputs must always take the form of written texts. We live in a literate professional culture, in which authority is associated with written authorship. From a counselling perspective, however, it is clear that experiential learning is, most of the time, a more powerful medium for communication and learning than reading and writing could ever be. There are many ways of using research findings. Even at academic conferences, it is not unusual for research papers to be presented as pieces of 'performance art'. In other settings, research can be translated into workshops or video documentaries. In the context of the day-to-day work of counselling agencies, the results of research can be incorporated into protocols and training manuals. The impact of practitioner research will depend, in the long run, not only on the adoption of a diversity of methodologies, but also on the exploration of a multiplicity of channels of communication and learning.

Suggestions for further reading

Everyone finds writing difficult. Because of this, a lot has been written about how to write. The following list offers advice and guidance around different aspects of the process of writing.

General writing strategies:

Becker, H.S. (2008) *Writing for Social Scientists: How to Start and Finish Your Thesis, Book or Article* (2nd edn). Chicago: University of Chicago Press.
Belcher, W.L. (2009) *Writing Your Journal Article in Twelve Weeks: A Guide to Academic Publishing Success*. Thousand Oaks, CA: Sage.

Canter, D. and Fairbairn, G. (2006) *Becoming an Author: Advice for Academics and Other Professionals*. Maidenhead: Open University Press.

Hartley, J. (2008) *Academic Writing and Publishing: A Practical Handbook*. London: Routledge.

Hunt, B. and Milsom, A. (2011) Academic writing: reflections from successful counsellor educators, *Journal of Humanistic Counselling*, 50: 56–60.

Kendall-Tackett, K.A. (2007) *How to Write for a General Audience: A Guide for Academics Who Want to Share Their Knowledge With the World and Have Fun Doing It*. Washington, DC: American Psychological Association.

Murray, R. (2009) *Writing for Academic Journals*. Maidenhead: Open University Press.

Silvia, P.J. (2007) *How to Write a Lot: A Practical Guide to Productive Academic Writing*. Washington, DC: American Psychological Association.

Guidelines for writing qualitative research articles:

Caulley, D.N. (2008) Making qualitative reports less boring: the techniques of writing creative nonfiction. *Qualitative Inquiry*, 14: 424–49 **(available on the companion website)**.

Choudhuri, D., Glauser, A. and Peregoy, J. (2004) Guidelines for writing a qualitative manuscript for the *Journal of Counseling & Development*. *Journal of Counseling and Development*, 82: 443–6.

Golden-Biddle, K. and Locke, K. (2006) *Composing Qualitative Research* (2nd edn). Thousand Oaks, CA: Sage.

Goodley, D., Lawthom, R., Clough, P. et al. (2004) *Researching Life Stories: Method, Theory and Analyses in a Biographical Age*. London: Routledge Falmer.

Knox, S., Schlosser, L.Z. and Hill, C.E. (2012) Writing the manuscript, in C.E. Hill (ed.), *Consensual Qualitative Research: A Practical Resource for Investigating Social Science Phenomena*. Washington, DC: American Psychological Association.

Ponterotto, J.G. and Grieger, I. (2007) Effectively communicating qualitative research. *The Counseling Psychologist*, 35: 404–30 **(available on the companion website)**.

Smith, L., Rosenzweig, L. and Schmidt, M. (2010) Best practices in the reporting of participatory action research: embracing both the forest and the trees. *The Counseling Psychologist*, 38: 1115–38 **(available on the companion website)**.

16

Building on Basic Research Competence: Further Possibilities

This book is intended for novice researchers. In my view, there are three keys to success as a novice researcher. The first is to read research papers. The second is to find someone who will take you on as an apprentice. And the third is to make something, to commit to planning and completing a research study that can be published. In this endeavour, the best chance of success is to start with a relatively straightforward project, using a tried and trusted design that is supported by many sources of guidance and inspiration. Earlier chapters have provided 'starter kits' for five different types of research product that represent the fundamental building blocks of research knowledge in counselling and psychotherapy: literature reviewing, practice-based outcome evaluation, qualitative interview-based inquiry, systematic case study research, and autoethnography. In an ideal world, everyone who undergoes training as a counsellor or psychotherapist would get first-hand experience and tuition in all of these types of research activity, before choosing one of them for their research dissertation or thesis.

Active participation in the research approaches highlighted in this book provides a point of entry into the basic research skills and competences. These include:

- being able to negotiate the design of a study, develop strategies for dealing with ethical issues, and work collaboratively with others to collect and analyse data;
- reading and understanding research articles in ways that it is able to appreciate their place in the overall literature, as well as evaluate their methodological strengths and limitations;
- the skill of using research to collect accounts of the experience of various aspects of therapy, and then to analyse, interpret and write up this material in ways that both give research participants a voice and address theoretical and practical issues;

- a basic capacity to understand and handle quantitative data;
- an ability to understand the issues involved in evaluating the effectiveness or outcomes of therapy; competence in designing and implementing a system for collecting outcome data; and awareness of the options that are available in terms of presenting the findings of such studies;
- critical understanding of the contribution of case study methodology and strategies for analysing case-based data;
- awareness of the role of self in research (researcher reflexivity) and in the potential value of inquiry that is based on analysis of personal experience.

The possession of a sufficient level of competence and hands-on experience in each of these areas provides a platform from which it is possible to undertake research that is methodologically more challenging. Any gaps in this basic repertoire mean that a researcher faced by complex research problems may lack sufficient knowledge of all the potential ways in which these problems could be investigated. For example, a researcher whose initial training missed out on case study research, or autoethnography (or any other methodology), is unlikely ever to read studies that use these approaches, and as a result they would never be in a position to see how the inclusion of such methods might make a valuable contribution to their programme of inquiry. In addition, being aware of the value of a diversity of methodological traditions introduces a kind of critical synergy. Each approach (literature reviewing, quantitative, qualitative, case study, personal experience) offers a standpoint that allows the limitations of other approaches to become visible.

Of course, the five types of research product introduced in this book do not, by any means, encompass the whole field of research in counselling and psychotherapy. Other research possibilities have been highlighted toward the end of several chapters, in the context of discussions of variants on the basic research models that have been introduced. For example, Chapter 12 closes with a discussion of how the methods and organisational skills required to carry out practice-based outcome research can be readily extended into the more ambitious and complex undertaking of a randomised controlled/clinical trial (RCT) or an action research project. It is not possible, in the space available, to even begin to attempt to describe all of the pathways that have been followed by therapy researchers in recent years. However, I would like to draw attention to three research traditions that I believe are particularly important for the future development of therapy theory and practice. I would not advise novice researchers to undertake these forms of research, because they call for a level of methodological sophistication that builds on the skills and competencies associated with my 'big 5' forms of inquiry.

Research that examines the use of language within therapy can be clearly seen to have major implications for both therapy practice (which mainly involves talking), and for the development of a critical perspective on all other forms of research (which use language to persuade readers of the veracity of their knowledge claims). There are three main traditions of qualitative inquiry into language use (McLeod, 2011). *Discourse analysis* considers the ways in which any form of language use involves the positioning of the subject (writer, speaker) in relation to the forms of knowledge and moral reasoning that exist within a culture. *Conversation analysis* looks specifically at naturally-occurring talk (for example, recordings of therapy sessions) in order to examine such processes as the construction of joint understanding/formulation of a problem, or the ways in which one speaker controls the other. *Narrative analysis* focuses on the ways in which stories are used to convey meaning in social interaction. Although these three methodological traditions draw on somewhat different sets of assumptions and analytic techniques, in terms of research practice there are many points of connection between them, and in terms of therapy practice these can each be regarded as interrogating a distinct but complementary facet of the massively complex topic of language use. Applying any of these approaches to the study of therapy talk, has the potential to yield new, powerful and disturbing insights, because this type of inquiry explores processes that are largely outside of conscious awareness. What makes these challenging is that the researcher needs to attain a sufficient level of understanding of narrative theory, discourse theory, or socio-linguistics and ethnomethodology. These fields of study are conceptually difficult (for most people) and are not readily reconciled with mainstream therapy theory.

A further key domain of therapy research relates to ethnographic studies that directly observe the interactions, culture, and way of life of groups of people. Historically, ethnographic participant observation was the earliest form of qualitative inquiry. Social anthropologists travelled to distant parts of the world to investigate the way of life of traditional, pre-modern communities. Later generations of ethnographers applied the same methods to the study of groups of people in modern industrial societies, such as street corner gangs and medical students in training. The great strength of ethnography is that it aims to develop an holistic understanding of a cultural group in terms of how everything fits together: history and myth, relationships and interactions, rituals, material objects and places, ways of thinking. The practice of contemporary qualitative research can be seen as built around fragments of ethnography: studies that analyse interviews, studies that analyse artefacts such as photographs, studies that look at language use. By contrast, ethnography holds all of this together. Such a strategy is only possible when the researcher is willing to spend extended periods of time in the field, and is also willing to tolerate the ambiguity and complexity of the kind of data that are generated. These factors mitigate against the use of ethnography by Master's or undergraduate students, or busy practitioners. The confidentiality of the therapeutic encounter can also be regarded as a barrier to ethnographic research. Despite these challenges, ethnographic research in counselling and psychotherapy does exist, and has proved highly fruitful (see McLeod, 2011, Chapter 5).

The third form of research possibility that I would particularly like to encourage is *action research*. The argument for the importance of action research, and some examples, are provided in McLeod (2011, 2013b). The big idea, in action research, is that data collection and analysis are integrated into practice, with the aim of finding ways to enhance the effectiveness of that practice. Action research therefore does not aim to generate general 'truths' or theories, but to make a difference at a local grass-roots level. In most action research situations it is helpful to collect both qualitative and quantitative data, because these different types of information offer complementary ways of getting close to practice. It is certainly the case that many therapists and therapy agencies already engage in informal (i.e., not formally disseminated) action research at some level. It is also certainly the case that many organisations claim to use research as part of a commitment to quality enhancement, but in reality do not utilise the information they collect to make any real difference to services. Adopting an action research approach requires a willingness to make a political shift, away from expert-led services and in the direction of the collaborative planning and design of services. This is a difficult thing to do, but in my view it represents a necessary direction of travel for counselling and psychotherapy. At the present time, it is hard for anyone who is considering an action research project to know what to do because there are so few published examples. There is a lot of work to be done in developing an understanding of what works (and does not work) in action research in counselling and psychotherapy, and how best the findings of such projects can be written up (Guiffrida et al., 2011). There is also an inherent tension here, because the fundamental purpose of action research is to make a practical difference and not to generate journal articles. But the absence of journal articles or other forms of reporting, limits the extent to which local accomplishments can inform and inspire colleagues in other places.

The aim and focus of this book have been on the issues, skills and options involved in *doing* research in counselling and psychotherapy. Doing research has been defined as making things – mainly journal articles, but also other tangible ways of disseminating research-based knowledge and contributing to a shared, collective knowledge network (the 'literature'). But what is this for? What can we do with all of these research products? These issues are discussed in the next book in this series: *Using Research in Counselling and Psychotherapy.*

References

Addis, M.E. and Krasnow, A.D. (2000) A national survey of practicing psychologists attitudes toward psychotherapy treatment manuals. *Journal of Consulting and Clinical Psychology*, 68: 331–39.

Agee, J. (2009) Developing qualitative research questions: a reflective process, *International Journal of Qualitative Studies in Education*, 22: 431–47.

Agnew-Davies, R., Stiles, W.B., Hardy, G.E. et al. (1998) Alliance structure assessed by the Agnew Relationship Measure (ARM). *British Journal of Clinical Psychology*, 37: 155–72.

Alaszewski, A. (2006) *Using Diaries for Social Research*. London: Sage.

Allen, M., Bromley, A., Kuyken, W. et al. (2009) Participants' experiences of mindfulness-based cognitive therapy: 'it changed me in just about every way possible', *Behavioural and Cognitive Psychotherapy*, 37: 413–30.

Allman, L.S., De La Rocha, O., Elkins, D.N. et al. (1992) Psychotherapists' attitudes toward clients reporting mystical experiences, *Psychotherapy*, 29: 564–9.

Alpers, G.W. (2009) Ambulatory assessment in panic disorder and specific phobia, *Psychological Assessment*, 21: 476–85.

Andersen, S.M. and Przbylinski, E. (2014) Cognitive distortion in interpersonal relationships: clinical implications of social cognitive research on person perception, *Journal of Psychotherapy Integration*, 24: 13–24.

Angus, L. (1996) An intensive analysis of metaphor themes in psychotherapy. In J.S. Mio and A. Katz (eds), *Metaphor: Pragmatics and Applications*. New York: Erlbaum.

Angus, L., Levitt, H. and Hardtke, K. (1999) The Narrative Processes Coding System: Research applications and implications for psychotherapy practice. *Journal of Clinical Psychology*, 55(10): 1255–70.

Angus, L.E. and Rennie, D.L. (1988) Therapist participation in metaphor generation, collaborative and noncollaborative styles, *Psychotherapy*, 25: 552–60.

Angus, L.E. and Rennie, D.L. (1989) Envisioning the representational world: the client's experience of metaphoric expressiveness in psychotherapy, *Psychotherapy*, 26: 373–9.

Anonymous (2011) Lessons learned from a long-term psychoanalysis on the telephone, *Journal of Clinical Psychology*, 67: 818–27.

Antoniou, P. and Cooper, M. (2013) Psychological treatments for eating disorders: What is the importance of the quality of the therapeutic alliance for outcomes? *Counselling Psychology Review*, 28: 32–46.

Archer, R., Forbes, Y., Metcalfe, C. et al. (2000) An investigation of the effectiveness of a voluntary sector psychodynamic counselling service, *British Journal of Medical Psychology*, 73: 401–12.

Armstrong, J. (2010) How effective are minimally trained/experienced volunteer mental health counsellors? Evaluation of CORE outcome data, *Counselling and Psychotherapy Research*, 10: 22–31.

Armstrong, R., Hall, B.F., Doyle, J. et al. (2011) 'Scoping the scope' of a Cochrane review, *Journal of Public Health,* 33: 147–50.

Ashworth, M., Evans, C. and Clement, S. (2008) Measuring psychological outcomes after cognitive behaviour therapy in primary care: a comparison between a new patient-generated measure, 'PSYCHLOPS' (Psychological Outcome Profiles) and 'HADS' (Hospital Anxiety Depression Scale). *Journal of Mental Health,* 14: 1–9.

Ashworth, M., Robinson, S., Evans, C. et al. (2007) What does an idiographic measure (PSYCHLOPS) tell us about the spectrum of psychological issues and scores on a nomothetic measure (CORE-OM)? *Primary Care and Community Psychiatry,* 12: 7–16.

Atkins, S., Lewin, S., Smith, H. et al. (2008) Conducting a meta-ethnography of qualitative literature: lessons learnt, *BMC Medical Research Methodology,* 8: 21. doi:10.1186/1471–2288-8-21

Attkisson, C.C. and Zwick, R. (1982) The client satisfaction questionnaire: psychometric properties and correlations with service utilization and psychotherapy outcome, *Evaluation and Program Planning,* 5: 233–7.

Attkisson, C.C. and Greenfield, T.K. (1994) 'Client Satisfaction Questionnaire-8 and Service Satisfaction Scale-30', in M.E. Maruish (ed.), *The Use of Psychological Testing for Treatment Planning and Outcome Assessment.* Hillsdale, NJ: Lawrence Erlbaum.

Aveyard, H. (2010) *Doing a Literature Review in Health and Social Care: A Practical Guide.* Maidenhead: Open University Press.

Bachelor, A. (1988) How clients perceive therapist empathy: a content analysis of 'received' empathy. *Psychotherapy,* 25: 277–40.

Bachelor, A., Laverdière, O., Gamache, D. at al. (2007) Clients' collaboration in therapy: Self-perceptions and relationships with client psychological functioning, interpersonal relations, and motivation. *Psychotherapy: Theory, Research, Practice, Training,* 44: 175–92.

Balfour, A. and Lanman, M. (2012) An evaluation of time-limited psychodynamic psychotherapy for couples: A pilot study. *Psychology and Psychotherapy: Theory, Research and Practice,* 85: 292–309.

Barker, C. and Pistrang, N. (2005) Quality criteria under methodological pluralism: implications for conducting and evaluating research, *American Journal of Community Psychology,* 35: 201–12.

Barker, C., Pistrang, N. and Elliott, R. (2002) *Research Methods in Clinical Psychology: An Introduction for Students and Practitioners* (2nd edn). Chichester: Wiley.

Barkham, M., Margison, F., Leach, C., et al (2001) Service profiling and outcomes benchmarking using the CORE OM: Toward practice based evidence in the psychological therapies. *Journal of Consulting and Clinical Psychology,* 69: 184–196.

Barkham, M., Mellor-Clark, J., Connell, J. et al. (2006) A core approach to practice-based evidence: a brief history of the origins and applications of the CORE-OM and CORE System. *Counselling and Psychotherapy Research,* 6: 3–15.

Barkham, M., Hardy, G.E. and Mellor-Clark, J. (eds) (2010) *Developing and Delivering Practice-based Evidence: A Guide for the Psychological Therapies.* Chichester: Wiley-Blackwell.

Barkham, M., Mellor-Clark, J., Connell, J. et al. (2010) 'Clinical Outcomes in Routine Evaluation (CORE) – The CORE Measures and System: Measuring, Monitoring and Managing Quality Evaluation in the Psychological Therapies', in M. Barkham, G.E. Hardy and J. Mellor-Clark (eds), *Developing and Delivering Practice-based Evidence: A Guide for the Psychological Therapies.* Chichester: Wiley-Blackwell.

Barkham, M., Stiles, W.B., Connell, J. et al. (2012) Psychological treatment outcomes in routine NHS services: what do we mean by treatment effectiveness?, *Psychology and Psychotherapy: Theory, Research and Practice*, 85: 1–16.

Barkham, M., Stiles, W.B., Connell, J. et al. (2008) Effects of psychological therapies in randomized trials and practice-based studies, *British Journal of Clinical Psychology*, 47: 397–415.

Barrett-Lennard, G.T. (1986) 'The Relationship Inventory now: issues and advances in theory, method and use', in L.S. Greenberg and W.M. Pinsof (eds), *The Psychotherapeutic Process: A Research Handbook*. New York: Guilford Press.

Beck, A.T., Steer, R.A. and Garbin, M.G. (1988) Psychometric properties of the Beck Depression Inventory: twenty-five years of evaluation, *Clinical Psychology Review*, 8: 77–100.

Beck, A.T., Ward, C.H., Mendelson, M. et al. (1961) Inventory for measuring depression, *Archives of General Psychiatry*, 4: 561–71.

Becker, H.S. (2008) *Writing for Social Scientists: How to Start and Finish Your Thesis, Book or Article* (2nd edn). Chicago: University of Chicago Press.

Belcher, W.L. (2009) *Writing Your Journal Article in Twelve Weeks: A Guide to Academic Publishing Success*. Thousand Oaks, CA: Sage.

Bentz, V.M. and Shapiro, J.J. (1998) *Mindful Inquiry in Social Research*. Thousand Oaks: Sage.

Berg, A.L., Sandahl, C. and Clinton, D. (2008) The relationship of treatment preferences and experiences to outcome in generalized anxiety disorder (GAD), *Psychology and Psychotherapy: Theory, Research and Practice*, 81: 247–59.

Bergman, M.M. (ed.) (2008) *Advances in Mixed Methods Research*. Thousand Oaks, CA: Sage.

Biddle, L., Cooper, J., Owen-Smith, A. et al. (2013) Qualitative interviewing with vulnerable populations: individuals' experiences of participating in suicide and self-harm based research, *Journal of Affective Disorders*, 145: 356–62.

Binder, P., Moltu, C., Hummelsund, D. et al. (2011) Meeting an adult ally on the way out into the world: adolescent patients' experiences of useful psychotherapeutic ways of working at an age when independence really matters, *Psychotherapy Research*, 21: 554–66.

Binder, P.E., Holgersen, H. and Nielsen, G.H. (2009) Why did I change when I went to therapy? A qualitative analysis of former patients' conceptions of successful psychotherapy, *Counselling and Psychotherapy Research*, 9: 250–6.

Binder, P.E., Holgersen, H. and Nielsen, G.H. (2010) What is a 'good outcome' in psychotherapy? A qualitative exploration of former patients' point of view, *Psychotherapy Research*, 20: 285–94.

Bjelland, I., Dahl, A.A., Haug, T.T., et al. (2002) The validity of the Hospital Anxiety and Depression Scale: an updated literature review. *Journal of Psychosomatic Research*, 52: 69–77.

Bloch, S., Rabstein, J., Crouch, E. et al. (1979) A method for the study of therapeutic factors in group psychotherapy. *British Journal of Psychiatry*, 134: 257–63.

Bloor, M., Frankland, J., Thomas, M. et al. (2000) *Focus Groups in Social Research*. London: Sage.

Bolton, G. (2013) *The Writer's Key: Creative Solutions for Life*. London: Jessica Kingsley.

Borawski, B.M. (2007) Reflecting on adversarial growth and trauma through autoethnography, *Journal of Loss and Trauma*, 12: 101–10.

Borck, C.R. (2011) The ontology of epistemological production: cases in ethnography and psychotherapy, *Qualitative Inquiry*, 17: 404–11.

Borenstein, M., Hedges, L.V., Higgins, J.P.T. et al. (2009) *Introduction to Meta-analysis*. Oxford: Wiley-Blackwell.

Borrill, J. and Foreman, E.I. (1996) Understanding cognitive change: a qualitative study of the impact of cognitive-behavioural therapy on fear of flying, *Clinical Psychology and Psychotherapy*, 3: 62–74.

Bowens, M. and Cooper, M. (2012) Development of a client feedback tool: a qualitative study of therapists' experiences of using the Therapy Personalisation Form, *European Journal of Psychotherapy and Counselling*, 14: 47–62.

Bowling, A. (2001) Measuring Disease: A Review of Disease-Specific Quality of Life Measurement Scales. 2nd edn. Maidenhead: Open University Press.

Bowling, A. (2004) *Measuring Health: A Review of Quality of Life Scales*. 3rd edn. Maidenhead: Open University Press.

Braud, W. (1998) 'Integral inquiry: complementary ways of knowing, being and expression', in W. Braud and R. Anderson (eds), *Transpersonal Research Methods for the Social Sciences: Honoring Human Experience*. Thousand Oaks, CA: Sage.

Braud, W. and Anderson, R. (eds) (1998) *Transpersonal Research Methods for the Social Sciences: Honoring Human Experience*. Thousand Oaks, CA: Sage.

Braun, V. and Clarke, V. (2006) Using thematic analysis in psychology. *Qualitative Research in Psychology*, 3: 77–101.

Bright, F.A.S., Boland, P., Rutherford, S.J. et al. (2012) Implementing a client-centred approach in rehabilitation: an autoethnography, *Disability and Rehabilitation*, 34: 997–1004.

Britten, N., Campbell, R., Pope, C. et al. (2002) Using meta ethnography to synthesise qualitative research: a worked example, *Journal of Health Services Research and Policy*, 7: 209–15.

Brooks, C.F. (2011) Social performance and secret ritual: battling against Obsessive-Compulsive Disorder, *Qualitative Health Research*, 21: 249–61.

Buckroyd, J. (2003) Using action research to develop an assessment system in a voluntary sector counselling service, *Counselling and Psychotherapy Research*, 3: 278–84.

Buzan, T. (2009) *The Mind Map Book: Unlock Your Creativity, Boost Your Memory, Change Your Life*. London: BBC Publications.

Caccia, J. and Watson, J.P. (1987) A counselling centre and a psychiatric out-patient clinic, *Bulletin of the Royal College of Psychiatrists*, 11: 182–4.

Cahill, J., Barkham, M. and Stiles, W.B. (2010) Systematic review of practice-based research on psychological therapies in routine clinic settings, *British Journal of Clinical Psychology*, 49: 421–53.

Cahill, J., Stiles, W.B., Barkham, M. et al. (2012) Two short forms of the Agnew Relationship Measure: The ARM-5 and ARM-12. *Psychotherapy Research*, 22: 241–55.

Cahill, P., O'Reilly, K., Carr, A. et al. (2010) Validation of a 28-item version of the Systemic Clinical Outcome and Routine Evaluation in an Irish context: the SCORE-28, *Journal of Family Therapy*, 32: 210–31.

Cairns, M. (2014) Patients who come back: clinical characteristics and service outcome for patients re-referred to an IAPT service, *Counselling and Psychotherapy Research*, 14: 48–55.

Callahan, J.L. and Ditloff, M. (2007) Through a glass darkly: reflections on therapist transformations, *Professional Psychology: Research and Practice*, 38: 547–53.

Cameron, J. (1994) *The Artist's Way: A Course in Discovering and Recovering your Creative Self*. London: Souvenir.

Canter, D. and Fairbairn, G. (2006) *Becoming an Author: Advice for Academics and Other Professionals*. Maidenhead: Open University Press.

Carroll, M. and Shaw, E. (2012) *Ethical Maturity in the Helping Professions: Making Difficult Life and Work Decisions*. Melbourne: PsychOz.

Carstensen, L.L., Turan, B., Scheibe, S. et al. (2011) Emotional experience improves with age: evidence based on over 10 years of experience sampling, *Psychology and Aging*, 26: 21–33.

Caulley, D.N. (2008) Making qualitative reports less boring: the techniques of writing creative nonfiction, *Qualitative Inquiry*, 14: 424–49.

Chadwick, P., Kaur, H., Swelam, M. et al. (2011) Experience of mindfulness in people with bipolar disorder: a qualitative study, *Psychotherapy Research*, 21: 277–85.

Chang, D.F. and Berk, A. (2009) Making cross-racial therapy work: a phenomenological study of clients' experiences of cross-racial therapy, *Journal of Counseling Psychology*, 56: 521–36.

Chang, D.F. and Yoon, P. (2011) Ethnic minority clients' perceptions of the significance of race in cross-racial therapy relationships, *Psychotherapy Research*, 21: 567–82.

Chapman, S. and Schwartz, J.P. (2012) Rejecting the null: research and social justice means asking different questions, *Counseling and Values*, 57: 24–30.

Charmaz, K. (2013) *Constructing Grounded Theory* (2nd edn). Thousand Oaks, CA: Sage.

Cheyne, A. and Kinn, S. (2001a) A pilot study for a randomised controlled trial of the use of the schedule for the evaluation of individual quality of life (SEIQoL) in an alcohol counselling setting. *Addiction Research and Theory*, 9(2): 165–78.

Cheyne, A. and Kinn, S. (2001b) Counsellors' perspectives on the use of the Schedule for the Evaluation of Individual Quality of Life (SEIQoL) in an alcohol counselling setting, *British Journal of Guidance and Counselling*, 29(1): 35–46.

Choudhuri, D., Glauser, A. and Peregoy, J. (2004) Guidelines for writing a qualitative manuscript for the *Journal of Counseling & Development*, *Journal of Counseling and Development*, 82: 443–6.

Christensen, H., Calear, A., Van Spijker, B. et al. (2014) Psychosocial interventions for suicidal ideation, plans, and attempts: a database of randomised controlled trials, *BMC Psychiatry*, doi:10.1186/1471-244X-14-86

Christopher, J.C., Chrisman, J.A., Trotter-Mathison, M.J. et al. (2011) Perceptions of the long-term influence of mindfulness training on counselors and psychotherapists: a qualitative inquiry, *Journal of Humanistic Psychology*, 51: 318–49.

Chui, H.T., Jackson, J.L., Liu, J. et al. (2012) 'Annotated bibliography of studies using Consensual Qualitative Research', in C.E. Hill (ed.), *Consensual Qualitative Research: A Practical Resource for Investigating Social Science Phenomena*. Washington, DC: American Psychological Association.

Clark, D.M., Fairburn, C.G. and Wessely, S. (2008) Psychological treatment outcomes in routine NHS services: a commentary on Stiles et al. (2007) *Psychological Medicine*, 28: 629–34.

Clark, L.A. and Watson, D. (1995) Constructing validity: basic issues in objective scale development, *Psychological Assessment*, 7: 301–19.

Clarke, H., Rees, A. and Hardy, G.E. (2004) The big idea: clients' perspectives of change processes in cognitive therapy, *Psychology and Psychotherapy: Theory, Research and Practice*, 77: 67–89.

Clement, P.W. (1994) Quantitative evaluation of 26 years of private practice, *Professional Psychology: Research and Practice*, 25: 173–6.

Clement, P.W. (2007) Story of 'Hope': successful treatment of Obsessive Compulsive Disorder, *Pragmatic Case Studies in Psychotherapy*, 3(4): 1–36.

Cohen, J. (1960) A coefficient of agreement for nominal scales, *Educational and Psychological Measurement*, 20: 37–46.

Cohen, L.H., Sargent, M.H. and Sechrest, L.B. (1986) Use of psychotherapy research by professional psychologists, *American Psychologist*, 41: 198–206.

Cohen, S., Kamarck, T. and Mermelstein, R. (1983) A global measure of perceived stress. *Journal of Health and Social Behavior*, 24: 386–96.

Collins, J., Gibson, A., Parkin, S. et al. (2012) Counselling in the workplace: how time-limited counselling can effect change in well-being, *Counselling and Psychotherapy Research*, 12: 84–92.

Comas-Dias, L. (2010) On being a Latina healer: voice, consciousness, and identity, *Psychotherapy Theory, Research, Practice, Training*, 47: 162–8.

Comtois, K.A. and Linehan, M.M. (2006) Psychosocial treatments of suicidal behaviors: A practice-friendly review. *Journal of Clinical Psychology*, 62: 161–70.

Cone, J.D. (2001) *Evaluating Outcomes: Empirical Tools for Effective Practice*. Washington, DC: American Psychological Association.

Connell, J., Barkham, M., Cahill, J. et al. (2009) *A Systematic Scoping Review of the Research on Counselling in Higher Education (HE) and Further Education (FE)*. Lutterworth: British Association for Counselling and Psychotherapy.

Connell, J., Barkham, M., Stiles, W.B. et al. (2007) Distribution of CORE-OM scores in a general population, clinical cut-off points, and comparison with the CIS-R, *British Journal of Psychiatry*, 190: 69–74.

Connell, J., Grant, S. and Mullin, T. (2006) Client initiated termination of therapy at NHS primary care counselling services, *Counselling and Psychotherapy Research*, 6: 60–7.

Connolly, M.B., Crits-Christoph, P., Shappell, S. et al. (1999) The reliability and validity of a measure of self-understanding of interpersonal patterns. *Journal of Counseling Psychology*, 46: 472–82.

Cooper, C.L. and Sadri, G. (1991) The impact of stress counselling at work, *Journal of Behavior and Personality*, 6: 411–23.

Cooper, H. (2010) *Reporting Research in Psychology: How to Meet Journal Article Reporting Standards*. Washington, DC: American Psychological Association.

Cooper, M. (2005) Therapists' experiences of relational depth: a qualitative interview study, *Counselling and Psychotherapy Research*, 5: 87–95.

Cooper, M. (2008) Essential Research Findings in Counselling and Psychotherapy: The Facts are Friendly. London: Sage.

Cooper, M., Stewart, D., Sparks, J. at al. (2013) School-based counseling using systematic feedback: a cohort study evaluating outcomes and predictors of change, *Psychotherapy Research*, 23: 474–88.

Cornelius III, E.T. (1983) The use of protective techniques in personnel selection, in K. Rowland and G. Ferris (eds), *Research and Human Resources Management*: Vol. 1. London: JAI Press.

Cornforth, S. (2011) 'Ethics for research and publication', in K. Crockett, M. Agee and S. Cornforth (eds), *Ethics in Practice: A Guide for Counsellors*. Wellington, NZ: Dunmore.

Cronbach, L. (1997) *Essentials of Psychological Testing* (5th edn). New York: Pearson.

Csikszentmihalyi, M. and Larson, R. (1987) Validity and reliability of the Experience Sampling Method, *Journal of Nervous and Mental Disease*, 175: 526–36.

Cumming, G. (2014) The new statistics: why and how, *Psychological Science*, 25: 7–29.

Curtis, R.C. (2011) Speaking freely: my experiences in individual psychotherapies, group therapies, and growth groups, *Journal of Clinical Psychology*, 67: 794–805.

Cushman, P. (1990) Why the self is empty: toward a historically-situated psychology, *American Psychologist*, 45: 599–611.

Cushman, P. (1992) 'Psychotherapy to 1992: a historically situated interpretation', in D.K. Freedheim (ed.), *History of Psychotherapy: a Century of Change*. Washington, DC: American Psychological Association.

Cushman, P. (1995) *Constructing the Self, Constructing America: A Cultural History of Psychotherapy.* Reading, MA: Addison-Wesley.

Danchev, D. and Ross, A. (2014) *Research Ethics for Counsellors, Nurses and Social Workers.* London: Sage.

Daniel, T. and McLeod, J. (2006) Weighing up the evidence: a qualitative analysis of how person-centred counsellors evaluate the effectiveness of their practice, *Counselling and Psychotherapy Research*, 6: 244–9.

Davidsen, A.S. (2009) How does the general practitioner understand the patient? A qualitative study about psychological interventions in general practice, *Psychology and Psychotherapy: Theory, Research and Practice*, 82: 199–217.

Davidson, C.V. and Davidson, R.H. (1983) 'The significant other as data source and data problem in psychotherapy outcome research', in M.J. Lambert, E.R. Christensen and S.S. DeJulio (eds), *The Assessment of Psychotherapy Outcome*. New York: Wiley.

Davidson, L., Stayner, D.A., Lambert, S. et al. (2001) 'Phenomenological and participatory research on schizophrenia: recovering the person in theory and practice', in D.L. Tolman and M. Brydon-Miller (eds), *From Subjects to Subjectivities: A Handbook of Interpretive and Participatory Methods*. New York: New York Universities Press.

Davis, J.H. (2003) 'Balancing the whole: portraiture as methodology', in P.M. Camic, J.E. Rhodes and L. Yardley (eds), *Qualitative Research in Psychology: Expanding Perspectives in Methodology and Design*. Washington, DC: American Psychological Association.

Deane, F.P., Spicer, J. and Todd, D.M. (1997) Validity of a simplified target complaints measure, *Assessment*, 4: 119–30.

Deeks, J.J., Dinnes, J., D'Amico, R. et al. (2003) Evaluating non-randomised intervention studies, *Health Technology Assessment*, 7 (27). Available at www.hta.nhsweb.nhs.uk/fullmono/mon727.pdf

Delamont, S. (2009) The only honest thing: autoethnography, reflexivity and small crises in fieldwork, *Ethnography and Education*, 4: 51–63.

Delgadillo, J., McMillan, D., Leach, C. et al. (2014) Benchmarking routine psychological services: a discussion of challenges and methods, *Behavioural and Cognitive Psychotherapy, Benchmarking Routine Psychological Services: A Discussion of Challenges and Methods*, 42: 16–30.

Denzin, N. and Lincoln, Y. (eds) (2005) *The SAGE Handbook of Qualitative Research* (3rd edn). Thousand Oaks, CA: Sage.

Derogatis, L.R. and Melisaratos, N. (1983) The Brief Symptom Inventory: an introductory report, *Psychological Medicine*, 13: 595–605.

DeVellis, R.F. (2011) *Scale Development: Theory and Applications* (3rd edn). Thousand Oaks, CA: Sage.

DiGiorgio, K.E., Arnkoff, D.B., Glass, C.R. et al. (2004) EMDR and theoretical orientation: a qualitative study of how therapists integrate Eye Movement Desensitization and Reprocessing into their approach to psychotherapy, *Journal of Psychotherapy Integration*, 14: 227–52.

Douglass, B.G. and Moustakas, C. (1985) Heuristic inquiry: the internal search to know, *Journal of Humanistic Psychology*, 25: 39–55.

Downs, S.H. and Black, N. (1998) The feasibility of creating a checklist for the assessment of the methodological quality both of randomised, and non-randomised, studies of health care interventions, *Journal of Epidemiology and Community Health*, 52: 377–84.

Dryden, W. and Spurling, L. (eds) (1989) *On Becoming a Psychotherapist*. London: Tavistock/Routledge.

Duckworth, J.C. (1990) 'The Minnesota Multiphasic Personality Inventory', in C.E. Watkins Jr., and V.L. Campbell (eds), *Testing in Counseling Practice*. Hillsdale, NJ: Lawrence Erlbaum.

Duffy, R.D., Torrey, C.L., Bott, E.M. et al. (2013) Time management, passion, and collaboration: a qualitative study of highly research productive counseling psychologists, *Counseling Psychologist*, 41: 881–917.

Duncan, B.L., Miller, S.D., Sparks, J.A. et al. (2003) The Session Rating Scale: preliminary psychometric properties of a "working" alliance measure. *Journal of Brief Therapy*, 3: 3–12.

Durham, R.C., Chambers, J.A., MacDonald, R.R. et al. (2003) Does cognitive-behavioural therapy influence the long-term outcome of generalized anxiety disorder? An 8–14 year follow-up of two clinical trials, *Psychological Medicine*, 33: 499–509.

Edwards, A.L. (1957) *The Social Desirability Variable in Personality Research*. New York: Dryden.

Elliott, R. (1984) 'A discovery-oriented approach to significant change events in psychotherapy: Interpersonal Process Recall and Comprehensive Process Analysis', in L.N. Rice and L.S. Greenberg (eds), *Patterns of Change: Intensive Analysis of Psychotherapy Process*. New York: Guilford.

Elliott, R. (1986) 'Interpersonal Process Recall (IPR) as a psychotherapy process research method', in L.S. Greenberg and W.M. Pinsof (eds), *The Psychotherapeutic Process: A Research Handbook*. New York: Guilford.

Elliott, R. (2002) Hermeneutic Single Case Efficacy Design, *Psychotherapy Research*, 12: 1–23.

Elliott, R., Fischer, C.T. and Rennie, D.L. (1999) Evolving guidelines for the publication of qualitative research studies in psychology and related fields, *British Journal of Clinical Psychology*, 38: 215–29.

Elliott, R., Slatick, E. and Urman, M. (2001) Qualitative change process research on psychotherapy: alternative strategies. *Psychologische Beiträge*, 43: 111–125.

Elliott, R., Partyka, R., Wagner, J. et al. (2009) An adjudicated Hermeneutic Single Case Efficacy Design study of experiential therapy for panic/phobia, *Psychotherapy Research*, 19: 543–57.

Elliott, R., Shapiro, D.A. and Mack, C. (1999) Simplified Personal Questionnaire procedure. Toledo, OH: University of Toledo, Department of Psychology.

Ellis, C. (2004) The ethnographic I: *a methodological novel about autoethnography*. Walnut Creek, CA: Altamira Press.

Ellis, C. (2007) Telling secrets, revealing lives: relational ethics in research with intimate others, *Qualitative Inquiry*, 13: 3–29.

Ellis, P.D. (2010) *The Essential Guide to Effect Sizes: Statistical Power, Meta-analysis, and the Interpretation of Research Results*. Cambridge: Cambridge University Press.

Elvish, R., Lever, S., Johnstone, J. et al. (2012) Psychological interventions for carers of people with dementia: a systematic review of quantitative and qualitative evidence. Lutterworth: British Association for Counselling and Psychotherapy.

Ely, M., Vinz, R., Downing, M. et al. (1997) *On Writing Qualitative Research: Living by Words*. London: Falmer.

Erford, B.T., Savin-Murphy, J.A. and Butler, C. (2010) Conducting a meta-analysis of counseling outcome research: twelve steps and practical procedures, *Counseling Outcome Research and Evaluation*, 1: 19–43.

Etherington, K. (2000) *Narrative Approaches to Working with Adult Male Survivors of Child Sexual Abuse: The Clients', the Counsellors' and the Researchers' Story*. London: Jessica Kingsley.

Etherington, K. (2002) Working together: editing a book as narrative research methodology, *Counselling and Psychotherapy Research*, 2: 167–76.

Etherington, K. (2004a) *Becoming a Reflexive Researcher: Using Our Selves in Research*. London: Jessica Kingsley.

Etherington, K. (2004b) Heuristic research as a vehicle for personal and professional development, *Counselling and Psychotherapy Research*, 4: 48–63.

Etherington, K. (2007) Ethical research in reflexive relationships, *Qualitative Inquiry*, 13: 599–616.

Evans, C., Mellor-Clark, J., Margison, F. et al (2000) CORE: Clinical Outcomes in Routine Evaluation. *Journal of Mental Health*, 9: 247–55.

Fairburn, C.G., Cooper, Z., Doll, H.A. et al. (2000) The natural course of bulimia nervosa and binge eating disorder in young women, *Archives of General Psychiatry*, 57: 659–65.

Fenner, P. (2011) Place, matter and meaning: extending the relationship in psychological therapies, *Health and Place*, 17: 851–7.

Fetherston, B. (2002) Double bind: an essay on counselling training, *Counselling and Psychotherapy Research*, 2: 108–25.

Field, A. (2013) *Discovering Statistics Using IBM SPSS Statistics* (4th edn). London: Sage.

Finlay, L. (2011) *Phenomenology for Therapists: Researching the Lived World*. Oxford: Wiley-Blackwell.

Fischer, C.T. (2009) Bracketing in qualitative research: conceptual and practical matters, *Psychotherapy Research*, 19: 583–90.

Fischer, C.T. (ed.) (2006) *Qualitative Research Methods for Psychologists: Introduction through Empirical Examples*. New York: Academic.

Fishman, D.B. (1999) *The Case for a Pragmatic Psychology*. New York: New York Universities Press.

Fitzpatrick, L., Simpson, J. and Smith, A. (2010) A qualitative analysis of mindfulness-based cognitive therapy (MBCT) in Parkinson's disease, *Psychology and Psychotherapy: Theory, Research and Practice*, 83: 179–92.

Flick, U. (2011) *Introducing Research Methodology: A Beginner's Guide to Doing a Research Project*. London: Sage.

Flory, J. and Emanuel, E. (2004) Interventions to improve research participants' understanding in informed consent for research: A systematic review, *Journal of the American Medical Association*, 292: 1593–601.

Fluckiger, C. and Holtforth, M.G. (2008) Focusing the therapist's attention on the patient's strengths: a preliminary study to foster a mechanism of change in outpatient psychotherapy, *Journal of Clinical Psychology*, 64: 876–90.

Flyvbjerg, B. (2001) *Making Social Science Matter: Why Social Inquiry Fails and How it can Succeed Again*. New York: Cambridge University Press.

Flyvbjerg, B. (2006) Five misunderstandings about case-study research, *Qualitative Inquiry*, 12: 219–45.

Frank, J.D. (1973) *Persuasion and Healing: A Comparative Study of Psychotherapy*. Baltimore: Johns Hopkins University Press.

Freeman, A. (2011) Manny's legacy: paying forward my personal therapy, *Journal of Clinical Psychology*, 67: 789–93.

Gabriel, L. (2009) 'Exploring the researcher-contributor research alliance', in L. Gabriel and R. Casemore (eds), *Relational Ethics in Practice: Narratives from Counselling and Psychotherapy*. London: Routledge.

Gabriel, L. and Casemore, R. (eds) (2009) *Relational Ethics in Practice: Narratives from Counselling and Psychotherapy*. London: Routledge.

Geller, J.D., Norcross, J.C. and Orlinsky, D.E. (eds) (2005) *The Psychotherapist's Own Psychotherapy: Patient and Clinician Perspectives*. New York: Oxford University Press.

Geller, S., Greenberg, L.S. and Watson, J.C. (2010) Therapist and client perceptions of therapeutic presence: the development of a measure, *Psychotherapy Research*, 20: 599–610.

Gelso, C.J., Baumann, E.C., Chui, H.T. et al. (2013) The making of a scientist–psychotherapist: the research training environment and the psychotherapist, *Psychotherapy*, 50: 139–49.

Gergen, K. (1997) Who speaks and who replies in human science scholarship? *History of the Human Sciences*, 10: 151–173.

Geschwind, N., Peeters, F., Drukker, M. et al. (2011) Mindfulness training increases momentary positive emotions and reward experience in adults vulnerable to depression: a Randomized Controlled Trial, *Journal of Consulting and Clinical Psychology*, 79: 618–28.

Gibbard, I. and Hanley, T. (2008) A five-year evaluation of the effectiveness of person-centred counselling in routine clinical practice in primary care. *Counselling and Psychotherapy Research*, 8: 215–22.

Gilbert, N., Barkham, M., Richards, A. et al. (2005) The effectiveness of a primary care mental health service delivering brief psychological interventions: a benchmarking study using the CORE system, *Primary Care Mental Health*, 3: 241–51.

Glaser, B.G. and Strauss, A. (1967) *The Discovery of Grounded Theory*. Chicago, IL: Aldine.

Glasman, D., Finlay, W.M.L. and Brock, D. (2004) Becoming a self-therapist: using cognitive-behavioural therapy for recurrent depression and/or dysthymia after completing therapy, *Psychology and Psychotherapy: Theory, Research and Practice*, 77: 335–51.

Goddard, A., Murray, C.D. and Simpson, J. (2008) Informed consent and psychotherapy: an interpretative phenomenological analysis of therapists' views, *Psychology and Psychotherapy: Theory, Research and Practice*, 81: 177–91.

Goldberg, D. and Williams, P. (1988) *A User's Guide to the General Health Questionnaire*. Slough: NFER-Nelson.

Goldberg, D.P. and Hillier, V.F. (1979) A scaled version of the General Health Questionnaire, *Psychological Medicine*, 9: 139–45.

Golden-Biddle, K. and Locke, K. (2006) *Composing Qualitative Research* (2nd edn). Thousand Oaks, CA: Sage.

Gomm, R., Needham, G. and Bullman, A. (eds) (2000) *Evaluating Research in Health and Social Care: A Reader*. London: Sage.

Gonçalves, M., Ribeiro, A.P., Mendes, I. et al. (2011) Tracking novelties in psychotherapy process research: the innovative moments coding system, *Psychotherapy Research*, 21: 497–509.

Gostas, M.W., Wiberg, B., Neander, K. et al. (2013) 'Hard work' in a new context: clients' experiences of psychotherapy, *Qualitative Social Work*, 12: 340–57.

Gottfredson, S.D. (1978) Evaluating psychological research reports: dimensions, reliability, and correlates of quality judgments, *American Psychologist*, 33: 920–34.

Gough, D., Oliver, S. and Thomas, J. (eds) (2012) *An Introduction to Systematic Reviews*. London: Sage.

Greenbaum, T.L. (1998) *The Handbook for Focus Group Research* (2nd edn). Thousand Oaks, CA: Sage.

Greenberg, L.S. and Pascual-Leone, A. (2006) Emotion in psychotherapy: a practice-friendly research review. *Journal of Clinical Psychology*, 62: 611–30.

Greenberg, L.S. and Pinsof, W.M. (eds) (1986) *The Psychotherapeutic Process: A Research Handbook*. New York: Guilford Press.

Greenhalgh, T., Robert, G., Macfarlane, F. et al. (2005) Storylines of research in diffusion of innovation: a meta-narrative approach to systematic review, *Social Science and Medicine*, 61: 417–30.

Guiffrida, D.A., Douthit, K.Z., Lynch, M.F. et al. (2011) Publishing action research in counseling journals, *Journal of Counseling and Development*, 89: 282–7.

Guillemin, M. and Gillam, L. (2004) Ethics, reflexivity and 'ethically important moments' in research, *Qualitative Inquiry*, 10: 261–80.

Haldeman, D.C. (2010) Reflections of a gay male psychotherapist, *Psychotherapy Theory, Research, Practice, Training*, 47: 177–85.

Halling, S., Leifer, M. and Rowe, J.O. (2006) 'Emergence of the dialogal approach: forgiving another', in C.T. Fischer (ed.), *Qualitative Research Methods for Psychologists: Introduction through Empirical Examples*. New York: Academic.

Hamill, M., Reid, M. and Reynolds, S. (2008) Letters in cognitive analytic therapy: the patient's experience, *Psychotherapy Research*, 18: 573–83.

Hanley, T. and Cutts, L. (2013) What is a systematic review? *Counselling Psychology Review*, 28: 3–6.

Hanson, J. (2005) Should your lips be zipped? How therapist self-disclosure and non-disclosure affects clients, *Counselling and Psychotherapy Research*, 5: 96–104.

Hanson, W.E., Creswell, J.W., Plano-Clark, V.L. et al. (2005) Mixed methods research designs in counseling psychology. *Journal of Counseling Psychology*, 52: 224–35.

Hartley, J. (2008) *Academic Writing and Publishing: A Practical Handbook*. London: Routledge.

Hatcher, R.L. and Gillaspy, J.A. (2006) Development and validation of a revised short form of the Working Alliance Inventory, *Psychotherapy Research*, 16: 12–25.

Haverkamp, B.E. (2005) Ethical perspectives on qualitative research in applied psychology, *Journal of Counseling Psychology*, 52: 146–55.

Hill, C.E. (ed.) (2012) *Consensual Qualitative Research: A Practical Resource for Investigating Social Science Phenomena*. Washington, DC: American Psychological Association.

Hill, C.E., Knox, S. and Hess, S.A. (2012) 'Qualitative meta-analyses of consensual qualitative research studies', in C.E. Hill (ed.), *Consensual Qualitative Research: A Practical Resource for Investigating Social Science Phenomena*. Washington, DC: American Psychological Association.

Hill, C.E., Sim, W.E., Spangler, P. et al. (2008) Therapist immediacy in brief psychotherapy: Case Study 2, *Psychotherapy: Theory, Research, Practice and Training*, 45: 298–315.

Hodge, S., Barr, W., Bowen, L. et al. (2012) Exploring the role of an emotional support and counselling service for people with visual impairments, *British Journal of Visual Impairment*, 31: 5–19.

Holliday, A. (2002) *Doing and Writing Qualitative Research*. London: Sage.

Holmqvist, R., Philips, B. and Barkham, M. (forthcoming) Developing practice-based evidence: Benefits, challenges, and tensions. *Psychotherapy Research*.

Horowitz, L.M., Turan, B., Wilson, K.R. et al. (2008) 'Interpersonal theory and the measurement of interpersonal constructs', in G.J. Boyle, G. Matthews and D.H. Saklofske (eds), *Sage Handbook of Personality Theory and Assessment: Vol. 2. Personality Measurement and Testing*. London: Sage.

Howard, G.S. (1983) Toward methodological pluralism, *Journal of Counseling Psychology*, 30: 19–21.

Howard, G.S. (1985) The role of values in the science of psychology. *American Psychologist*, 40: 255–65.

Hunt, C. (2000) *Therapeutic Dimensions of Autobiography in Creative Writing*. London: Jessica Kingsley.

Innerhofer, B. (2013) The relationship between children's outcomes in counselling and psychotherapy and attachment styles. *Counselling Psychology Review*, 28: 6–76.

Iwi, D.J., Watson, P., Barber, N. et al. (1998) The self-reported well-being of employees facing organisational change: effects of an intervention, *Occupational Medicine*, 48(6): 361–9.

Jackson, J.L., Chui, H.T. and Hill, C.E. (2012) The Modification of Consensual Qualitative Research for Case Study Research: An Introduction to CQR-C', in C.E. Hill (ed.), *Consensual Qualitative Research: A Practical Resource for Investigating Social Science Phenomena*. Washington, DC: American Psychological Association.

Jennings, L. and Skovholt, T.M. (1999) The cognitive, emotional and relational characteristics of master therapists, *Journal of Counseling Psychology*, 48: 3–11.

Jokela, M., Singh-Manoux, A., Shipley, M. J. et al. (2011) Natural course of recurrent psychological distress in adulthood, *Journal of Affective Disorders*, 130: 454–61.

Josselson, R. (1996) 'On writing other people's lives, self-analytic reflections of a narrative researcher', in R. Josselson (ed.), *Ethics and Process in the Narrative Study of Lives*. Thousand Oaks, CA: Sage.

Josselson, R. (2013) *Interviewing for Qualitative Inquiry: A Relational Approach*. New York: Guilford.

Karakurt, G., Dial, S., Korkow, H. et al. (2013) Experiences of marriage and family therapists working with intimate partner violence. *Journal of Family Psychotherapy*, 24: 1–16.

Kasper, L.B., Hill, C.E. and Kivlighan, D.E. (2008) Therapist immediacy in brief psychotherapy: Case Study 1, *Psychotherapy: Theory, Research, Practice and Training*, 45: 281–97.

Kerr, C.E., Josyula, K. and Littenberg, R. (2011) Developing an observing attitude: an analysis of meditation diaries in an MBSR clinical trial, *Clinical Psychology and Psychotherapy*, 18: 80–93.

Kidd, J.D. and Finlayson, M.P. (2010) Mental illness in the nursing workplace: a collective autoethnography, *Contemporary Nurse*, 36: 21–33.

King, A. (2011) When the body speaks: tummy rumblings in the therapeutic encounter. *British Journal of Psychotherapy*, 27: 156–74.

King, M., Semylen, J., Killaspy, H. et al. (2007) *A Systematic Review of Research on Counselling and Psychotherapy for Lesbian, Gay, Bisexual and Transgender People*. Lutterworth: British Association for Counselling and Psychotherapy.

Kitchner, K.S (1984) Intuition, critical evaluation and ethical principles: the foundation for ethical decisions in counseling psychology. *Counseling Psychologist*, 12: 43–55.

Klein, M.H., Mathieu-Coughlan, P. and Kiesler, D.J. (1986) 'The Experiencing Scales', in L.S. Greenberg and W.M. Pinsof (eds), *The Psychotherapeutic Process: A Research Handbook*. New York: Guilford.

Klein, M.H., Mathieu, P.L., Gendlin, E.T. et al. (1969) *The Experiencing Scale: A Research and Training Manual, Vol. 1*. Madison: University of Wisconsin Bureau of Audiovisual Instruction.

Knox, R. (2008) Clients' experiences of relational depth in person-centred counselling, *Counselling and Psychotherapy Research*, 8: 118–24.

Knox, S., Adrians, N., Everson, E. et al. (2011) Clients' perspectives on therapy termination, *Psychotherapy Research*, 21: 154–67.

Knox, S., Goldberg, J.L., Woodhouse, S.S. et al. (1999) Clients' internal representations of their therapists, *Journal of Counseling Psychology*, 46: 244–56.

Knox, S., Hess, S.A., Petersen, D.A. et al. (1997) A qualitative analysis of client perceptions of the effects of helpful therapist self-disclosure in long-term therapy, *Journal of Counseling Psychology*, 44: 274–83.

Knox, S. and Hill, C.E. (2003) Therapist self-disclosure: research-based suggestions for practitioners. *Journal of Clinical Psychology*, 59: 529–39.

Knox, S., DuBois, R., Smith, J. et al. (2009) Clients' experiences giving gifts to therapists. *Psychotherapy: Theory, Research, Practice, Training*, 46: 350–361.

Knox, S., Schlosser, L.Z. et al. (2012) 'Writing the manuscript', in C.E. Hill (ed.), *Consensual Qualitative Research: A Practical Resource for Investigating Social Science Phenomena*. Washington, DC: American Psychological Association.

Kottler, J. and Carlson, J. (2005) *The Client Who Changed Me: Stories of Therapist Personal Transformation*. New York: Routledge.

Kraus, D. and Castonguay, L.G. (2010) 'Treatment Outcome Package (TOP) – Development and use in naturalistic settings', in M. Barkham, G.E. Hardy and J. Mellor-Clark (eds), *Developing and Delivering Practice-based Evidence: A Guide for the Psychological Therapies*. Chichester: Wiley-Blackwell.

Kraus, D.R., Castonguay, L., Boswell, J.F. et al. (2011) Therapist effectiveness: Implications for accountability and patient care. *Psychotherapy Research*, 21: 267–76.

Kroenke, K., Spitzer, R.L. and Williams, J.B. (2001) The PHQ-9: validity of a brief depression severity measure. *Journal of General Internal Medicine*, 16: 606–13.

Krueger, R.A. and Casey, M.A. (2008) *Focus Groups: A Practical Guide for Applied Research* (4th edn). Thousand Oaks, CA: Sage.

Kuhnlein, I. (1999) Psychotherapy as a process of transformation: the analysis of postthera-peutic autobiographical narrations, *Psychotherapy Research*, 9: 274–88.

Kvale, S. and Brinkmann, S. (2009) *InterViews: Learning the Craft of Qualitative Research Interviewing*. Thousand Oaks, CA: Sage.

Lambert, M.J. (2007) What we have learned from a decade of research aimed at improving psychotherapy outcome in routine care, *Psychotherapy Research*, 17: 1–14.

Lambert, M.J. (2010) 'Yes, it is time for clinicians to routinely monitor treatment outcome', in B.L. Duncan, S.D. Miller, B.E.Wampold and M.A. Hubble (eds), *The Heart and Soul of Change: Delivering What Works in Therapy* (2nd edn). Washington, DC: American Psychological Association.

Lambert, M.J. and Finch, A.E. (1999) 'Outcome Questionnaire', in M.E. Maruish (ed.), *The Use of Psychological Testing for Treatment Planning and Outcome Assessment* (2nd edn). Mahwah, NJ: Lawrence Erlbaum.

Lambert, M.J., Hansen, N.B. and Harmon, S.C. (2010) 'Outcome Questionnaire System (The OQ System): development and practical applications in healthcare settings', in M. Barkham, G.E. Hardy and J. Mellor-Clark (eds), *Developing and Delivering Practice-based Evidence: A Guide for the Psychological Therapies*. Chichester: Wiley-Blackwell.

Larsen, D., Flesaker, K. and Stege, R. (2008) Qualitative interviewing using Interpersonal Process Recall: investigating internal experiences during professional-client conversation, *International Journal of Qualitative Methods*, 7: 18–37.

Leach, C. and Lutz, W. (2010) 'Constructing and disseminating outcome data at the service level: case tracking and benchmarking', in M. Barkham, G.E. Hardy and J. Mellor-Clark (eds), *Developing and Delivering Practice-based Evidence: A Guide for the Psychological Therapies*. Chichester: Wiley-Blackwell.

Leech, N.L., Onwuegbuzie, A.J. and O'Conner, R. (2011) Assessing internal consistency in counseling research. *Counseling Outcome Research and Evaluation*, 2: 115–25.

Lees, J. (2001) Reflexive action research: Developing knowledge through practice. *Counselling and Psychotherapy Research*, 1: 132–8.

Leitch, R. (2006) Outside the spoon drawer, naked and skinless in search of my professional esteem: the tale of an 'academic pro', *Qualitative Inquiry*, 12: 353–64.

Lepper, G. and Riding, N. (2006) *Researching the psychotherapy process: a practical guide to transcript-based methods*. Basingstoke: Palgrave Macmillan.

Levitt, H.M., Butler, M. and Hill, T. (2006) What clients find helpful in psychotherapy: developing principles for facilitating moment-to-moment change, *Journal of Counseling Psychology*, 53: 314–24.

Levy, R.A. and Ablon, J.S. (eds) (2009) *Handbook of Evidence-Based Psychodynamic Psychotherapy: Bridging the Gap Between Science and Practice.* New York: Humana.

Levy, R.A., Ablon, J.S. and Kächele, H. (eds) (2012) *Psychodynamic Psychotherapy Research: Evidence-Based Practice and Practice-Based Evidence.* New York: Humana.

Liamputtong, P. (2007) *Researching the Vulnerable: A Guide to Sensitive Research Methods.* London: Sage.

Liddle, B.J. (1996) Therapist sexual orientation, gender, and counseling practices as they relate to ratings of helpfulness by gay and lesbian clients, *Journal of Counseling Psychology,* 43(4): 394–401.

Liddle, B.J. (1997) Gay and lesbian clients' selection of therapists and utilization of therapy, *Psychotherapy,* 34: 11–18.

Lietaer, G. (1992) 'Helping and hindering processes in client-centered/experiential psychotherapy: a content analysis of client and therapist postsession perceptions', in S.G. Toukmanian and D.L. Rennie (eds), *Psychotherapy Process Research: Paradigmatic and Narrative Approaches.* London: Sage.

Lilienfeld, S.O., Wood, J.M. and Howard, N. (2000) The scientific status of projective techniques, *Psychological Science in the Public Interest,* 1: 27–66.

Lilliengren, P. and Werbart, A. (2005) A model of therapeutic action grounded in the patients' view of curative and hindering factors in psychoanalytic psychotherapy, *Psychotherapy: Theory, Research, Practice, Training,* 3: 324–99.

Lindgren, A., Werbart, A. and Philips, B. (2010) Long-term outcome and post-treatment effects of psychoanalytic psychotherapy with young adults, *Psychology and Psychotherapy: Theory, Research and Practice,* 83: 27–43.

Llewelyn, S. (1988) Psychological therapy as viewed by clients and therapists, *British Journal of Clinical Psychology,* 27: 223–38.

Llewelyn, S.P., Elliott, R., Shapiro, D.A. et al. (1988) Client perceptions of significant events in prescriptive and exploratory periods of individual therapy, *British Journal of Clinical Psychology,* 27: 105–14.

Logan, D.E. and Marlatt, G.A. (2010) Harm reduction therapy: A practice-friendly review of research. *Journal of Clinical Psychology,* 66: 201–14.

Lott, D.A. (1999) *In Session: The Bond between Women and their Therapists.* New York: W.H. Freeman.

Luborsky, L., Diguer, L., Seligman, D.A. et al. (1999) The researcher's own therapy allegiances: a 'wild card' in comparisons of treatment efficacy, *Clinical Psychology: Science and Practice,* 6: 95–106.

Lueger, R.J. and Barkham, M. (2010) 'Using benchmarks and benchmarking to improve quality of practice and services', in M. Barkham, G.E. Hardy and J. Mellor-Clark (eds), *Developing and Delivering Practice-based Evidence: A Guide for the Psychological Therapies.* Chichester: Wiley-Blackwell.

Lundahl, B. and Burke, B.L. (2009) The effectiveness and applicability of motivational interviewing: a practice-friendly review of four meta-analyses. *Journal of Clinical Psychology,* 65: 1232–45.

Lupton, E. (2011) *Graphic Design Thinking: Beyond Brainstorming.* New Jersey: Princeton Architectural Press.

Macaskill, N. and Macaskill, A. (1992) Psychotherapists-in-training evaluate their personal therapy: results of a UK survey, *British Journal of Psychotherapy,* 9: 133–8.

MacCormack, T., Simonian, J., Lim, J. et al. (2001) 'Someone who cares': a qualitative investigation of cancer patients' experiences of psychotherapy, *Psycho-Oncology,* 10: 52–65.

Macdonald, S., Lothian, S. and Wells, S. (1997) Evaluation of an employee assistance program at a transportation company, *Evaluation and Program Planning*, 20(4): 495–505.

Macdonald, W., Mead, N., Bower, P. et al. (2007) A qualitative study of patients' perceptions of a 'minimal' psychological therapy, *International Journal of Social Psychiatry*, 53: 23–33.

Mackrill, T. (2007) Using a cross-contextual qualitative diary design to explore client experiences of psychotherapy. *Counselling and Psychotherapy Research*, 7: 233–9.

Mackrill, T. (2008) Solicited diary studies of psychotherapeutic practice – pros and cons. *European Journal of Psychotherapy and Counselling*, 10: 5–18.

Mackrill, T., Elklit, A. and Lindgaard, H. (2012) Treatment-seeking young adults from families with alcohol problems: what have they been through? What state are they in?, *Counselling and Psychotherapy Research*, 12: 276–86.

Mains, J.A. and Scogin, F.R. (2003) The effectiveness of self-administered treatments: A practice-friendly review of the research. *Journal of Clinical Psychology*, 59: 237–46.

Mair, M. (1989) *Between Psychology and Psychotherapy, A Poetics of Experience*. London: Routledge.

Malterud, K. (2011) *Kvalitative metoder i medisinsk forskning: En innføring [Qualitative methods in medical research: An introduction]* (3rd edn). Oslo: Universitetsforlaget.

Marriott, M. and Kellett, S. (2009) Evaluating a cognitive analytic therapy service; practice-based outcomes and comparisons with person-centred and cognitive-behavioural therapies, *Psychology and Psychotherapy: Theory, Research and Practice*, 82: 57–72.

Martin, C., Godfrey, M., Meekums, B. et al. (2011) Managing boundaries under pressure: a qualitative study of therapists' experiences of sexual attraction in therapy, *Counselling and Psychotherapy Research*, 11. 248–56.

Marzillier, J. (2010) *The Gossamer Thread: My Life as a Psychotherapist*. London: Karnac.

Mason, O. and Hargreaves, I. (2001) A qualitative study of mindfulness-based cognitive therapy for depression, *British Journal of Medical Psychology*, 74: 197–212.

McCaslin, M.L. and Scott, K.W. (2003) The five-question method for framing a qualitative research study, *The Qualitative Report*, 8: 447–61.

McClelland, D.C. (1980) 'Motive dispositions: the merits of operant and respondent measures', in L. Wheeler (ed.), *Review of Personality and Social Psychology*. Beverley Hills, CA: Sage.

McKenna, P.A. and Todd, D.M. (1997) Longitudinal utilization of mental health services, a time-line method, nine retrospective accounts, and a preliminary conceptualization, *Psychotherapy Research*, 7: 383–96.

McKenzie, K., Murray, G.C., Prior, S. et al. (2011) An evaluation of a school counselling service with direct links to Child and Adolescent Mental Health (CAMH) services, *British Journal of Guidance and Counselling*, 39: 67–82.

McLaughlin, C., Holliday, C., Clarke, B. et al. (2013) Research on counselling and psychotherapy with children and young people: a systematic scoping review of the evidence for its effectiveness from 2003–2011. Lutterworth: British Association for Counselling and Psychotherapy.

McLeod, J. (1999) *Practitioner Research in Counselling*, London: Sage.

McLeod, J. (2001) An administratively created reality: some problems with the use of self-report questionnaire measures of adjustment in counselling/psychotherapy outcome research, *Counselling and Psychotherapy Research*, 1: 215–26.

McLeod, J. (2003) *Doing Counselling Research* (2nd edn). London: Sage.

McLeod, J. (2010a) *Case Study Research in Counselling and Psychotherapy*. London: Sage.

McLeod, J. (2010b) The effectiveness of workplace counselling: a systematic review. *Counselling and Psychotherapy Research*, 10: 238–48.

McLeod, J. (2011) *Qualitative Research in Counselling and Psychotherapy*. 2nd edn. London: Sage.

McLeod, J. (2013a) *An Introduction to Counselling* (5th edn). Maidenhead: Open University Press.

McLeod, J. (2013b) *An Introduction to Research in Counselling and Psychotherapy*. London: Sage.

McLeod, J. (2013c) Increasing the rigor of case study evidence in therapy research, *Pragmatic Case Studies in Psychotherapy*, 9: 382–402.

McLeod, J. and Cooper, M. (2011) A protocol for systematic case study research in pluralistic counselling and psychotherapy, *Counselling Psychology Review*, 26: 47–58.

McLeod, J., Johnston, J. and Griffin, J. (2000) A naturalistic study of the effectiveness of time-limited counselling with low-income clients, *European Journal of Psychotherapy, Counselling and Health*, 3: 263–78.

McLeod, J., Thurston, M. and McLeod, J. (2014) 'Case studies methodologies', in A. Vossler and N. Moller (eds), *The Counselling and Psychotherapy Research Handbook*. London: Sage.

Mellor-Clark, J., Barkham, M., Connell, J. et al. (1999) Practice based evidence and standardized evaluation: Informing the design of the CORE system. *European Journal of Psychotherapy, Counselling and Health*, 2: 357–374.

Mellor-Clark, J., Twigg, E., Farrell, E. et al. (2013) Benchmarking key service quality indicators in UK Employee Assistance Programme Counselling: a CORE System data profile, *Counselling and Psychotherapy Research*, 13: 14–23.

Michael, C. and Cooper, M. (2013) Post-traumatic growth following bereavement: A systematic review of the literature. *Counselling Psychology Review*, 28: 18–33.

Michell, J. (1999) *Measurement in Psychology: Critical History of a Methodological Concept*. New York: Cambridge University Press.

Michell, J. (2000) Normal science, pathological science and psychometrics, *Theory and Psychology*, 10: 639–67.

Miller, S.D., Duncan, B.L. and Hubble, M.A. (2005) Outcome-informed clinical work. In J.C. Norcross and M.R. Goldfried (eds) *Handbook of Psychotherapy Integration*. New York: Oxford University Press.

Miller, S.D., Duncan, B.L., Sorrell, R. et al. (2005) The partners for change outcome management system, *Journal of Clinical Psychology*, 61: 199–208.

Miller, T., Birch, M., Mauthner, M. et al. (eds) (2012) *Ethics in Qualitative Research* (2nd edn). Thousand Oaks, CA: Sage.

Milligan, C., Bingley, A. and Gatrell, A. (2005) Digging deep: using diary techniques to explore the place of health and well-being amongst older people, *Social Science and Medicine*, 61: 1882–92.

Minami, T., Wampold, B., Serlin, R.C. et al. (2007) Benchmarks for psychotherapy efficacy in adult major depression, *Journal of Consulting and Clinical Psychology*, 75: 232–43.

Minami, T., Wampold, B., Serlin, R.C. et al. (2008) Benchmarking the effectiveness of psychotherapy treatment for adult depression in a managed care environment: a preliminary study, *Journal of Consulting and Clinical Psychology*, 76: 116–24.

Mishler, E.G. (1986) *Research Interviewing, Context and Narrative*. Cambridge, MA: Harvard University Press.

Moerman, M. and McLeod, J. (2006) Person-centred counselling for alcohol-related problems: the client's experience of self in the therapeutic relationship, *Person-Centered and Experiential Psychotherapies*, 5: 21–35.

Moore, S. (2006) Voluntary sector counselling: has inadequate research resulted in a misunderstood and underutilised resource?, *Counselling and Psychotherapy Research*, 6: 221–6.

Morone, N.E., Lynch, C.S., Greco, C.M. et al. (2008) 'I felt like a new person': the effects of Mindfulness Meditation on older adults with chronic pain: qualitative narrative analysis of diary entries, *The Journal of Pain*, 9: 841–8.

Morris, B. (2005) *Discovering Bits and Pieces of Me: Research Exploring Women's Experiences of Psychoanalytical Psychotherapy*. London: Women's Therapy Centre (available at www.womenstherapycentre.co.uk/news/news.html).

Morrison, K.H., Bradley, R. and Westen, D. (2003) The external validity of controlled clinical trials of psychotherapy for depression and anxiety: a naturalistic study, *Psychology and Psychotherapy: Theory, Research and Practice*, 76: 109–32.

Morrow-Bradley, C. and Elliott, R. (1986) Utilization of psychotherapy research by practicing psychotherapists, *American Psychologist*, 41: 188–97.

Moustakas, C. (1967) 'Heuristic research', in J. Bugental (ed.) *Challenges of Humanistic Psychology*. New York: McGraw-Hill.

Moustakas, C. (1990) *Heuristic Research: Design, Methodology and Applications*. Thousand Oaks, CA: Sage.

Mullin, T., Barkham, M., Mothersole, G. et al. (2006) Recovery and improvement benchmarks for counselling and the psychological therapies in routine primary care, *Counselling and Psychotherapy Research*, 6: 68–80.

Muran, J.C. and Barber, J.P. (eds) (2010) *The Therapeutic Alliance: An Evidence-based Approach to Practice*. New York: Guilford.

Murray, R. (2009) *Writing for Academic Journals*. Maidenhead: Open University Press.

Nezu, A.M. and Nezu, C.M. (eds) (2007) *Evidence-based Outcome Research: A Practical Guide to Conducting Randomized Controlled Trials for Psychosocial Interventions*. Cary, NC: Oxford University Press.

Nielsen, K. (2008) On learning psychotherapy from clients, *Nordic Psychology*, 60: 163–82.

Nilsson, T., Svensson, M., Sandell, R. et al. (2007) Patients' experiences of change on cognitive-behavioral therapy and psychodynamic therapy: a qualitative comparative study, *Psychotherapy Research*, 17: 553–66.

Nunnally, J.C. and Bernstein, I. (1993) *Psychometric Theory* (3rd edn). New York: McGraw-Hill.

Ogles, B.M., Lambert, M.J. and Fields, S.A. (2002) *Essentials of Outcome Assessment*. Chichester: Wiley.

Ogrodniczuk, J.S., Sochting, I., Piper, W.E. et al. (2012) A naturalistic study of alexithymia among psychiatric outpatients treated in an integrated group therapy program, *Psychology and Psychotherapy: Theory, Research and Practice*, 85: 278–91.

Okiishi, J., Lambert, M.J., Nielsen et al. (2003) Waiting for supershrink: an empirical analysis of therapist effects. *Clinical Psychology and Psychotherapy*, 10: 361–373.

Oluyori, T. (2013) A systematic review of qualitative studies on shame, guilt and eating disorders. *Counselling Psychology Review*, 28: 47–59.

O'Neill, P. (1998) *Negotiating Consent in Psychotherapy*. New York: New York University Press.

Osborn, M. and Smith, J.A. (2008) The fearfulness of chronic pain and the centrality of the therapeutic relationship in containing it: an Interpretative Phenomenological Analysis, *Qualitative Research in Psychology*, 5: 276–88.

Netto, G., Gaag, S., Thanki, M. et al. (2001) *A Suitable Space: Improving Counselling Services for Asian People*. Bristol: The Policy Press.

Paterson, B.L., Dubouloz, C., Chevrier, J. et al. (2009) Insights from a metasynthesis project, *International Journal of Qualitative Methods*, 8: 22–33.

Paterson, C. (1996) Measuring outcome in primary care: a patient-generated measure, MYMOP, compared to the SF-36 health survey. *British Medical Journal*, 312: 1016–20.

Paterson, C. and Britten, N. (2000) In pursuit of patient-centred outcomes: a qualitative evaluation of MYMOP, Measure Yourself Medical Outcome Profile. *Journal of Health Service Research and Policy*, 5: 27–36.

Perren, S., Godfrey, M. and Rowland, N. (2009) The long-term effects of counselling: the process and mechanisms that contribute to ongoing change from a user perspective, *Counselling and Psychotherapy Research*, 9: 241–9.

Philips, B., Werbart, A., Wennberg, P. et al. (2007) Young adults' ideas of cure prior to psychoanalytic psychotherapy, *Journal of Clinical Psychology*, 63: 213–32.

Philips, S.B. (2004) Client satisfaction with university Employee Assistance Programs, *Employee Assistance Quarterly*, 19: 59–70.

Plano Clark, V.L. and Creswell, J.W. (eds) (2008) *The mixed methods reader*. Thousand Oaks, CA: Sage.

Ponterotto, J.G. (2005) Qualitative research in counseling psychology: a primer on research paradigms and philosophy of science. *Journal of Counseling Psychology*, 52: 126–36.

Ponterotto, J.G. and Grieger, I. (2007) Effectively communicating qualitative research, *The Counseling Psychologist*, 35: 404–30.

Post, B.C. and Wade, N.G. (2009) Religion and spirituality in psychotherapy: a practice-friendly review of research. *Journal of Clinical Psychology*, 65, 131–46.

Poulsen, S., Lunn, S. and Sandros, C. (2010) Client experience of psychodynamic psychotherapy for bulimia nervosa, *Psychotherapy Theory, Research, Practice, Training*, 47: 469–83.

Proulx, K. (2008) Experiences of women with Bulimia Nervosa in a mindfulness-based eating disorder treatment group, *Eating Disorders*, 16: 52–72.

Råbu, M., Halvorsen, M.S. and Haavind, H. (2011) Early relationship struggles: a case study of alliance formation and reparation, *Counselling and Psychotherapy Research*, 11: 23–33.

Rasmussen, B. and Angus, L. (1996) Metaphor in psychodynamic psychotherapy with borderline and non-borderline clients: a qualitative analysis, *Psychotherapy*, 33: 521–30.

Ratts, M.J. (2009) Social justice counseling: toward the development of a fifth force among counseling paradigms, *Journal of Humanistic Counseling*, 48: 160–72.

Rennie, D.L. (1990) 'Toward a representation of the clients experience of the psychotherapy hour', in G. Lietaer, J. Rombauts and R. Van Balen (eds), *Client-Centered and Experiential Therapy in the Nineties*. Leuven: University of Leuven Press.

Rennie, D.L. (1992) 'Qualitative analysis of the clients experience of psychotherapy, the unfolding of reflexivity', in S.G. Toukmanian and D.L. Rennie (eds), *Psychotherapy Process Research, Paradigmatic and Narrative Approaches*. London: Sage.

Rennie, D.L. (1994a) Clients' deference in psychotherapy, *Journal of Counseling Psychology*, 41: 427–37.

Rennie, D.L. (1994b) Storytelling in psychotherapy, the clients' subjective experience, *Psychotherapy*, 31: 234–43.

Rennie, D.L. (1994c) Clients' accounts of resistance in counselling, a qualitative analysis, *Canadian Journal of Counselling*, 28: 43–57.

Rennie, D.L. (1994d) 'Strategic choices in a qualitative approach to psychotherapy process research, a personal account', in L. Hoshmand and J. Martin (eds), *Method Choice and Inquiry Process: Lessons from Programmatic Research in Therapeutic Psychology*. New York: Teachers Press.

Rennie, D.L. (2000) 'Experiencing psychotherapy, grounded theory studies', in D. Cain and J. Seeman (eds), *Handbook of Research in Humanistic Psychotherapies*. Washington, DC: American Psychological Association.

Rennie, D.L. and Fergus, K.D. (2006) Embodied categorizing in the grounded theory method: methodical hermeneutics in action, *Theory and Psychology*, 16: 483–503.

Rice, L.N. (1992) From naturalistic observation of psychotherapy process to micro theories of change, in D.L Rennie and S.G. Toukmanian (eds), *Psychotherapy Process Research: Narrative and Paradigmatic Approaches*. London: Sage.

Rice, L.N. and Kerr, G.P. (1986) Measures of client and therapist voice quality, in L.S. Greenberg and W.M. Pinsof (eds), *The Psychotherapeutic Process: A Research Handbook*. New York: Guilford Press.

Richardson, L. and Reid, C. (2006) 'I've lost my husband, my house and I need a new knee … why should I smile?': action research evaluation of a group cognitive behavioural therapy program for older adults with depression, *Clinical Psychologist*, 10: 60–6.

Riessman, C.K. (2008) *Narrative Methods for the Human Sciences*. Thousand Oaks, CA: Sage.

Riva, J., Malik, K.M.P., Burnie, S.J. et al. (2012) What is your research question? An introduction to the PICOT format for clinicians, *Journal of the Canadian Chiropractic Association*, 56: 167–71.

Roberts, J. (1996) Perceptions of the significant other of the effects of psychodynamic psychotherapy, implications for thinking about psychodynamic and systems approaches, *British Journal of Psychiatry*, 168: 87–93.

Robson, C. (2011) *Real World Research: A Resources for Social Scientists and Practitioner-Researchers* (3rd edn). Oxford: Blackwell.

Rodgers, B. (2006) Life space mapping: preliminary results from the development of a new method for investigating counselling outcomes, *Counselling and Psychotherapy Research*, 6: 227–32.

Rodgers, B. and Elliott, R. (2014) 'Qualitative psychotherapy outcome research', in O. Gelo, A. Pritz and B. Rieken (eds), *Psychotherapy Research: General Issues, Outcome and Process*. Vienna: Springer-Verlag.

Rodgers, N.M. (2011) Intimate boundaries: therapists' perception and experience of erotic transference within the therapeutic relationship, *Counselling and Psychotherapy Research*, 11: 266–74.

Rogers, C.R. and Dymond, R.F. (eds) (1954) *Psychotherapy and Personality Change*. Chicago: University of Chicago Press.

Rogers, C.R., Gendlin, E.T., Kiesler, D.J. et al. (eds) (1967) *The Therapeutic Relationship and its Impact: A Study of Psychotherapy with Schizophrenics*. Madison: University of Wisconsin Press.

Rogers, D., McLeod, J. and Sloboda, J. (1995) Counsellor and client perceptions of the effectiveness of time-limited counselling in an occupational counselling scheme, *Counselling Psychology Quarterly*, 8(3): 221–31.

Rojon, C., McDowall, A. and Saunders, M.N.K. (2011) On the experience of conducting a systematic review in Industrial, Work, and Organizational Psychology: Yes, it is worthwhile, *Journal of Personnel Psychology*, 10: 133–8.

Rossouw, G., Smythe, E. and Greener, P. (2011) Therapists' experience of working with suicidal clients, *Indo-Pacific Journal of Phenomenology*, 11: 1–12.

Rowan, N. and Wolff, D. (2007) Using qualitative methods to inform scale development, *The Qualitative Report*, 12: 450–66.

Royal College of Psychiatrists (2011) National Audit of Psychological Therapies for Anxiety and Depression, National Report 2011. London: Royal College of Psychiatrists.

Rust, J. and Golombok, S. (2008) *Modern Psychometrics: The Science of Psychological Assessment* (3rd edn). London: Routledge.

Sandelowski, M. and Leeman, J. (2012) Writing usable qualitative health research findings. *Qualitative Health Research*, 22: 1404–13.

Santiago-Rivera, A.L., Altarriba, J., Poll, N. et al. (2009) Therapists' views on working with bilingual Spanish–English speaking clients: a qualitative investigation, *Professional Psychology: Research* and Practice, 40: 436–43.

Saxon, D., Ivey, C. and Young, T. (2008) Can CORE assessment data identify those clients less likely to benefit from brief counselling in primary care?, *Counselling and Psychotherapy Research*, 8: 223–30.

Scheeres, K., Wensing, M., Knoop, H. et al. (2008) Implementing cognitive behavioral therapy for chronic fatigue syndrome in a mental health center: a benchmarking evaluation, *Journal of Consulting and Clinical Psychology*, 76: 163–71.

Schielke, H.J., Fishman, J.L., Osatuke, K. et al. (2009) Creative consensus on interpretations of qualitative data: the Ward method, *Psychotherapy Research,* 19: 558–65.

Schindler, A., Hiller, W. and Witthöft, M. (2013) What predicts outcome, response, and drop-out in CBT of depressive adults? A naturalistic study, *Behavioural and Cognitive Psychotherapy*, 41: 365–70.

Schjelderup, H. (1955) Lasting effects of psychoanalytic treatment, *Psychiatry*, 18: 109–33.

Schnellbacher, J. and Leijssen, M. (2009) The significance of therapist genuineness from the client's perspective, *Journal of Humanistic Psychology*, 49: 207–28.

Sealy, P.A. (2012) Autoethnography: reflective journaling and meditation to cope with life-threatening breast cancer, *Clinical Journal of Oncology Nursing*, 16: 38–41.

Self, R., Oates, P., Pinnock-Hamilton, T. et al. (2005) The relationship between social deprivation and unilateral termination (attrition) from psychotherapy at various stages of the health care pathway, *Psychology and Psychotherapy: Theory, Research and Practice*, 78: 95–111.

Semeonoff, B. (1976) *Projective Techniques*. Chichester: Wiley.

Shaw, I. (2008) Ethics and the practice of qualitative research, *Qualitative Social Work*, 7: 400–14.

Sheach Leith, V.M. (2009) The search for meaning after pregnancy loss: an autoethnography, *Illness, Crisis and Loss*, 17: 201–21.

Shedler, J., Mayman, M. and Manis, M. (1993) The illusion of mental health. *American Psychologist,* 48, 1117–31.

Sieber, J.E. and Tolich, M.B. (2013) *Planning Ethically Responsible Research* (2nd edn). Thousand Oaks, CA: Sage.

Sin, N.L. and Lyubomirsky, S. (2009) Enhancing well-being and alleviating depressive symptoms with positive psychology interventions: A practice-friendly meta-analysis. *Journal of Clinical Psychology,* 65: 467–87.

Sloboda, J.A., Hopkins, J.S., Turner, A. et al. (1993) An evaluated staff counselling programme in a public sector organisation, *Employee Counselling Today*, 5: 10–16.

Smith, B. (1999) The abyss: exploring depression through a narrative of the self, *Qualitative Inquiry*, 5: 264–79.

Smith, JA. (2011) 'We could be diving for pearls': the value of the gem in experiential qualitative psychology. *Qualitative Methods in Psychology Bulletin*, 12: 6–15.

Smith, J.A., Flowers, P. and Larkin, M. (2009) *Interpretative Phenomenological Analysis: Theory, Method and Research*. London: Sage.

Smith, K., Shoemark, A., McLeod, J. et al. (2014) Moving on: a case analysis of process and outcome in person-centred psychotherapy for health anxiety, *Person-Centered and Experiential Psychotherapies*, 13: 111–27.

Smith, L., Rosenzweig, L. and Schmidt, M. (2010) Best practices in the reporting of participatory action research: embracing both the forest and the trees, *Counseling Psychologist*, 38: 1115–38.

Snape, C., Perren, S., Jones, L. et al. (2003) Counselling – why not? A qualitative study of people's accounts of not taking up counselling appointments, *Counselling and Psychotherapy Research*, 3: 239–45.

Solomon, S.D. and Johnson, D.M. (2002) Psychosocial treatment of posttraumatic stress disorder: A practice-friendly review of outcome research. *Journal of Clinical Psychology*, 58: 947–59.

Sparkes, A.C. (1996) The fatal flaw: a narrative of the fragile body-self, *Qualitative Inquiry*, 2: 463–94.

Sparkes, A.C. (2000) Autoethnography and narratives of self: reflections on criteria in action, *Sociology of Sport Journal*, 17: 21–43.

Sparkes, A.C. (2002) 'Autoethnography: self indulgence or something more?', in A. Bochner, A. and C. Ellis (eds), *Ethnographically Speaking: Autoethnography, Literature, and Aesthetics*. London: Altamira. pp. 209–32.

Sparkes, A.C. (2013) 'Autoethnography: self-indulgence or something more?' in P. Sikes (ed.), *Autoethnography*. London: Sage. pp. 175–94.

Sparkes, A.P. (2012) Fathers and sons: in bits and pieces, *Qualitative Inquiry*, 18: 174–85.

Speedy, J. (2008) *Narrative Inquiry and Psychotherapy*. Basingstoke: Palgrave Macmillan.

Sperry, L. (2008) The place of values in counseling research: an introduction, *Counseling and Values*, 53: 2–7.

Spielberger, C.D., Gorsuch, R.L. and Lushene, R. (1970) *Manual for the State–Trait Anxiety Inventory*. Palo Alto, CA: Consulting Psychologists Press.

Spitzer, R.L., Kroenke, K., Williams, J.B., et al. (2006) A brief measure for assessing generalized anxiety disorder: the GAD-7. *Archives of Internal Medicine*, 166(10): 1092–7.

Stiles, W.B. (2001) Assimilation of problematic experiences, *Psychotherapy: Theory, Research, Practice and Training*, 38: 462–5.

Stiles, W.B. (2002) 'Assimilation of problematic experiences', in J.C. Norcross (ed.), *Psychotherapy Relationships That Work*. New York: Oxford University Press.

Stiles, W.B. (1993) Quality control in qualitative research, *Clinical Psychology Review*, 13: 593–618.

Stiles, W.B., Barkham, M., Connell, J. et al. (2008) Responsive regulation of treatment duration in routine practice in United Kingdom primary care settings: replication in a larger sample, *Journal of Consulting and Clinical Psychology*, 76: 298–305.

Stiles, W.B., Barkham, M., Mellor-Clark, J. et al. (2008) Effectiveness of cognitive-behavioural, person-centred, and psychodynamic therapies in UK primary-care routine practice: replication in a larger sample, *Psychological Medicine*, 38: 667–88.

Stiles, W.B., Barkham, M., Twigg, E. et al. (2006) Effectiveness of cognitive-behavioural, person centred, and psychodynamic therapies as practiced in UK National Health Service settings, *Psychological Medicine*, 36: 555–66.

Stiles, W.B., Elliott, R., Llewelyn, S. et al. (1990) Assimilation of problematic experiences by clients in psychotherapy, *Psychotherapy*, 27: 411–20.

Stiles, W.B., Gordon, L.E. and Lani, J.A. (2002) 'Session evaluation and the Session Evaluation Questionnaire', in G. S. Tryon (ed.), *Counseling Based on Process Research: Applying what we Know*. Boston, MA: Allyn & Bacon.

Stiles, W.B., Leach, C., Barkham, M. et al. (2003) Early sudden gains in psychotherapy under routine clinic conditions: practice-based evidence, *Journal of Consulting and Clinical Psychology*, 71: 14–21.

Stiles, W.B., Meshot, C.N., Anderson, T.M. et al. (1992) Assimilation of problematic experiences: the case of John Jones, *Psychotherapy Research*, 2(2): 81–101.

Stiles, W.B., Morrison, L.A., Haw, S.F. et al. (1991) Longitudinal study of assimilation in exploratory psychotherapy, *Psychotherapy*, 28: 195–206.

Stinckens, N. and Elliott, R. (2014) Dealing with anxiety in a short-term therapy: keeping it company or going beyond, *Person-Centered and Experiential Psychotherapies*, 13: 94–110.

Stinckens, N., Elliott, R. and Leijssen, M. (2009) Bridging the gap between therapy research and practice in a person-centered/experiential therapy training program: the Leuven Systematic Case Study Protocol, *Person-Centered and Experiential Psychotherapies*, 8: 143–62.

Stratton, P., Bland, J., Janes, E. et al. (2010) Developing an indicator of family function and a practicable outcome measure for systemic family and couple therapy: the SCORE, *Journal of Family Therapy*, 32: 232–58.

Stratton, P., McGovern, M., Wetherell, A. et al. (2006) Family therapy practitioners researching the reactions of practitioners to an outcome measure, *Australian and New Zealand Journal of Family Therapy*, 27: 199–207.

Stulz, N., Lutz, W., Leach, C. et al. (2007) Shapes of early change in psychotherapy under routine outpatient conditions, *Journal of Consulting and Clinical Psychology*, 75: 864–74.

Suh, C.S., Strupp, H.H. and O'Malley, S.S. (1986) The Vanderbilt process measures: the Psychotherapy Process Scale (VPPS) and the Negative Indicators Scale (VNIS). In L.S. Greenberg and W.M. Pinsof (eds), *The Psychotherapeutic Process: A Research Handbook*. New York: Guilford.

Sullivan, K.I. and Davila, J. (2014) 'The problem is with my partner': treating couples when one partner wants the other to change, *Journal of Psychotherapy Integration*, 24: 1–12.

Sussman, S. (2001) The significance of psycho-peristalsis and tears within the therapeutic relationship, *Counselling and Psychotherapy Research*, 1: 90–100.

Telford, C., McCarthy-Jones, S., Corcoran, R. et al. (2012) Experience Sampling Methodology studies of depression: the state of the art, *Psychological Medicine*, 42: 1119–29.

Tennant, R., Hiller, L., Fishwick, R. et al. (2007) The Warwick-Edinburgh Mental Well-being Scale (WEMWBS): development and UK validation. *Health and Quality of Life Outcomes*, 5: 63.

Thompson, A.R. and Russo, K. (2012) Ethical dilemmas for clinical psychologists in conducting qualitative research, *Qualitative Research in Psychology*, 9: 32–46.

Thompson, V.L.S., Bazile, A. and Akbar, M. (2004) African Americans' perceptions of psychotherapy and psychotherapists, *Professional Psychology: Research and Practice*, 35: 19–26.

Thurston, M., McLeod, J. and McLeod, J. (2014) 'How to use case study methodology with single client therapy data', in A. Vossler and N. Moller (eds), *The Counselling and Psychotherapy Research Handbook*. London: Sage.

Thurston, M., Thurston, A. and McLeod, J. (2012) Counselling for sight loss: using Hermeneutic Single Case Efficacy Design methods to explore outcome and common factors, *Counselling Psychology Review*, 27: 56–70.

Timulak, L. (2007) Identifying core categories of client identified impact of helpful events in psychotherapy – a qualitative meta-analysis, *Psychotherapy Research*, 17: 305–14.

Timulak, L. (2008) Research in Counselling and Psychotherapy. London: Sage.

Timulak, L. (2009) Qualitative meta-analysis: a tool for reviewing qualitative research findings in psychotherapy, *Psychotherapy Research*, 19: 591–600.

Timulak, L. and Creaner, M. (2010) 'Qualitative meta-analysis of outcomes of person-centred/experiential therapies', in M. Cooper, J.C. Watson and D. Holledampf (eds), *Person-centred and Experiential Psychotherapies Work*. Ross-on-Wye: PCCS.

Timulak, L. and Creaner, M. (2013) Experiences of conducting qualitative meta-analysis, *Counselling Psychology Review*, 28: 94–104.

Timulak, L. and McElvaney, R. (2013) Qualitative meta-analysis of insight events in psychotherapy, *Counselling Psychology Quarterly*, 26: 131–50.

Timulak, L., Buckroyd, J., Klimas, J. et al. (2013) *Helpful and Unhelpful Aspects of Eating Disorders Treatment Involving Psychological Therapy: A Meta-synthesis of Qualitative Research Studies*. Lutterworth: British Association for Counselling and Psychotherapy (BACP).

Tinsley, H.E. and Weiss, D.J. (1975) Interrater reliability and agreement of subjective judgements, *Journal of Counseling Psychology*, 22: 358–76.

Tolich, M. (2010) A critique of current practice: ten foundational guidelines for autoethnographers, *Qualitative Health Research*, 20: 1599–610.

Toto-Moriarty, T. (2013) A retrospective view of psychodynamic treatment: perspectives of recovered bulimia nervosa patients, *Qualitative Social Work*.

Toukmanian, S.G. and Rennie, D.L. (eds) (1992) *Psychotherapy Process Research: Paradigmatic and Narrative Approaches*. London: Sage.

Trauer, T. (ed.) (2010) Outcome Measurement in Mental Health: Theory and Practice. New York: Cambridge University Press.

Traux, C.B. and Carkhuff, R.R. (1967) *Toward Effective Counseling and Psychotherapy: Training and Practice*. Chicargo: Aldine.

Unsworth, G., Cowie, H. and Green, A. (2011) Therapists' and clients' perceptions of routine outcome measurement in the NHS: A qualitative study. Counselling and Psychotherapy Research,

Valente, V. and Marotta, A. (2005) The impact of yoga on the professional and personal life of the psychotherapist, *Contemporary Family Therapy*, 27: 65–80.

Valkonen, J., Hanninen, V. and Lindfors, O. (2011) Outcomes of psychotherapy from the perspective of the users, *Psychotherapy Research*, 21: 227–40.

Van den Hoonard, W.C. (2002) *Walking the Tightrope: Ethical Issues for Qualitative Researchers*. Toronto: University of Toronto Press.

Van Dierendonck, D., Schaufeli, W.B. and Buunk, B.P. (1998) The evaluation of an individual burnout program: the role of inequity and social support, *Journal of Applied Psychology*, 83: 392–407.

Wagner, J. and Elliott, R. (2001) The Simplified Personal Questionnaire. Unpublished manuscript, University of Toledo, Department of Psychology.

Ward, E.C. (2005) Keeping it real: a grounded theory study of African American clients engaged in counseling at a community mental health agency, *Journal of Counseling Psychology*, 52: 471–81.

Watts, R.E. (2011) Developing a conceptual article for publication in counseling journals, *Journal of Counseling and Development*, 89: 308–12.

Weatherhead, S. and Daiches, A. (2010) Muslim views on mental health and psychotherapy, *Psychology and Psychotherapy: Theory, Research and Practice*, 83: 75–89.

Weersing, V.R. (2005) Benchmarking the effectiveness of psychotherapy: program evaluation as a component of evidence-based practice, *Journal of the American Academy of Child and Adolescent Psychiatry*, 44: 1058–62.

Weersing, V.R. and Weisz, J.R. (2002) Community clinic treatment for depressed youth: benchmarking usual care against CBT clinical trials, *Journal of Consulting and Clinical Psychology*, 70: 299–310.

Werbart, A. and Wang, M. (2012) Predictors of not starting and dropping out from psychotherapy in Swedish public service settings, *Nordic Psychology*, 64: 128–46.

Werbart, A., Levin, L., Andersson, H. et al. (2013) Everyday evidence: outcomes of psychotherapies in Swedish public health services, *Psychotherapy*, 50: 119–30.

West, M. and Reynolds, S. (1995) Employee attitudes to work-based counselling services, *Work and Stress*, 9: 31–44.

Westbrook, D. and Kirk, J. (2005) The clinical effectiveness of cognitive behaviour therapy: outcome for a large sample of adults treated in routine practice, *Behaviour Research and Therapy*, 43: 1243–61.

Whybrow, D. (2013) Psychiatric nursing liaison in a combat zone: an autoethnography, *Journal of Psychiatric and Mental Health Nursing*, 20: 896–901.

Wilkinson, H. (ed.) (2001) *The Perspectives of People with Dementia: Research Methods and Motivations*. London: Jessica Kingsley.

Winter, D., Bradshaw, S., Bunn, F. et al. (2009) *Counselling and Psychotherapy for the Prevention of Suicide: A Systematic Review of the Evidence*. Lutterworth: British Association for Counselling and Psychotherapy.

Wittchen, H.-U. and Fehm, L. (2003) Epidemiology and natural course of social fears and social phobia, *Acta Psychiatrica Scandinavica*, 108: 4–18.

Wolcott, H.F. (1990) *Writing up Qualitative Research*. London: Sage.

Woo, H. and Heo, N. (2013) A content analysis of qualitative research in select ACA journals (2005–2010), *Counseling Outcome Research and Evaluation*, 4: 13–25.

Woodward, L.E., Murrell, S.A. and Bettler, R.F., Jr (2005) Stability, reliability and norms for the Inventory of Interpersonal Problems, *Psychotherapy Research*, 15: 272–86.

Worthington, R.L. and Whittaker, T.A. (2006) Scale development research: a content analysis and recommendations for best practices, *Counseling Psychologist*, 34: 806–38.

Zigmond, A.S. and Snaith, R.P. (1983) The hospital anxiety and depression scale. *Acta Psychiatrica Scandinavica*, 67: 361–70.

Index